NIPPON

Dolls & Playthings

IDENTIFICATION AND VALUES

Joan Van Patten

&

Linda Lau

COLLECTOR BOOKS

A Division of Schroeder Publishing Co., Inc.

The current values in this book should be used only as a guide. They are not intended to set prices, which vary from one section of the country to another. Auction prices as well as dealer prices vary greatly and are affected by condition as well as demand. Neither the authors nor the publisher assumes responsibility for any losses which might be incurred as a result of consulting this guide.

On the Cover:

Front cover, clockwise from top right:
Pincushion doll, 3" tall, $250.00 – 300.00 (Plate 435).
Pumpkin candy container, 2¼" tall, $100.00 – 125.00 (Plate 663).
Halloween doll, 4½" tall, $165.00 – 200.00 (Plate 661).
Child's tea set, $325.00 – 375.00 (Plate 550).
Figural all-bisque doll, 4½" tall, $175.00 – 225.00 (Plate 172).
Morimura Brothers Dolly, 7" tall, $245.00 – 275.00 (Plate 95).
Louis Wolf & Co. bisque-head doll, 17" tall, $450.00 – 550.00 (Plate 351).

Back cover:
Clown doll, 7" tall (including hat), $140.00 – 175.00 (Plate 192).

Cover design: Beth Summers   **Book design: Sherry Kraus**

Searching For A Publisher?

We are always looking for knowledgeable people considered experts within their fields. If you feel that there is a real need for a book on your collectible subject and have a large comprehensive collection, contact Collector Books.

Collector Books
P.O. Box 3009
Paducah, KY 42002-3009

www.collectorbooks.com

Copyright © 2001 by Joan Van Patten & Linda Lau

Contents

Acknowledgments

Collector Books is noted for publishing the finest books on antiques and collectibles, and we are very happy to be part of that family. We are especially grateful to Billy Schroeder for the opportunity to have this book published. Without his approval, this book would never have been written. Lisa Stroup, our editor, and Amy Hopper, her assistant, always do a super job on every project they take on, and we want to thank them for their help. We also want to thank all the others at Collector Books who do so much to make these books extra special.

Next we want to thank our good friends, BJ and Lewis Longest. BJ and Lewis spent countless hours photographing many of the items featured in this book including dolls and tea sets from their wonderful collection. They are truly special people and graciously give their time and energy. Lewis is a professional photographer, and we were fortunate to have him and BJ as contributors. More importantly, we are fortunate to have them as friends.

Another collector we wish to give special thanks to is Dawn Fisher. She has an awesome collection of Nippon dolls and playthings. We were given complete access to her collection and were allowed to photograph anything and everything we wanted. We spent a wonderful weekend with Dawn enjoying her gracious hospitality. She is a great friend, and we really appreciate her contribution to this book. We also want to express our appreciation to Dawn's sister, Ann Land, who helped us the day we photographed Dawn's collection.

We are indebted to several Japanese contributors who provided historical information, patent copies, and translations. Mr. Keishi Suzuki and Mr. Tadashi 'Tony' Kawamura from Noritake Co., Ltd. provided the information found in the section devoted to the history of the Noritake Company.

Mr. Ikuo Fukunaga of Morimura Brothers initially provided an account of the development of Morimura Brothers' doll production. This valuable information was the starting point for our research on Morimura Brothers dolls. He later provided a detailed history of the early Morimura Brothers Company.

Mrs. Aki Kato researched and translated the Japanese patents you see in this book which yielded Nippon doll information that we otherwise would not have had access to.

Mr. H. Suzuki of Froebel-Kan, Ltd. sent us the history of that company and their involvement with Morimura Brothers doll production.

A special thanks to Dave Przech for his support and encouragement with this project.

Others that we would like to thank for photos are Joyce and Charles Briggs, Marie and John Simm, Chuck Dillon, Agnes Sura, Polly Frye, Gay and Raymond Doggett, Carol Hale, David Bausch, Mark Griffin, and Earl Smith.

A generous thank you to each and every person who was part of this project. We could not have done it without you! Doll and plaything collectors are truly special people. We hope you enjoy this book.

Introduction

"An investment in knowledge always pays the best interest."

Franklin

Our pleasure and skill increase when we know more about what we collect. To fully appreciate the items we purchase, one needs to have questions answered; a sense of their history is needed. How were the pieces made? How and who designed and manufactured them? Why were they made? Who sold them? Who bought them? These are a few of the questions that this book hopes to address about Nippon dolls and playthings.

What is Nippon?

Nippon is not the name of a type of ware or the manufacturer as some think, but rather the country of origin. It comes from a Chinese phrase meaning "the source of the sun" and is the name the Japanese people called their country. The word "Nippon" is synonymous with the word "Japan," the Land of the Rising Sun, and so it is that the rays from this Japanese sun continue to light up the lives of so many Nippon enthusiasts.

It was not necessary for items entering the United States prior to 1891 to be backstamped with their country of origin. However, in October of 1890, the McKinley Tariff Act was passed by Congress and stated the following:

> *That on and after the first day of March, eighteen hundred and ninety-one, all articles of foreign manufacture, such as are usually or ordinarily marked, stamped, branded or labeled, and all packages containing such or other imported articles, shall respectively, be plainly marked, stamped, branded or labeled in legible English words, so as to indicate the country of their origin; and unless so marked, stamped, branded or labeled they shall not be admitted to entry.*

Thus the Nippon era began, lasting until 1921 when the government reversed its position and decided that Nippon was a Japanese word, the English equivalent of which was Japan. Customs agents were then instructed that as of September 1, 1921, merchandise from Japan, the marking of which was governed by this provision, would not be released when bearing only the Japanese word "Nippon" to indicate the country of origin. Items made after this period were to be marked "Japan" or "Made in Japan."

Research indicates though that not all imported goods were marked as dictated by law. There were loopholes in the law which allowed for some unmarked items to enter this country. For instance, at some ports of entry, goods were allowed into the country if merely the box or container was stamped with the name of the country of origin. Novice Nippon porcelain collectors would probably fare better by purchasing only marked pieces, as it is sometimes difficult to distinguish between genuine Nippon era items and the later Japanese wares. Doll and toy collectors must be especially careful of this since buying unmarked dolls, toys, and holiday items is problematic. For example, we know that the Japanese copied many of the German all-bisque dolls. Therefore, an unmarked all-bisque doll may have had its origin in either Japan or Germany. Toy and holiday items were made in

Japan for many years from the Nippon era into the "Made in Japan" era. If the item is unmarked, it's impossible to tell in which era it was made.

A Quick Look at Nippon Porcelain

When doll collectors hear the word "Nippon," they usually think of the bisque dolls that were produced during the World War I era. However, when other collectors think of "Nippon," they often associate it with the beautiful hand painted porcelain items that the Japanese manufactured for the American market. While this book is dedicated to Nippon dolls and playthings, we feel that in order to fully understand and appreciate the Nippon era of dolls and playthings it is helpful to know something about the Nippon porcelain.

During the years 1870 – 1900 the American export trade nearly tripled. There was an increasing demand for a greater world market. This era in U.S. history knew strikes and depressions, as well as buoyancy and free spending. Items that had previously been available only to the wealthy were now available to the ever-growing middle class. The late Victorian Age was a time for ostentation, ornate, fancy, even exotic items, a time when knick-knacks abounded. In fact, most Americans during this time period adopted the attitude "nothing succeeds like excess," and this is reflected in the range of porcelain items found today. It was a time of past elegance. Japanese art reached peaks of popularity in Europe and, during the late Victorian age, the pieces became gaudier and gaudier until almost every square inch was covered with decoration. The people of this era identified decoration with beauty, the more ornate and intricate the design the better. On many of the Nippon wares, the design tends to cover the whole article, which appealed to the English at this particular time in history and, as a result, much of this inexpensive porcelain was imported from Japan. During this so-called "Gilded Age" there was incredible business expansion. It was a time of skyscrapers, steam engines, railroads, telephones, and telegraphs.

The period of 1891 to 1921 (the Nippon era) was certainly one of great importance and social change in our country's history. The United States in 1907 faced financial panic; the San Francisco earthquake and fire almost overnight destroyed a major U.S. city; the Wright Brothers' first flight made everyone, including Japanese porcelain decorators, begin to think that air travel was really possible; and the sinking of the Titanic in 1912 and the first ship passing through the Panama Canal in 1914 kept ocean travel in the news. But it was women's suffrage and World War I that would have the greatest and longest lasting impact on the United States and the world in general.

The Japanese have always had an eagerness to learn from others and Japanese painters went abroad to study and learn the ways of the New World. It has been said that the Japanese are "conscious cultural borrowers," they seem to have the capacity to borrow and adapt, making it something new and quintessentially Japanese. The Japanese government also hired foreign experts to come to Japan to train their people. The artists began imitating the European styles or tried to combine both those of the Eastern and Western manner. There were no copyright laws and the Japanese copied whatever they admired. They were highly skilled and capable of quickly learning new techniques. They had previously copied the master artists from China but in order to satisfy this new Western market, they now copied the arts of many other countries.

The Japanese porcelain items were less expensive to purchase than pieces coming from Germany or Austria and around the end of the nineteenth and early into the twentieth century were very popular in the United States. This country was very receptive to the inexpensive porcelain and, as a result, much was imported. Many of the items were sold in gift shops, at summer resorts, boardwalks, fairs, five and ten cent stores, carnivals, penny arcades and even at the local grocery store.

It is interesting to note how much Nippon porcelain items actually sold for during this period. Old catalogs list vases for 59¢ each, a nine piece tea set for $2.29, game plates were 95¢ a dozen, and a dozen cups and saucers were sold as low as $1.49.

Of course, other prices were also low along with the wages of this time period. Bedroom suites sold for $14.95, ladies dresses were $1.48, and one could buy house paint for 39¢ a gallon. This paint came with a ten year guarantee, and a large two story home could be painted for about $4.00. Wouldn't we all love to find such bargains today!

Twenty to thirty years ago a box full of Nippon porcelain could be purchased for just a few dollars. Today, this is no longer the case. Nippon has been elevated to one of the most sought after collectibles on the antique market. Among the favorite pieces of collectors have been vases, humidors, bowls, chocolate sets, plaques, the list goes on and on. Most of these items have been fully or partially handpainted, and many can be considered works of art because they are so breathtakingly beautiful.

We have included photos of a few of the types of Nippon porcelain that were manufactured for the American market. Nippon porcelain is known for its gaudy florals and beautiful scenes, much of which is trimmed in gold. As you will see in the photos, the Japanese utilized many different techniques — heavy gold, moriage, cobalt, molded in relief, just to name a few — in the manufacture of their products. A few of these techniques, such as the hand painted flowers and scenes or the molded-in-relief items, were also used on children's porcelain. It is hoped that these items will give the reader a better understanding of the types of products that the Japanese were making in addition to dolls and playthings. We know that one company, Morimura Brothers, manufactured both porcelain items and bisque dolls, and it could be that other Japanese porcelain firms also manufactured bisque dolls.

Demitasse set. Aqua background features flying swans, gold and jeweling.

Large 24" palace vase.

Beautiful small cobalt, gold, and floral pitcher.

Molded in relief owl decorated vase.

Moriage (clay slip decoration) basket vase.

Humidor decorated with hand-painted mums and heavy gold beading.

Our Focus on Nippon Dolls and Playthings

In 1914 when hostilities in Europe escalated into World War I, German doll and toy production was curtailed and ultimately halted. This opening gave the Japanese an opportunity to begin producing and exporting all types of dolls and toys, including copies of the popular German character dolls.

Since the Japanese already had experience in creating porcelain products and because dolls play an important role in Japanese society, it was a natural step that they would want to take advantage of the German inability to produce and export dolls. The Japanese, after all, saw an opportunity to satisfy the American consumer's appetite for dolls of all kinds.

These items, as you will read in other chapters, were mass-produced, sold relatively cheaply (although the prices on some of the bisque-head dolls appear to be high when one considers how much the average yearly salary was at that time), and, for the most part, were meant to be played with. Many were broken or thrown away, so actually it's amazing that so many have survived all these years.

The dictionary describes a doll as a "child's toy baby" but purchasing these older dolls is hardly child's play to the serious collector. It can be a very expensive hobby although the majority of Nippon-marked examples are still within the reach of most pocketbooks.

The original owners may long have outgrown these toys, but the collector certainly has not. In fact, when the collecting fever goes unchecked, avid collectors often find themselves surrounded by hundreds of little people in every room of the house!

Although some Nippon era (1891 – 1921) dolls and playthings have been featured in *Collector's Encyclopedia of Nippon Porcelain, First through Sixth Series*, these wonderful items have not received the attention they are due. That is about to change with the publication of this book.

The intent of this book is to show the wide variety of dolls and playthings manufactured during the Nippon era and to provide information about the history of Nippon dolls and playthings. We have not tried to show every doll or toy made. That would be impossible, but we have tried to include at least one example of the types of dolls and toys that we know about. Every year collectors find previously undocumented examples, which is part of the fun of collecting Nippon dolls and playthings. You never know what you will find next.

We have also tried to provide historical information as it relates to the manufacture and importation of Nippon dolls and playthings. Whenever possible, we have included advertisements, articles, and patents because we feel that these items can provide you with a real sense of what was actually available and of interest during that time.

There is little information to be found on Nippon dolls in any of the current doll books, and much of the information found in early doll reference books is either inaccurate or incomplete. We were astounded by the amount of information we have been able to gather over the last few years. And now we are anxious to share this information with other collectors.

Our advice is to be informed and enlightened, read anything and everything you can on the subject. Go to the library, frequent museums, antique shops, malls and shows, subscribe to weekly and monthly trade magazines and newspapers. Check the Internet for auctions of these items; also question other collectors and dealers.

Truly great collections require work, knowledge and discipline. Also patience! They do not happen overnight. There is a big difference between having an accumulation and a "collection." An accumulation is merely a hodgepodge of items, a mixture collected with little rhyme or reason, often just for quantity. The "true" collector, however, doesn't collect just to collect for quantity, but has a purpose in mind along with an eye for quality.

Beware, Nippon dolls and playthings can be addictive, but they can also be the beginning of a timeless heritage and who can begin to guess how many generations to come will see and love these items as we do today. As collectors we never truly "own" these treasures, we are merely caretakers for future generations.

Nippon-marked dolls are not only popular in the United States, but Japanese collectors are now buying all kinds and many are being returned to the country of manufacture. In fact, the Yumeji Takehisa Ikaho Memorial Museum in Japan held an exhibit of Nippon dolls in 1996. There are 325 dolls in the museum's collection, 130 of which are Morimura Brothers dolls. The dolls were acquired from collectors living in the United States who wanted them to go back home. Now they are referred to as "dolls of illusion" because most Japanese have never seen them although they were manufactured there.

The museum also has a display of old Noritake wares and a number of old Noritake salesman pages on display as well.

The Memorial Museum is named after a Japanese artist who was popular during the time period that the old Noritake pieces and dolls were manufactured. He created wonderful prints and paintings featuring beautiful women as the basic theme of his work.

The doll collection includes both small and large dolls, and the following photos show the collection before the dolls made their long journey back home to Japan.

Nippon,
The Land of the Rising Sun

Nippon, "Land of the Rising Sun," is a country of Oriental splendor. Legend tells us that the Japanese people descended from the Sun Goddess thousands of years ago, the sun being adored by the primitive Japanese. Nippon is the Japanese word for "Japan." Japan, the oldest monarchy in the world, is a chain of volcanic islands bordered by the Sea of Japan and the Pacific Ocean, off the coast of China. Its coast is deeply indented and the country consists of four main islands and thousands of smaller ones that span a length of about 1,300 miles. It is a land of contrasts and contradictions — the bustle of Tokyo and the serenity of Kyoto. A land of tranquil palaces, temples, and shrines. Waterfalls and lakes shimmer in the spectacular scenery of the snowcapped mountains. Ancient trees, lakes, valleys, and rivers, the sun glittering over Mt. Fuji, and yet it also can be a violent land at times, a land of earthquakes, typhoons, floods, and volcanoes. This is the homeland of Nippon dolls and playthings.

In 1638 Japan was closed to all Europeans and cut off from the rest of the world. This was done to hopefully secure Japan from the Europeans and quell the rebellious Japanese peasants. The Japanese were forbidden to build any ship larger than a coasting boat. They could not go abroad and no foreigner could enter. The law of the land decreed a death penalty for any foreigner entering Japan and the people of Japan lived in almost total isolation for 214 years until Commodore Matthew Perry, USN, steamed into Yedo Bay in 1853. Yedo was later renamed Tokyo, meaning eastern capitol, and this period of isolation in Japan is often referred to by historians as the Yedo period.

Perry arrived with four fighting ships, two steam frigates, the Mississippi (the flagship), and the Susquehanna, and two sloops named the Saratoga and the Plymouth. He was sent to deliver President Fillmore's letter that was written in the hope of establishing trade and friendship between the United States and Japan. The United States needed harbors in which to dock its ships for repairs and supplies and wanted better treatment for shipwrecked sailors. Upon arrival in Nippon, Perry sent messages to the Japanese dignitaries but received only short and unsatisfactory answers in return. They attempted to send minor officials to deal with him but he refused. At one point he even threatened to land with armed forces if an answer was not soon forthcoming. Reluctantly, he withdrew his boats and troops for the winter with the promise of returning in the spring for his answer. This time, upon his arrival in February 1854, he was met in a much friendlier fashion. This was more likely due to the fact that he now appeared with 10 ships instead of four. They were all powered by steam and mounted with many large guns. The Japanese referred to them as the "Black Ships" because of the clouds of black smoke they produced. These clouds could be seen all over the countryside, and the Japanese were undoubtedly impressed with the display of force. Perry proceeded to play upon their fears. This time they put up no resistance and before long trade negotiations were underway. The Kanagawa treaty, opening the small ports of Shimoda near the Bay of Yedo and Hakodate in the north was signed on March 31, 1854. Soon treaties with other European countries followed. By 1865 Japan was opened to world trade and ensuing contacts with the West brought a flood of European art to her shores. Japan had thus been rediscovered, her isolation was ended, and a new life begun.

The Japanese have a long history with the making of pottery and porcelain-type products. According to carbon dating, pottery making can be dated back to around 2500 B.C.E.

in Japan. So it should be no surprise that once Japan was open for trading, one area they would concentrate on would be the making of porcelain products. The Japanese have always had an eagerness to learn from others, and now native painters went abroad to study and learn the ways of the new world. It has been said that the Japanese are "conscious cultural borrowers," they seem to have the capacity to borrow and adapt, making it something new and quintessentially Japanese. They merely reshape everything to suit their needs.

During this period the Japanese government also hired thousands of foreign experts to come to Japan to train their people. The artists began imitating the European styles or trying to combine both those of the Eastern and Western manners. There were no copyright laws and the Japanese copied whatever they admired. They were highly skilled and capable of quickly learning new techniques. They had previously copied the master artists from China but in order to satisfy this new Western market, they now copied the arts of many other countries. Occidental decoration was being painted on Oriental wares.

The Japanese first exhibited in the West at the International Exhibition in London in 1862. They also exhibited at the Centennial Exhibition of 1876 in Philadelphia, the Paris Exhibition in 1878, and the Columbian Exposition in Chicago in 1893 had a large exhibit of Japanese items. The new styles and patterns took the West by storm and for a number of years everyone went Japanese mad. The country of Nippon now began to enjoy unprecedented prosperity.

In 1868 Emperor Mutsuhito mounted the throne, beginning the Meiji period, meaning enlightened rule, which was to continue until his death in 1912. The feudal system was suppressed in 1871, marking the rise of the upper middle classes led by the powerful trading families. Previously, the merchant had been placed at the bottom of the social scale but now began to dominate economic life.

During this time, however, Japan also found herself with a minimum of land and an over abundance of labor. There were approximately 40 million people living in Japan in 1891; by 1909 this figure had risen to 50 million. Industry kept growing and the search for overseas markets for goods became vital. Low wages were paid to almost all of the workers, with employers claiming this was necessary to enable them to compete more effectively. Japan's prices were thus kept low, enabling her to sell goods all over the world.

It was against this backdrop that the Nippon era, as we know it, began in 1891 with the enactment of the McKinley Tariff Act. The McKinley Tariff Act stated that all wares coming into the United States from foreign countries had to be marked with the country of origin in legible English words. The Japanese began marking their wares with the word "NIPPON" which is the Japanese word for Japan. They would continue to do so until 1921 when they were forced to begin using "JAPAN" as the country of origin.

The decade from 1912 to 1926 greeted a new emperor in Japan, Yoshihito, who took the name of Taisho, meaning great peace. This was a period much like the one that had preceded it. Increased trade continued with Japan, and she found herself adapting easily to the foreign cultural influences. It was during this decade that the majority of Nippon dolls and toys were produced.

The Japanese have always had a reverence for dolls. They are treasured and a sacred part of the household with the dolls being treated as a real child. To the Japanese a new doll is only a doll, but if it has received the love of generations, it takes on a soul. Old dolls are not just thrown out but are either burned or thrown into running water or dedicated to the God Kojin.

Sacred to Kojin is the enoki tree and the tree is often found on the grounds of temples. By the tree is a little shrine and there the remains of the worn out dolls are laid. Seldom, if ever, are the dolls given to Kojin in the owner's lifetime.

In ancient Japan, wooden dolls were used as a protective amulet against illness. For wives who felt betrayed by their husbands, dolls were made of straw in his likeness and pierced with nails. The doll was then placed under the husband's place of nightly rest in the hope that this would make the husband have a change of heart.

Japan is a country noted for producing beautiful ceremonial dolls. The third of March each year is designated as the Dolls' Festival which has been celebrated for over 900 years. It is a time when little girls set up displays of their dolls, many of which are heirlooms, having been passed down from generation to generation. The Japanese believe that these dolls reflect Oriental life and traditions. This occasion, Girls' Day (also known as the Peach Festival) is called *Hina Matsuri* in Japanese and honors the daughters of the family while two months later a similar festival is held on May 5th which is called Children's Day (originally Boys' Day). These doll festivals are occasions where friends and relatives gather to view the displays and enjoy refreshments.

Several days before the festival begins the house is thoroughly cleaned and the dolls are taken from their boxes where they have been safely stored all year. The dolls, which usually number 15, are placed in the best room of the house. They are then arranged in a special order on steps that have been covered with a red cloth. The dolls' stand is a tier of shelves or steps called *hina-dan*. The top shelf has miniature folding screens. In front of these screens are placed dolls representing the Emperor and Empress dressed in ancient costumes. The second step becomes the garden steps of the palace of Kyoto. This step and the remaining ones have court attendants, ministers, ladies in waiting, court musicians, and dancers. Miniature furniture and trees are also placed on the shelves. The bottom shelves contain decorative miniatures. Peach blossoms are arranged carefully around the dolls. These flowers represent happiness in marriage and also stand for feminine qualities, peacefulness, softness, and mildness.

The young girls in the family are encouraged to invite their friends and relatives to enjoy the display and refreshments during the three-day ceremony. The girls are responsible for planning the menu and shopping. Tiny fish, small vegetables, cakes, and teas are served.

Japanese store windows are also decorated with peach and cherry blossoms at this time.

The fifth of May is set aside as a special holiday when displays of figures of Japanese heroes and warriors abound. Children's Day (originally Boys' Day) *Kodomoni-Hi,* sees carp shaped flags flown in front of houses where boys live because the carp is symbolic of strength.

The boys' display usually consists of three to four steps covered with a green cloth. The top step has banners showing drawings of famous battles. Placed on the steps are dolls that represent Samurai warriors and dolls in ancient dress. Horses are also included. Vases of iris flowers are used in the display as the iris is sword-like and the Japanese associate them with warriors. The dolls are given to boys for display and are not used as toys. They are put away after the festival and stored until the next year. Refreshments are also served at this occasion.

It is not known when the Japanese first began producing dolls for children's play or to be sold commercially. We do know, however, that they have a long history of dollmaking. It is reported that one family in Hakata began making dolls in 1596 and was still making them in 1955. *Collector's Encyclopedia of Dolls* makes note that *La Poupee Modele* reported in 1863 that a true Japanese doll was a real curiosity in the Western World. It is likely that the Japanese dolls mentioned in the *La Poupee Modele* report were exhibited at the 1862 International Exhibition in London.

In the next chapter, "History of Nippon Playthings," we will take a closer look at the

Nippon years of doll and toy production.

THE JAPANESE DOLL FESTIVAL.

DOLLS play so important a part in the lives of the little girls of Japan that a whole day is set apart in their honor. On the third of April big dolls and little, lordly dolls and poorly clad, are brought out from the boxes and drawers, where they are stored from generation to generation by every Japanese family, and displayed in the best room of the house for the delight of the little daughter of the family.

For this is girls' day, when for once in their lives the little girls of Japan are more important than the boys. All are gaily dressed in holiday kimonos, and devote themselves to entertaining the family dolls, offering them both food and drink. Then they strap the dolls on their backs, as Japanese mothers strap their babies, and take them for an airing.

This picture shows the celebration of the Doll Festival by the children of the Shinai Mission Kindergarten at Beppu, Japan. The program of the Methodist Centenary Movement, to carry out which $105,000,000 is now being raised for the building of schools, orphanages, hospitals and churches, will aid in giving Japanese girls a more important place in the family and national life in Japan.

History of Nippon Playthings

The Nippon era began in 1891 with the enactment of the McKinley Tariff Act. In October 1890, Congress passed the McKinley Tariff Act named for Rep. William McKinley who sponsored it. McKinley drafted this bill at the insistence of the Easterners in the United States who wanted more protection for U.S. manufacturers. The tariff act of the Fifty-First Congress stated the following:

> *Chapter 1244, Section 6: That on and after the first day of March, eighteen hundred and ninety-one, all articles of foreign manufacture, such as are usually or ordinarily marked, stamped, branded or labeled, and all packages containing such or other imported articles, shall, respectively, be plainly marked, stamped, branded or labeled in legible English words, so as to indicate the country of their origin; and unless so marked, stamped, branded, or labeled they shall not be admitted to entry.*

Therefore, all articles coming into the U.S. from Japan had to be marked with the country of origin. Nippon, which means "Land of the Rising Sun" is the Japanese word for Japan so it was only natural that they used "Nippon" as the country of origin on their export wares. Of course, they were not precluded from using "Japan" on exported items, and it is likely that many items produced during the Nippon era were marked "Japan." In this book we are focusing on those items that are marked "Nippon" or items which we can definitely place in the Nippon era such as the Morimura Brothers dolls.

It is difficult to write about the history of Nippon dolls and toys without focusing on the World War I era beginning in 1914. We know that the Japanese were exporting dolls and toys prior to World War I but there is very little documentation available about what types of items the Japanese were exporting or who in Japan was producing dolls and toys. A 1920 *Playthings* article had this to say about the Japanese pre-World War I toy industry:

> *The toy industry is a comparatively recent development in Japan. Statistics of production prior to 1913 are of little value, due to the smallness of the trade prior to that time. The production of toys was valued at approximately $5,975,230.00 in 1913 and had increased to $8,170,216.00 by 1918.*

The table shown at the top of page 17 was published by *Playthings* in 1917 and shows the low dollar amounts for Japanese dolls and toys imported into the United States prior to 1917.

Notice that it wasn't until 1916 that Japan imported more than $5,000 worth of dolls in a year. This table also shows that in 1916 there was a significant drop in German dolls imported into the United States.

Table 3.

Imported from—	Fiscal year ended June 30—					
	1911a	1912	1913	1914	1915	1916
DOLLS.						
Austria-Hungary	....	$5,435	$6,641	$4,592	$805	$3,119
Belgium	....	8,348	4,190	668	6,085	....
France	....	12,578	8,776	12,286	5,699	6,166
Germany	....	1,384,372	1,537,964	1,791,913	1,661,511	617,333
Italy	....	200	48	58	73	4,242
Netherlands	....	3,457	2,409	338	17,251	33,199
United Kingdom	....	3,238	1,010	2,484	1,177	162
Japan	....	4,189	1,505	2,925	4,250	7,471
All other countries	....	475	641	1,232	1,280	587
Total, dolls	....	1,422,292	1,563,184	1,816,496	1,698,131	672,270
OTHER TOYS.						
Austria-Hungary	$155,757	174,646	178,662	177,809	113,922	25,572
Belgium	48,966	45,142	57,062	69,092	22,531	....
France	224,517	169,591	156,316	206,194	156,507	98,551
Germany	7,078,880	5,596,757	5,362,810	5,926,941	5,125,764	1,758,663
Italy	1,650	2,161	4,627	2,900	1,325	1,321
Netherlands	25,638	1,622	5,216	8,696	47,083	19,405
Norway	42	3	2,477	30	40	5
Russia in Europe	4,474	2,971	3,890	143	196	151
Switzerland	10,449	10,413	10,214	9,896	7,766	1,671
United Kingdom	113,160	145,098	286,657	421,182	435,420	137,448
Canada	2,886	744	1,017	7,774	3,608	4,329
Brazil	1,251	....				
Japan	295,641	320,241	301,249	434,006	470,345	494,248
All other countries	1,524	1,901	2,174	2,860	2,725	3,407
Total, other toys	7,964,835	6,471,290	6,372,371	7,267,523	6,387,232	2,544,774
Grand total	7,964,835	7,893,582	7,935,555	9,084,019	8,085,363	3,217,044

a Dolls included with " other toys."

We will probably never know for sure what types of dolls or toys were produced by Japan in the years prior to World War I. A review of *Playthings* published prior to World War I provides us no information — there were no articles or advertisements for Japanese made items. Nor does there appear to be any documentation available in Japan as much of it was destroyed during World War II. It is likely that the dolls being imported were lesser quality all-bisque dolls or the traditional Japanese souvenir dolls. Butler Brothers Fall 1908 catalog had the following descriptive listing for Japanese dolls:

3½ in. clay body, painted features, felt topknot, gay paper dress. 1 gro. in box. Gro. 72¢.

Papier mache dolls, 3½ in., painted features, felt topknot, asstd. colors, crimped paper dress, with voices, ½ gro. in box. Gro. 98¢.

4½ in., papier mache head with hair, imit. glass eyes, painted features, strong crepe paper asstd. color kimonos with tinsel sash. 1 doz. in box. Doz. 25¢.

7½ in., like above with cloth kimonos, 2 doz. in box. Asstd. Doz. 27¢.

Ht. 6 in., glazed clay head, feet and hands, painted features, good topknot, gaudy paper dress, 1 doz. in pkg. Doz. 35¢.

8 in. like above with crepe cloth kimonos, Doz. 75¢.

9½ in. glass eyes, painted features, natural hair, fancy cloth kimonos, with voices,1 doz. in box. Doz. 89¢.

11 in. papier mache head, painted features, glass eyes, real hair, free arms and legs, fancy figured crepe paper kimono, moving head, each with voice, 1 doz. in box. Doz. 89¢.

We have advertisements from another 1908 Butler Brothers catalog showing that a wide range of Easter items were being produced, and it's possible that other holiday items were being made as well. As for other types of toys, it's likely these were lesser quality toys and novelties made of wood, metal, and papier-mache.

In 1914 when hostilities in Europe escalated into World War I, German doll and toy production was severely curtailed although it would be several years before German imports were cut off entirely. World War I gave the Japanese an opportunity to expand into lucrative American markets, and they were quick to do so. A 1917 Japanese doll patent states that its design "would make the doll strong enough to be suitable for exporting" and Froebel-Kan was already working on a process for making glass doll eyes (which was also patented in 1917). A 1915 Morimura Brothers advertisement announced that they were "in a position to supply the American trade with original, quaint, well made and profitable merchandise from Japan" including dolls, wooden toys, toy tea sets, holiday novelties, stuffed animals, and celluloid toys.

The table to the right published by *Playthings* in March 1917 shows the dramatic increase in Japanese exports from 1914 through 1916. Of particular note is the number of countries that Japan was exporting toys to, including England, Canada, and Australia.

Although German doll and toy factories had been converted to wartime activities, the Germans had large supplies of completed dolls and toys in warehouses. American importers and distributors continued to obtain as many of these items as they could. After the sinking of the passenger ship, *the Lusitania*, in May 1915, the U.S. turned against Germany, the war escalated, and anti-German sentiment became the order of the day. In an August 1915 *Playthings* Julius Baer of Louis Wolf and Company reported that "nearly half of all the dolls and toys sold in America at Christmas are made in Germany and if these shipments, now ready, are not permitted to go through, the supply will be much less than normal…At our assembling plant in Sonnenberg we have 20,000 cases of dolls and toys, all finished and ready to be shipped, but since the blockade has

THE JAPANESE TOY TRADE.

JAPAN'S exports have increased when compared to previous years. For example, the following list shows what the nine months' trade in 1916 is when compared to twelve months in 1914 and 1915:

Countries.	1914. Yen.	1915. Yen.	To Sept. 1916. Yen.
China	229,463	204,353	200,593
Kwantung	33,259	43,443	35,348
Hongkong	178,189	79,582	81,037
India	281,862	510,674	762,797
Str. Settlements	91,403	56,098	127,846
D. India	83,409	93,332	238,989
Philippines	27,827	78,319	59,620
England	332,167	1,596,648	1,292,046
France	15,296	14,581	24,443
Germany	64,907	......	......
United States	828,889	1,100,709	1,624,975
Canada	42,715	96,497	263,446
Australia	73,945	521,056	675,162
Others	186,481	138,176	333,099
Total	2,489,792	4,533,486	5,722,399

The above shows the marked increase of Japan's export to foreign markets.

Most of the toys sent to England are of tin and celluloid.

The articles shipped to America are imitation of German makes, such as dolls and wooden goods.

Not only the above products, but all kinds of toys, are now made, and the quality, too, has improved.

been in force it's useless to ship further orders…." Even so, some German dolls and toys still made their way into the United States probably because Germany had dolls and toys stored in Dutch warehouses. A George Borgfeldt advertisement from October 1915 states "Immense shipments just arrived from Rotterdam…." It would not be until 1917 when the United States entered the war that German imports were completely stopped.

The sinking of the *Lusitania* and the U.S. entrance into World War I created havoc for some American doll and toy importers as they had to quickly find alternate sources for merchandise. Many importers had already gone to Japan for merchandise, but those that had not yet done so were soon on boats heading to Japan. A February 1917 Playthings notice provides this insight: "the 1 or 2 buyers who had intended to make trips to the European toy centers have abandoned the idea now that the break has come between the United States and Germany. Many of the buyers…are now in the Eastern Markets." Indeed, after the German imports were halted, both importers and large department stores rushed to Japan to secure shipments of dolls and toys.

Getting playthings from Japan was no easy task however. There was a language barrier and a lack of knowledge as to the American lifestyle. The Japanese workmen did not always understand what the importers wanted and some items had to be returned to Japan; therefore, it was necessary for samples to be taken over to Japan and some Japanese companies secured American expertise to help to supervise production.

JAPANESE TOYS.

HALF the stock in a leading Tokio toy factory has been taken by a New York concern, and several American toy experts are now on their way to Japan to direct the manufacture of the goods, according to a bulletin issued by the Japan Society. It adds that Americans are better able to judge the tastes of their countrymen than are the Japanese, and that toys made under the supervision of these experts are certain to be in greater demand. A new $500,000 concern, the Nitto Toy Manufacturing Company, has chosen several Japanese juvenile story writers as its advisers. Improvements in the designs of Japanese toys are therefore to be expected.

There also appears to have been problems in shipping the large amount of merchandise to the United States. This news note from the July 1917 *Playthings* gives some information on the shipping situation:

And, as these next two notices indicate, even a year or more later Japan was still having problems getting merchandise shipped over to the U.S.

Julius I. Baer of Louis Wolf & Company has sent to "Playthings" a very interesting clipping from the "Japan Advertiser" published in Tokio, Japan. According to this well-known Japanese newspaper, there are now more than eighty thousand tons of goods valued at more than seventy-five million yen, awaiting shipment at Yokohama. A conference has been held in which many important Japanese shipping magnates took part for the purpose of discussing means of providing vessels to carry these goods. It is stated that fifty thousand tons of toys, valued at five million yen, are included in the figures given above.

The Solomon-Heineman Co., 524 Market street, reports that it is one of the very few firms on the Pacific Coast fortunate enough to get Japanese toys this season, and they expect to be able to deliver 90 per cent. of their orders. Last year it was 100 per cent., but traffic conditions were not so congested then as now. A. A. Solomon reports that for several weeks back Japanese merchandise has been arriving on every steamer, and so far they have been fortunate enough to secure permits to ship all their orders.

Buyers of Japanese toys report that makers of playthings in Japan are showing irom a 75 to a 100 per cent. increase in the output of these goods this year over last, and if they had been able to secure space on the steamers, it would undoubtedly have been a 100 per cent. increase.

Haber Brothers, with new and larger showrooms at 91-93 Fifth avenue, are especially well prepared this year to supply their popular Japanese lines from stock and on import. Huge quantities of their Jap playthings were held over from pre-restrictions days—and with the resumption of import trading in these toys the buyer benefits. Bisque dolls, bisque doll heads, wood and metal novelties, accordeons, paper specialties and all the well known lines can be procured.

January 1919 Playthings *notice.*

Even with these problems, it was only a matter of time before all of the major doll and toy importers — Haber Brothers, Louis Wolf & Company, George Borgfeldt, Foulds & Freure, Inc. to name a few — were advertising Japanese dolls, toys, and holiday items. In just two years Japan had become a major exporter of dolls and toys. In fact, in 1918 so many Japanese dolls and toys were being imported that an embargo was placed against Japan because they were "flooding the market" with dolls and toys. This embargo did little good since most of the import companies were American. Also some distributors imported only the doll heads, assembling and dressing the dolls here. The embargo was quickly lifted and Nippon dolls and toys were again arriving in the U.S.

During the height of the Nippon doll and toy era, all of the major doll and toy importers as well as many smaller import and novelty companies were importing and distributing Nippon playthings. Major retailers such as Montgomery Ward, Gimbels, and Marshall Field & Company were also quick to procure Nippon playthings. Gimbels, in December 1917, proudly announced "The Dolls Are Here!" and went on to say "those in our Japanese bureau worked like beavers to get the dolls for us...."

Morimura Brothers, a leading Japanese import company, was one of the first companies to begin doll production. In 1917 they established the Nippon Gangu (Japan Toy) Company and constructed a factory in Nagoya for the sole purpose of making Morimura bisque dolls. Other companies such as The Tajimi Co. and Yamato Importing Co. began producing their own line of dolls and, there were a number of manufacturers of celluloid toys including Ando Togoro, Sekiguchi Co. Ltd., and Aiba Kintoro. Little is known about what other companies were producing Nippon era playthings. We do know that, except for bisque, celluloid, and better grade metal toys, much of the toy production was still a household industry with many items made by hand, not machine. This curtailed production because of a shortage of labor and also led to the manufacture of toys that were not of a uniform quality. There was little, if any, quality control performed by the Japanese manufacturers so even items of a substandard quality were shipped out.

By 1920 the Nippon era of playthings (especially dolls) was quickly drawing to a close. As this November 1920 notice indicates, with the war over and European doll and toy makers back in business there was now a glut of dolls and toys on the market. This over abundance appears to have made the Japanese dolls and toys easily expendable.

> ***"Big Doings" at the Emporium***
>
> No shortage of goods can be observed anywhere. As one goes from store to store, it seems to be a case of "an embarrassment of riches," so large and varied are the different displays. Dolls seem to be the most featured of all the lines. Stores like the Emporium and the City of Paris have Parisian fine ladies and exquisite dancers in addition to baby dolls, and dolls in all kinds of attractive designs and clothes. The dolls from Nippon are retailing in some of the cheaper stores for fifteen cents, clothes and all. As an instance of the abundance of toys, it may be mentioned that a large auction house, this week, is advertising that it has $10,000 worth of Japanese toys to be auctioned off, the auctions going on daily.

November 1920.

Japan was facing competition from the return of Germany to the doll market as well as from the United States in the form of composition dolls which were continuing to grow in popularity. As the following October 1920 *Playthings* statement indicates, there was even an anti-Japanese movement forming in the United States:

> *Large quantities of toys have come and are coming from Japan, but there is not a cordial feeling on the Pacific Coast for playthings made under Japanese labor conditions. Apropos of a ship, laden with toys, that recently reached Seattle from Yokohama, Senator J. M. Inman exhorted Americas not to patronize articles "made under the cheapest labor conditions." He emphasized the fact that American manufacturers cannot compete with the wages paid to toy-makers in Japan.*

Morimura Brothers announced that they were having problems meeting manufacturing goals "which are due to the constant increase in wage scales as well as almost prohibitive prices of raw materials." Morimura Brothers stopped producing and exporting dolls and toys when it closed Nippon Gangu (Japan Toy) in 1921. The other Nippon doll companies were experiencing similar problems and the advertisements in 1921 all reflect a similar theme: Nippon dolls at "Greatly Reduced Prices."

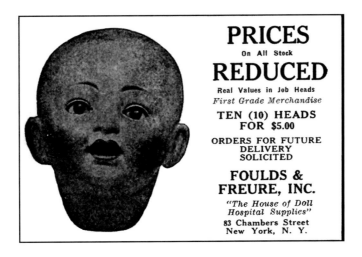

In March 1921 the United States government decided that the word "Nippon" was a Japanese word and that, as of September 1, 1921, goods from Japan must be marked "Japan" in place of "Nippon." This brought an end to the Nippon era of dolls and toys even though Japan would continue to manufacture many types of toys, dolls, and holiday items for years to come. Perhaps the best information on the history of Nippon playthings is that which was written during the Nippon era. We are including in this section several *Playthings* articles in their entirety. These articles provide a great deal of insight into the Nippon doll and toy industry of that time.

The Japanese Toy Trade

JAPANESE toys now find their largest sale in the United States and England. No department of Japanese industry has made more progress since the outbreak of the great war than the toy trade. The Japan Magazine has an article on the subject that will interest those Americans who buy toys for their own or other people's children. Its author, S. Kamiyama, is an authority on the subject. He says: "Four years ago, the export of Japanese toys was limited to a few varieties, such as dolls, bamboo models and the like. A great change has taken place. Last year the total value of toys exported from Japan amounted to $4,200,000, and in 1918 will exceed $5,000,000! Thus the 'land of dolls and flowers,' as Japan has been so charmingly called, has been transformed into a country creating playthings of every description for the children of foreign lands, as well as for its own. One might have supposed that owing to the cheapness of labor in Japan it long ago would have become the largest source of supply for the toy trade; but until the shutting off of the German supply the toymakers of Nippon never attempted seriously to enter foreign markets. Present increase in exportation is due wholly to efforts of Government authorities to find markets for Japanese toys in foreign markets. And only a beginning has been made!

Seizing an Opportunity.

"Officials in the department of foreign trade saw that great possibilities lay in the toy business and stimulated the manufacturers in every possible manner. They supplied samples from all parts of the toymaking world, most of which have been successfully imitated. In addition, the workmanship, peculiar to Japan, has been encouraged and improved. The largest export has been sent to the United States, amounting in value last year to $1,216,030. England comes next, taking a total value of $659,462 in 1917. The value of exports to British India and the Straits Settlements was $457,485, and to Australia, $447,664.

Japanese toymakers have risen to their opportunity with remarkable promptitude and efficiency. In another year they will meet the demands of western markets which they cannot wholly supply at present. In 1907 the extent of the exportation of toys from Japan was only $394,904; in 1917, as stated above, it exceeded $4,200,000—ten times what it was ten years ago!

Various Kinds of Toys.

"In addition to common toys made of earthenware, wood and cotton, the Japanese now fashion them from rubber, metal and celluloid. They are especially apt in mechanical toys. The story of imports of toys is in reserve order. From a value of $54,406 in 1906, imports decreased to $21,045 in 1916, and the figures for the year 1917, though not yet available, are much less. Japan may regard herself as one of the leading toy countries of the world, and it is a trade that may be expected to continue. In various other lines Japan has also gained a leading place during the war, but whether this prosperity will continue when competition revives after the war is another question. In toys, however, Japan is not likely to have any serious rivals. The toy trade has been created for Japan by the war, but it will not be destroyed by cessation of the war. The reason, as already suggested, is that material and labor are much cheaper in Japan than in any western country.

"Most wooden toys in Japan are manufactured by hand in the mountain regions of the country, where wood is plentiful and cheap. Individuals or families make them in their houses for the dealers. The chief centers for toys made in factories are Toyko, Osaka, Koyto, Nagoya and Kanagawa.

More Care and Better Workmanship.

"Some complaints have been received as to the comparative frailty of Japanese-made toys. Every attention has been paid to remedying this defect, and in future no such complaints will be justified. Toys are now made in more durable manner and of better materials, with great improvements in designs and finishings. The value of exports in toys sent from the various ports is as follows: Yokohama, $2,307,595; Kobe, $1,349,586; Osaka, $264,514; Nagasaki, $1,171, and others $250,392.

January 1919

"Viewing the destination of exports of toys from Japan more in detail it may be said that the largest supplies have gone to the following countries: British India, Straits Settlements, China, Dutch East Indies, England, France, United States, Canada and Argentine Republic. Australia, New Zealand and South Africa have also taken considerable quantities of Japanese toys. It is remarkable how the tastes of various countries differ as to the kinds of toys. Europeans like best such toys as bamboo flutes, dolls, earthenware, fans, wooden toys, cotton birds and animals, while the Americans prefer Christmas toys, such as birds, baskets, celluloid and paper, toy chairs, furniture suites and wooden dolls. Australia likes flutes, leaf work, glass toys, rubber dolls, toy mirrors, musical instruments. Dutch India imports chiefly such toys as metal leaf ornaments, paper and celluloid goods. India desires clay dolls, animal toys, and South America wants toy umbrellas, lanterns, bamboo models and dolls; while China prefers toy insects, rubber dolls, warships and electric cars."

JAPAN AND THE WORLD TRADE.
By F. H. Haywood of Morimura Bros.

September 1919

JAPAN has been the wonder and surprise of this age.

It seems only a few years since the most we knew about Japan and its country and people was the traveling circus or show troupe with its Japanese family of performers in mystery and surprise, but in a few short years, practically since the world war started, Japan has been in reality a nation of mystery and surprise for it has developed and grasped a world wide trade which it had taken Germany and other nations nearly a half century to perfect and develop.

Nations and peoples have been amazed at the ingenuity and adaptability of this race. Not only have they won a high place in world commerce of toys and dolls, but also in silks, textiles, electrical equipment and various other miscellaneous industries.

What is Japan's future outlook as to the world trade now that competition will again take place from all the European countries?

At present she holds first place in exports of dolls and toys, the same being over four million dollars for the year 1917, and she will not throw away the knowledge which has come to her. They have studied this market thoroughly as well as the competition which is liable to come from all other sources in the future, and they entered into the manufacture of these lines with the idea and intention that when the time came to meet all competition they would be able to retain their markets. While the new lines developed were at first poorly made, flimsy and crude in design, they have improved wonderfully in the manufacture of bisque head dolls, bisque baby dolls, celluloid dolls and toys, china tea sets, fancy designed Christmas tree ornaments and beads and especially harmonicas—these items now being perfectly tuned and finished in the largest harmonica factory in the world.

As a result of the war Japan is better equipped in every way to challenge the bid of European countries for foreign trade supremacy in toys and dolls. As the lines developed took the place of German merchandise their natural competitor is Germany, therefore what is the outlook as to their ability to beat German competition?

Cheaper labor, cheaper raw materials (practically all of which are produced in Japan), equal tariff conditions, possibly slightly higher freight rates, but national unity and determination not to lose this great opportunity.

As to Germany's position, while goods already manufactured before or during the war may be sent out at fairly low value especially on account of the present low price of the German Mark, a real shortage of raw materials such as copper, leather, textiles, etc., precludes any great volume of manufacturing for many months, and it is reliably reported that German labor is in bad shape, due to lack of work as well as shortage of foodstuffs and clothing. When they do begin to produce the manufacturer will be confronted with an eight-hour day for labor, greatly advanced wages, advanced costs of materials, excessive taxes and increased freights, all of which will help maintain high prices. Therefore, for a long time to come German competition will be neglegible.

Japan does not attempt to compete with American made toys, and such toys as they manufacture are not made in America, so that Japan looks to America for its future big market and co-operation to help meet German competition.

Finally I might state that many dealers are showing a tendency to delay their purchases awaiting developments from European countries. It looks as if they will experience the same sad results as in 1918, waiting for "prices to drop." Then, buyers were finally obliged to go into the market and purchase at advanced prices and deliveries were also delayed. Under present conditions it is necessary to give Japan from 6 to 7 months to execute and deliver an order. The labor situation there is acute and labor is very scarce, due to the heavy demand for all kinds of help.

That Japan is regarded as a stable and permanent market is evidenced by the big influx of importers from all countries, especially the United States, increasing so fast that the Hotels are overcrowded, two or six sleeping in a room and even the halls and billiard rooms are used for buyers' accommodations.

Now is the time to place orders for 1920 delivery, whether wanted for the first six months delivery, or the last six months of the year, as buyers placing late orders, even as late as February, have discovered to their sorrow that all of the desirable lines are usually sold up. Fortunately many of the larger dealers have studied the situation and are already coming into the market to place for 1920. The man who waits for developments is letting his wide awake competitor get ahead of him. This is the time of opportunity, and those shrewd enough to anticipate their future needs will always be able to supply the merchandise to their customers and make progress.

THE TOY INDUSTRY IN JAPAN.
By Vice Consul H. T. Goodier, Yokohama.

THE toy industry is a comparatively recent development in Japan. Statistics of production prior to 1913 are of very little value, due to the smallness of the trade prior to that time. The production of toys was valued at approximately $5,975,230 in 1913 and had increased to $8,170,216 by 1918. During this period the imports of toys into Japan decreased from $48,886 in 1913 to $29,685 in 1918. The imported toys consist mostly in better grade mechanical devices, etc., which, although the initial cost is greater, last longer than the domestic article. The Japanese toy is attractive to the eye, but is likely to break or become damaged in a short while. Among the countries exporting toys to Japan in 1913, Germany was first, with $30,997. The United States followed with a value of $10,651. The trade with Germany ceased during the latter years of the war, but the imports from the United States increased from $10,651 in 1913 to $28,340 in 1918. This would lead one to believe that possibly there is room for a further development of this trade, especially in view of the increased wealth of Japan and the growing demand for better goods.

The toy industry in Japan is still in the household stage, save for celluloid, porcelain, and metal toys of the better grades. Thus the industry is mainly a hand and not a machine trade, which prevents uniformity of product and keeps profits down to a level lower than those offered in other endeavors. This tends to curtail production through shortage of labor. Even in the making of "factory" toys, which has shown by far the greatest development since 1913, the number of employees is reported to have increased only from 4,692 in 1913 to 7,622 in 1917.

Kind of Toys—Production Centers—Capitalization.

The principal toys made in Japan are of celluloid, porcelain, clay, rubber, metal (tin and nickel principally), wood, cotton and paper. The production of wooden toys in 1918 was valued at $782,220; of porcelain toys, $808,267; celluloid, $2,191,822; metal, $723,580.

The centers of production are Tokyo for celluloid, metal and rubber toys and dolls; Osaka for celluloid, cotton and paper toys and dolls; Kyoto for porcelain toy tea sets, other porcelain toys, dolls, paper and cotton toys; Nagoya for porcelain and clay toys, wooden toys, etc.; and Yokohama for wooden, mosaic work, and other toys of a similar nature.

The finished articles made in the homes are collected at various depots by middlemen, some of whom also export directly. Manufacturers seldom export direct, except a few of the larger ones, who have capital. The industry as a whole seems to be suffering from a lack of ready money, which may account for the non-centralization in large plants and the poor quality of the products. It is rarely that any large supply of toys of any variety is kept in stock. Toys are mostly made upon individual order from sample, and sold usually upon a thirty days' payment basis.

Two new companies are at present projected, the Nitto Gangu Kabushiki Kaisha, proposed capital, $489,500; and the Taisho Gangu Kabushiki Kaisha, with a proposed capital of $249,250. The companies now operating are capitalized at $15,000 to $50,000.

Difficulties of Export Trade—Export Statistics by Countries.

For a time porcelain doll heads constituted an important item in exports. However, inferior quality, an earlier predilection to give Mongolian features to the faces, and various other faults reacted unfavorably. At present celluloid toys are the principal item. Out of a total export of toys from Japan of $5,079,728 in 1918, $1,102,261 represented the value of celluloid articles. A considerable share of this export consisted of cheap toys for the five and ten cent store trade.

On account of the import restrictions placed on toys during 1917 and 1918 by the United States and Great Britain, and the loss of trade from Europe—exports to Spain showing the only increase to a European country—the Japanese exporter endeavored strongly to get increased trade in China, Hongkong, British India, Dutch East Indies, Peru, Chile, Argentina, Brazil, Egypt, South Africa, Australia and New Zealand.

The following table shows the exports of toys from Japan, by principal countries of destination, for the years 1913, 1915, 1917 and 1918:

Countries of Destination.	1913	1915	1917	1918
Great Britain	$165,585	$795,929	$71,924	$119,274
United States	413,191	548,702	1,889,563	808,566
China	114,387	101,869	240,941	527,674
Hongkong	88,827	37,677	76,000	178,064
British India	140,508	254,570	337,836	532,382
Dutch East Indies	41,579	46,525	144,634	267,732
Peru	3,377	3,549	39,147	74,734
Chile	4,630	2,424	77,493	142,579
Argentina	9,527	13,714	72,720	319,157
Brazil	.....	.....	31,850	114,698
Egypt	4,010	2,067	4,554	41,224
South Africa	1,446	4,903	60,974	254,722
Australia	36,861	259,755	578,859	920,764
New Zealand	.....	.....	57,010	130,857
Other	217,233	188,257	508,639	647,301
Total	$1,241,161	$2,259,942	$4,192,144	$5,079,728

Chronology of Events
in the History of Nippon Playthings

March 1891   McKinley Tariff Act passed in 1890; as of March 1891 all articles of foreign manufacture must be marked in legible English words with the country of their origin.

March 1913   Rose O'Neill issued a design patent for Kewpie; all-bisque dolls begin a period of unparalleled popularity.

December 1913   Kusutaroh Nakamura files for a Japanese patent on the "structure" of a cloth body doll with bisque shoulderplate head, arms and feet; patent No. 30441, issued on February 12, 1914, states that this design would "make the doll strong enough to be suitable for exporting."

August 1914   Germany enters World War I and German production of dolls and toys is severely limited.

1914   Froebel-Kan and Morimura Brothers begin development of glass sleep eyes.

May 1915   A German U-Boat sinks the passenger ship the *Lusitania* and U.S. sentiment turns against Germany.

June 1915   Morimura Brothers announces that their doll and toy department has been "greatly enlarged to accommodate the enormous demand for these goods."

January 1916   George Borgfeldt announces "Japanese Playthings will necessarily be a big factor in the 1916 business... Early Import Orders...are advised."

Haber Brothers advertises they are direct importers of Japanese dolls, toys, tea sets, and novelties.

February 1917   A news notice in *Playthings* states that "the 1 or 2 buyers who had intended to make trips to the European toy centers have abandoned the idea now that the break has come between the United States and Germany. Many of the buyers...are now in the Eastern Markets."

Carl Silverman introduces a new line of character babies called Blue Ribbon Babies which are manufactured in Japan.

April 1917   The United States enters the war against Germany; German imports are totally cut off.

June 1917	Foulds & Freure, Inc. advertises that they have a supply of Japanese bisque doll heads and that more shipments are on the way.
December 1917	The Tajimi Co. introduces Baby Lucy to the trade, advertising "Our Perfected Character Doll...Pronounced by all to be the Best Yet Produced in Japan." By this time most doll and toy distributors including Louis Wolf & Co., B. Illfelder & Co., George Borgfeldt, Haber Brothers, and S. Lisk & Brother were advertising Japanese dolls, toys and novelties.
1918	U.S. places an embargo against the importation of Japanese dolls but dolls continue to flood in primarily because most of the doll import companies are American.
November 1918	World War I ends; however, anti-German sentiment still runs high and many doll and toy distributors refuse to sell German-made toys.
June 1918	Foulds & Freure, Inc. advertises a large shipment of Japanese bisque head dolls, mostly character dolls, including 30 large show dolls measuring 30 to 42 inches in height.
December 1918	News note from *Playthings* states "Morimura Brothers are showing some remarkable dolls for the 1919 season...The Japanese dolls are manufactured in Japan under the personal supervision of Morimura Brothers."
1919	Louis Wolf & Co. advertises Japanese bisque dolls modeled after old German designs.
May 1919	Haber Brothers' doll, Best Baby, is refused entry into the U.S. because it looks too much like Kewpie; in 1920 Rose O'Neill and George Borgfeldt would win their infringement suit against Haber Brothers.
September 1919	Morimura Brothers advertise that they have all types of dolls including bisque head toddlers and babies; all-bisque dolls, china limb dolls, and celluloid dolls; they also advertise toy tea sets, celluloid novelties, papier mache animals, fur dogs, and toy nursing and sewing sets.
October 1919	Yamato Importing Co. announces imported Japanese bisque dolls modeled on European lines with fine facial expressions.
1920	After a falling out with the Fulper Co., E. I. Horsman turns to the Japanese to produce bisque heads for the Horsman line of bisque-head dolls.

January 1920	Morimura Brothers, due to the heavy demand for their dolls and toys, laments, "It is a difficult task to meet such demand with the manufacturing conditions as are now prevailing in Japan, which are due to the constant increase in wage scales as well as prohibitive prices of raw materials."
March 1920	Yamato Importing Co. advertises that they are the only "genuine bisque doll manufacturer in Japan."
April 1920	Baer Notion and Toy Co. announces "a large assortment of Japanese dolls is anticipated, outdoor toys are expected for the summer holiday, and the fall stock will include electrical and mechanical toys."
March 1921	The U.S. government decides that the word "Nippon" is a Japanese word and that as of September 1, 1921, goods from Japan must be marked "Japan" in place of "Nippon."
September 1921	The Nippon era ends; dolls and toys must be marked with "Japan;" some items imported during the transition are marked with both "Nippon" and "Japan."
January 1922	Morimura Brothers is out of the doll and toy business having sold their Miscellaneous Imports Department to Langfelder, Homma, and Hayward, Inc.

Nippon Playthings
"Marching Off To War"

The years preceding World War I were a time of change both politically and socially. Socialism was the social movement of the day. Population was increasing at a rapid rate. It was a time of new technology. Life was more secure, safer, longer, more comfortable, and cleaner for most people. The sense of distance among people shrank. Organized religion was in retreat. In France there were struggles between the right and the left. Germany was challenging England's control of the world's seas and markets. War seemed inevitable.

War finally broke out in the aftermath of the assassination of Archduke Franz Ferdinand, heir to the Austro-Hungarian throne by a Bosnian nationalist. In 1914 Germany declared war on Russia and France and also invaded Belgium. Britain, Serbia and Montenegro declared war on Germany. Austria declared war on Russia and Belgium; France and Britain declared war on Austria. It wasn't long before most of the European countries were at war with each other.

In 1915 Germany sank the passenger ship *Lusitania*. This would further strain relations between the United States and Germany and would cause many to boycott German products.

Meanwhile, war was continuing in Europe with Italy joining in by declaring war on Austria, Hungary, and Turkey. Then, in 1916, the war escalated even further with Germany declaring war on Portugal and Italy declaring war on Germany.

In 1917 Cuba and China entered the fracas when Cuba declared war on Germany and China declared war on Germany and Austria. By now it was clear that the U.S. would have to enter the conflict. The U.S. felt that the entire future of civilization depended on the outcome of this military struggle. War fervor had attained a terrific intensity in the U.S. and in 1917 the U.S. declared war on Hungary, Austria, and Germany.

Because the U.S. (and the world) was so preoccupied with the war effort some all-bisque and celluloid Nippon dolls were manufactured to represent miniature soldiers, medics, aviators, military police, and even Red Cross nurses. Larger dolls were often sold dressed as soldiers, sailors, and nurses. And this type of war patriotism was not limited to dolls. There were children's tea sets produced with soldiers and sailors and feeding dishes with nurses and soldiers decorating them. One particularly patriotic tea set displays a soldier carrying the American flag. These Nippon dolls and toys are a reflection of a time in history when war and patriotism were on the minds of men, women, and children alike.

Today it seems unthinkable that we would make dolls or toys that promoted or popularized a war effort, but in that era patriotism was extremely high and even touched children. When war fever took over the U.S., little girls were encouraged to get rid of their German dollies and replace them with more suitable dolls made by Japanese or American companies. Many doll hospitals advertised that they could easily provide replacement doll heads, and no doubt some German doll heads were replaced with Nippon doll heads.

This was a time when many would not patronize stores that sold German products. In fact, thousands of customers closed their accounts at F.A.O. Schwarz, the large New York toy store, because they imported and sold German products. Many stores took advantage of the situation to appeal directly to children and their parents with military or patriotic displays:

This is a time, then, for the toy dealer to feature tents, guns, swords and soldier equipment for the larger boys; rough rider, cowboy, and boy scout play suits and tin and wooden soldiers of all descriptions for the little ones.

Above all, use quantities of bunting and let Old Glory fly, for this is the time of times when the youngsters should be taught to proud of the American flag.

Playthings, May 1917

LITTLE MOTHER DROWNS GERMAN DOLLS.

Sadly, But with Her Duty Plain, Takes Play Babies to Fountain and Drowns Them.

SOMEWHERE in San Francisco a stven-year-old lassie is grieving for three darlings of her heart, but grieving with a patriotic pride that she was able to put duty above her love. Yesterday, and because they were German dolls, she took her beloved play children to the fountain in the Civic Center, and, there drowned them all. The watchman saw the little girl loitering about the fountain, apparently reluctant to leave, but it was not until after she had departed that he found what she had been doing. Then he fished out the drowned babies. They had been pretty and expensive dolls, but already their hair was dropping from their heads and the color was running from there bare forms. Nevertheless, there still remained stamped plainly on the back of each the legend that had sentenced it to a sacrificial death, "Made in Germany."—*San Francisco Chronicle.*

Some suggested that toy departments put on patriotic plays in order to attract customers and make a statement about the store's patriotism.

In October 1918 *Playthings* ran an article entitled "Arrival of Hun Toys, They Raise a Storm of Protest." In this article both wholesalers and retailers go to great lengths to explain that they do not have German toys nor do they believe it good business to stock them:

You can put us down as not going to take any of these German toys. I think it would be the worst sort of policy — suicidal — for a shop to attempt to foist these German products on the American public at this time.

Frederick Loeser & Company
Brooklyn, New York

At the meeting of the American Relief Legion there were numerous suggestions on how to deal with the possible importation of German products and how to keep these products out of the hands of the public. One plan advocated was to collect all German-made toys and on a selected date — to be called "National Destruction Day" — make a huge bonfire in various localities and burn all of the toys! This feeling of patriotism and anti-German sentiment would remain for several years after the end of the war.

The war continued until November 11, 1918, when the armistice was signed between the Allies and Germany. The Allied conference at Versailles agreed on peace terms with Germany, and in 1919 the German peace treaty was signed. At this time the European countries set about rebuilding their cities and industries and soon after Germany, as well as other European countries, was back in the doll and toy business.

PLAYTHINGS   October, 191

WARNS AGAINST GERMAN TOYS

Chairman of Defense Society Boycott Committee Tells of German Trade Plans.

That the arrival in New York of 10,000,000 pounds of toys, every piece ...to bear the words "Made in Ger-...ssibly set a precedent ...ta to be sent un-

THROW GERMAN TOYS INTO BAY, CRY WOMEN

Women's Clubs Meeting in Riot Over German Toys

Many Favor Raid on Vessel and Dumping of Dolls and Noaks Arks. "Made in Germany" Into Waters of Bay— Committee to Act.

DESTROY GERMAN MADE TOYS' CRY GROWS IN VIGOR

Women Urge City to Do A with Playthings Made in Enemy Country.

WOMEN OPEN FIGHT TO BAR GERMAN TOYS

Another Boston Tea Party Advocated at City Federation Meeting.

WANT WILSON TO STEP IN

News That Tons of Goods "Made Germany" Have Been Landed Brings Angry Protests

here was the usual moment of great ...itement near the end of the meeting the New York City Federation of men's Clubs, which held its forty-venth convention at the Hotel Astor ...esterday. It has become the custom ...r the federation conventions, which are big, brilliant, all-day affairs, to roll along peacefully to the latter part of the afternoon, when some member suddenly spring...something of moment to which ...stately rises.

GERMAN TOYS CALLED MENACE

'INTO THE OCEAN WITH HUN TOYS,' WOMEN'S SLOGAN

"Down with All Made in Germany Articles," Urge Member of Federation at Meeting.

Boston's famous tea party will look like a ...mild affair in the perspective of the proposed act of the members of the New York City Federation of Women's Clubs, who yesterday were urged to dump the entire shipment of "Made in Germany" toys re-...received here, into the bay.

WOMEN WANT GERMAN TOYS PITCHED IN RIVER

Meeting of Club Women in Uproar Over Arrival of Cargo From Rotterdam

The reception that is likely to be accorded German toys should any of the shipment from Rotterdam, which has arrived here, appear in any of the stores, may be judged from what occurred at a meeting of the New York City Federation of Women's Clubs, which met at the Hotel Astor yesterday. The 2,000 women who attended the meeting were prepared for anything, not excluding a "toy-party" to which the historic "tea party" by which our American ancestors first showed their estimate of their foe.

ASKS AMERICANS TO SHUN ALL TOYS 'MADE IN GERMANY'

REFUSE TO ACCEPT GERMAN-MADE TOYS

'Made in U.S.A.' to Rule Gifts of Christmas Toys

'INTO THE OCEAN WITH HUN TOYS, WOMEN'S SLOGAN

...th All Made in Ger-cles," Urge Members ...eration at Meeting.

ADMISSION OF GERMAN TOYS CALLED MISTAKE

Flood of Cheap Goods by Way of Neutral Lands Feared.

WOMEN OPEN FIGHT TO BAR GERMAN TOYS

Another Boston Tea Party Advocated at City Federation Meeting.

WANT WILSON TO STEP IN

News That Tons of Goods "Made In Germany" Have Been Landed Brings Angry Protests

"TORCH FOR THE TOYS," CRIES A CLUB LEADER

"If Uncle Sam refuses to protect ... people from the shame of ... of German-made toys on sale ... in this crisis of the world's ... ry, the women have no choice."

Women Unite To Keep Out German Toys

Modern "Boston Tea Party" Threatened if Goods Reach Public

A BAS "MADE IN GERMANY."

Isn't it rather premature, this economic invasion Germany seems to be making? And through such a sweet medium! Such a delicate idea, this, dumping toys, with the hated "Made in Germany" stamp in a neutral country, so that after the war, or perhaps before, they may flood the world's market again—subtle propaganda. There is a comic element in the arrival at this port of about 10,000,000 pounds of German toys, consigned to local importers, with old-world names. Now that the toys are here what can the importer do with them? Sell them, you will undoubtedly say, before you stop to think. True, that might have been the plan, ...out the boycott committee of the American Defense Society is not willing that there be put into the hands of American children "toys made by the German hands which drip with the blood of countless innocent non-com-

GERMAN MADE TOYS REFUSED BY OWNERS

Butler Brothers Will Not Accept 109 Cases and See Teuton Propaganda.

DIDN'T ORDER SHIPMENT

Some Firms, However, May Accept Consignments and Store Them Till After War.

Wants Loyal Americans to Boycott German Toys

GERMAN CUNNING SEEN IN SENDING TOYS TO AMERICA

000 worth of German made ...hina arriving here unex-...ednesday on a Holland-...e steamship will never, it ...rday, be hung on American ...rees or arouse the interest ...l youngsters from glittering ...ws.

...the largest wholesale toy ...e country has refused to ac-...re of the consignment and ...sted other firms will take ...on. The toys were bought

A sign of the times.

All-bisque doll dressed as sailor.

All-bisque doll dressed as Red Cross nurse.

All-bisque figural medic and nurse.

Child's creamer.

All-bisque aviators with Nippon aviation plaque.

Celluloid aviator.

Child's tea set.

Plate from a child's tea set.

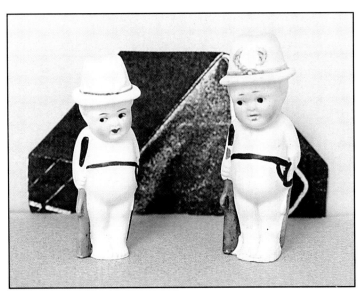

All-bisque figural soldiers.

All-bisque figural foreign legionnaire.

All-bisque figural dough boy.

Nippon Playthings
Wholesalers and Retailers

In this chapter we will take a look at some of the companies which we know sold, either wholesale or retail, Nippon playthings. Many of the companies identified here are the major doll and toy import firms, usually located in New York City, that had a significant impact on the sales of Nippon playthings.

Today, names such as George Borgfeldt, Foulds & Freure, Haber Brothers, Louis Wolf & Company, and S. Lisk and Brother are unknown to many collectors, but these companies played a major role in the design, development, manufacture, and sale of Nippon playthings. Because many of them actually went to Japan to assist in the transfer of knowledge regarding what Americans wanted in their dolls and toys, the quality of Nippon dolls and toys improved. Of course, this was somewhat self-serving because the American importers/ distributors had a lot to lose if they couldn't provide the American public with the dolls, toys, and novelties they wanted. It was to the benefit of these importers/ distributors to make sure that the Japanese could provide suitable products. That is why many of these firms sent some type of expertise and provided samples to the Japanese. It was, after all, Louis Wolf & Company who advertised Japanese dolls modeled after German designs; it is probable that an American company provided samples of the German dolls for the Japanese to copy. Therefore, it was the importers and distributors who greatly affected the Nippon playthings market. Had they not gone to Japan for these products, had they not provided samples, and had they not been willing to work with the Japanese in overcoming production obstacles, then it's possible that the retailers would not have had any Nippon playthings to sell and we would not have any Nippon playthings to collect.

Most, if not all, of the importer/distributor advertisements shown in this chapter are from *Playthings,* a popular toy trade periodical of that time period. By no means have we identified all the Nippon playthings importers and distributors. There were probably hundreds, if not thousands, of different companies across the United States importing dolls and toys including local area wholesalers and novelty companies, many of which we will never even know the names.

Known Importers/Distributors of Nippon Playthings

George Borgfeldt & Co.
Baltimore Bargain House
Butler Brothers
Foulds & Freure
Haber Brothers, Inc.
P. F. Hare & Co.
E. I. Horsman
B. Illfelder & Co.

Japan Import & Export
   Commission Co.
S. Lisk & Brother
Morimura Brothers
Nagai & Co.
Nippon Novelty Co.
Carl Silverman
Soloman-Heineman Co.

Son Brothers & Co.
Strobel and Wilkens Co.
The Taiyo Trading Co.
   (formerly known as The
   Tajimi Co.)
Louis Wolf & Co.
Yamato Importing Co.

These importers and distributors did not sell directly to the public but provided merchandise to the many retailers that were selling dolls, toys, and novelties at that time. Major department stores such as Gimbel's, Marshall Field and Company, John Wanamaker, and Lord and Taylor were selling Nippon playthings in the larger cities. Catalogs such as Montgomery Ward and Sears Roebuck and Company reached all areas of the country.

Some of these larger chains went directly to Japan to buy their merchandise, but most used the services of importers/ distributors. Of course, Nippon playthings were also sold in five and dime stores, candy stores, craft shops, general stores, toy stores, and local family-owned department stores.

Unfortunately, there is little documentation available as to what retail stores actually sold Nippon dolls and when they sold them. The information we do have came from sources such as old catalogs, advertisements in newspapers, and *Playthings*.

It is fortunate for researchers that several large retailers used catalogs as their primary means of selling during this time period. These catalogs provide us with the best indication of what was available to the public and the retail selling price. Today we are accustomed to Sears and Montgomery Ward having stores in all areas of the country. But during the Nippon era, these companies sold only through catalogs, as they had not yet opened any retail stores. Therefore, their catalogs are excellent documentation of the products of that era.

Interestingly, Sears Roebuck and Company does not appear to have sold Nippon dolls. A review of their catalogs for the years 1915 through 1921 shows that in 1915 they were selling a number of different bisque-head dolls but by 1917 were not offering any for sale. Instead they offered a selection of celluloid and composition dolls which they continued to offer, along with rubber and cloth dolls, until fall/winter 1920 when they provided a small note in their catalog that they had Fulper bisque-head dolls. In 1921 they began to advertise "imported" bisque-head dolls which most likely were the German dolls that were returning to the market. It is unclear why they did not sell Nippon dolls because they did advertise Japanese toy tea sets.

Montgomery Ward did sell Nippon dolls, toy tea sets, and probably other types of Nippon toys (although their catalogs don't specifically identify them as such). Their first advertisement for bisque-head dolls and toy tea sets appears in their November-December 1918 grocery catalog. In this catalog they advertise two dolls with this caption: "After a lapse of years I am again in your midst. Although I have been miles away my thoughts have always been with my American sisters." This was no doubt a reference to the fact that Ward had not advertised bisque head dolls in their fall/winter 1917 – 1918 catalog nor did they have any in their fall/winter 1918 – 1919 catalog. Apparently, at some point late in 1918 they had been able to obtain two styles of Nippon bisque-head dolls. This explains why they were in the November-December 1918 grocery catalog but not the fall/winter 1918 – 1919 catalog. Wards would continue to advertise Nippon dolls and toys for the next two years, 1919 and 1920.

The Charles William Stores (New York City) catalog from 1916 – 1917 has at least one wooden Nippon toy in it — a quacking duck. We believe it to be Nippon because we have an example of that toy with its original Nippon sticker. The Charles William Stores also advertised what appear to be Morimura Brothers dolls and toy tea sets in their 1920 fall/winter catalog. The advertisement for the tea sets makes note that the cover of the box bears a label with table etiquette lessons for little hostesses. These in all likelihood are Morimura Brothers' "The Little Hostess" tea sets (see chapter on Children's Porcelain).

Throughout this book you will see advertisements from the Nippon playthings manufacturers, importers/distributors, and retailers. We believe that these advertisements provide an invaluable reference as to the dolls, toys, and novelties that were available during the Nippon era.

GEO. BORGFELDT & CO.

TOYS   1916   DOLLS

Full Lines = Domestic and Import
Ready About February First

AMERICAN TOYS AND DOLLS

Our Domestic Lines have been greatly extended. Many new factories have been added. Our Display is replete with new things, ideas that will put "ginger" into your Spring Toy and Doll business.

If you have had the impression that our Toys are exclusively imported, an inspection of the American Toy and Doll Department will prove a revelation.

JAPAN

Japanese Playthings will necessarily be a big factor in the 1916 business. We have made extraordinary preparations, and the genius of the Orient is in fullest evidence here.

Early Import Orders for Japan are advised in view of the heavy demand sure to come.

EUROPE

Full Import Sample Lines of European Dolls and Toys are here, including many new things from neutral countries. Notwithstanding the War, and the consequent shortage elsewhere, OUR DISPLAY IS COMPLETE.

IMPORT STOCK

We are very fortunate in being able to offer to our friends, for Immediate Delivery, liberal stocks of imported Toys and Dolls.

These include full representation of celebrated Steiff Stuffed Toys and Animals, and the world-known Spear's Games. Surprises also await you here in the famous Richter Anchor Blocks, of which we have FULL LINES.

GEO. BORGFELDT & CO.

16th St. at Irving Pl.   **New York City**

Chicago   San Francisco   Boston   Toronto   Montreal

January 1916

January 1917

December 1917 Gimbels Department Store ad in the New York Times.

The Morimura
Brothers Connection

Morimura Brothers was perhaps the largest of the Nippon doll and toy importers, and they were a leader in the development, manufacture, and export of Nippon dolls, being one of the first companies in Japan to realize the potential of the doll and toy market in the United States. They are also the best known of the Nippon doll and toy manufacturers since they marked many of their dolls and toys with their distinctive "spider" symbol and usually the letters "MB." The spider symbol was originally used in 1906 as a backstamp for Morimura Brothers Nippon-marked Noritake porcelain. As described in Noritake's *Chronology of the Backstamps,* the design symbolized a mixture of calligraphy. The design represented the difficulty that was anticipated when Morimura Brothers started business with foreigners whose customs and ways of thinking were different from theirs and a pair of spears to break through the difficult situation. The circle meant to settle everything harmoniously.

Because Morimura Brothers is still in business as a Japanese import-export company, we have been able to obtain information from them about the history of their company as well as the history and years of their doll production.

The following information was provided by Mr. Ikuo Fukunaga who works for Morimura Shoji (Morimura Brothers, Inc. in English):

Morimura Shoji is a worldwide, import-export company. They currently import various kinds of aluminum and titanium products for aircraft from the United States, bauxite from Brazil, quartz from India, magnesium from Norway, whiskey malt from the United Kingdom and so on. They also export fine ceramics products and car parts to many countries and distribute tabular alumina produced by Moralco exclusively as the sole agent in the domestic market.

Morimura Brothers (Morimura Gumi in Japanese) many, many years ago gathered a number of potters and craftsmen to produce various ceramics under the Morimura Gumi name. For example, the Kawahara factory in Tokyo, Ishida factory in Kyoto, Saigo factory in Nagoya, and so on were all producing works for Morimura Gumi.

At that time (from the 1890s to 1920s) there were excellent designers such as Matsutaro Waki, Toranosuke Miyanaga, Yukio Takema, Tadao Waki, and Cyril W. Leigh (an Englishman) working at Morimura Brothers in New York. They drew very fascinating and very fashionable designs that would appeal to American customers.

Such designs were sent to Morimura Gumi in Tokyo. The people at Morimura Gumi took these designs to the Morimura Gumi factories and gave exact instructions to the potters and craftsmen who had never been in America or Europe. They took the steps necessary to ensure that the potters and craftsmen produced Morimura "fine" china.

At the beginning of the twentieth century Morimura Gumi decided to centralize their operation in Nagoya and moved their various craftsmen to this location. In 1904, Morimura Gumi set up their own factory, Nippon Toki (now called the Noritake Company) to produce the porcelain under their own brand name, Noritake China. Noritake is the name of the place where the factory was built.

The fine china fired in this period is referred to as "old Noritake" especially the "Nippon back-stamped porcelain." Morimura Gumi exported china of very high quality.

In the middle of the eighteenth century, Ichizaemon Morimura the First arrived in Edo (now called Tokyo) from Enshu (which means a place far away from Kyoto, the old capital of Japan). Edo was the capital of Japan in the Tokugawa era and was gradually becoming a prosperous city in the eighteenth century. The Morimura family began business at a place called Kyobashi near

Ginza. Their first venture was to produce saddles and harnesses for horses.

Ichizaemon Morimura the Sixth, the hero of the Morimura Gumi story, succeeded to the family business and it was his good fortune to be in the right place at the right time. The old Japan was about to give way to a new age of opportunity. This new tide was created by an American naval officer, Commodore Perry. Perry commanded an American fleet, the East India Squadron. In June 1853 the Perry squadron entered Edo Bay (now called Tokyo Bay). These ships known as "Kuro Fune" in Japanese, black ships in English, broke more than two hundred years of national isolation. Commodore Perry demanded that Japan be opened to international trade.

With this step, the floodgates were opened and Japan was drawn out of isolationism. In 1854 Japan concluded a treaty with America which was called The Treaty of Peace and Amity between the United States of America and the Empire of Japan. This was the first treaty Japan concluded with a foreign country. In 1859 Japan opened three ports, Yokohama, Kobe, and Nagasaki, to trade.

On July 4, 1859, American Independence Day, a consulate was set up at the Honkaku Temple to Kanagawa near Yokohama. A young American by the name of Eugene Miller Van Reed was one of the delegation members. He was an assistant to the consul, General Dorr. Soon after this, Van Reed opened his own company in the Yokohama foreign settlement and began to live there.

Maybe if Ichizaemon Morimura had not met this American Van Reed there would not have been Morimura Gumi or any Nippon porcelain. Ichizaemon was a man of enterprise who went to Yokohama soon after the opening of this treaty port to seek a business opportunity. In a short time Ichizaemon became a trader who bought foreign goods at Yokohama to sell them in Edo. He visited Van Reed's firm many times. He heard from Van Reed about America and the world in general. This information motivated him to think about a business venture overseas.

Eugene Van Reed was born in 1835 in Reading, Pennsylvania. The date of his birth is not recorded on his gravestone at the Oak Hill Memorial Park, San Jose, California. The reason why Van Reed came to Japan may be due to a chance meeting in his youth. In September 1850 a Japanese cargo ship the Gumiyoshi Maru *was wrecked in a storm on its way from Osaka to Edo. The ship drifted in the Pacific for more than fifty days. Seventeen sailors were eventually rescued by the American merchant ship the* Oakland *and brought to San Francisco.*

Eugene Van Reed, who was fifteen years old at the time, and his father had moved from Reading to San Francisco. There Eugene Van Reed met a Japanese boy by the name of Hikozo Hamada, one of the shipwrecked sailors, two years younger than himself. He learned elementary Japanese from Hikozo and took an interest in Japan, an unknown country.

Fortunately the Japanese boy Hikozo came across what is called a long-legged uncle, or a patron by the name of Thunders, a banker from Baltimore. Thunders brought this boy to his house to educate him in Baltimore in 1853. Hikozo attended a mission school and was baptized as a Catholic. After this he became known as Joseph Heco and was the first Japanese to be naturalized as an American citizen in 1858.

In June 1858 Joseph Heco visited Reading to see Eugene Van Reed. Joseph Heco wrote in his autobiography The Narrative of a Japanese, *"I was given a heart-warming welcome in Reading." It was a trip to say goodbye to Van Reed. In July, soon after this, Joseph Heco left Baltimore and on September 26, 1858, set sail for Japan from San Francisco, on board the surveying schooner* Fenimore Cooper.

*Eugene Miller Van Reed (1835 – 1873),
Hikozo Hamada / Joseph Heco (1837 – 1897)*

After Joseph Heco left America, Van Reed felt an even greater desire to see Japan for himself. Van Reed asked his friend, Jacob Knabb, who was the chief editor of the Berks and Schuykill Journal, *a Reading newspaper, to appoint him as a correspondent for the newspaper. After getting*

The Morimura Brothers Connection

Van Reed riding his horse on the grounds of his house at No. 33 in the Foreign Settlement in Yokohama.

Knabb's approval Van Reed hurried back to San Francisco.

On February 2, 1859, he took passage on a clipper called the Sea Serpent *from* San Francisco. Margaret, Van Reed's younger sister, said in her later years, "My brother started for Japan being urged by the spirit of adventure." On April 6, Van Reed arrived in Hong Kong, where he wrote "California to Japan." This article appeared in the newspaper, Berks and Schuykill Journal, *on June 25.*

Ichizaemon Morimura, who learned various things about the foreign world, such as the state of affairs in America, from Van Reed, persuaded his younger brother Toyo to enter the Keio Gijyuku University with the idea of making him proficient in English. Ichizaemon thought that English would be necessary if they were to begin a foreign trade venture.

In the spring of 1876, Ichizaemon and his brother Toyo established a small company, Morimura Gumi, at their family store, Ginza, Tokyo. On March 10, Toyo went on board an American liner, the Oceanic, *with four colleagues who wished to learn American business under the supervision of Momotaro Sato, who had stayed many years in America. He had learned business at commercial schools and had already set up his own company on Front Street in Manhattan.*

On April 10, 1876, the Oceanic *group arrived in New York. After finishing a short course at the Eastman Business College, Poughkeepsie, New York, Toyo Morimura established a retail store, Hinode Shokai meaning "Rising Sun Firm" at 258 Sixth Street, New York City, in partnership with Momotoro Sato and another colleague, each of whom invested $3,000.00.*

Two years later in 1878 this partnership was dissolved and Toyo became independent. Morimura Gumi in Tokyo was reorganized and became Morimura Brothers. Morimura Gumi in Tokyo collected various Japanese goods such as antiques, china, bronzes, fans, dolls, and so on and forwarded them to Hinode Shokai and Morimura Brothers. These Japanese goods sold very well for good prices. Morimura Brothers in New York City began to get prosperous and this situation continued until World War II.

The fine china line, a new business of Morimura Gumi and Morimura Brothers, began in about 1887. Japan had a long tradition of producing fine quality china and Morimura Gumi enlisted the services of many factories and craftsmen around the country.

Noritake dinnerware of a pure white color produced by Nippon Toki, was introduced in 1914 after a ten-year trial and error period, with great success. From this point on Nippon Toki began to produce less and less hand-painted fine china.

By coincidence this was the year that saw the outbreak of war in Europe. This prevented American merchants from importing bisque dolls from Europe, which were mainly produced in France and Germany. The American market ran short of stock and this created a favorable situation for Morimura Gumi to establish a factory for producing bisque dolls in Nagoya.

1897 photo of the Morimura Bros. store in New York City.

The Morimura Brothers Connection

Top left to right: Kaisaku Morimura, 2nd president of Morimura Gumi; Yasukata Murai, general manager of Morimura Bros., Inc.; Kazuchika Okura, the first president of Nippon Toki.

Bottom left to right: Magobe Okura, general manager of Morimura Gumi; Ichitaro Morimura, the founder of Morimura Gumi; Saneyoshi Hirose, president of Morimura Bank.

As a first step Morimura Gumi set up a ceramic research laboratory for the production of ceramic toys on the site of Nippon Toki factory in March 1916. And, in 1917, Morimura Gumi established Nippon Gangu (Japan Toy) Company with a capital of 200,000 yen and constructed a factory for making Morimura bisque dolls at Sanbon Aze 1,616, Sakou-cho, Nishi-ku, Nagoya. Hirose Jikko was made president and Yamachi Torataro general manager.

On this project Morimura Gumi worked in concert with Froebel-Kan (Froebel House in English) a playthings shop in Kanda, Tokyo, which still exists at Kanda Ogawa-cho 3-1, Chou-ku, Tokyo. Froebel House provided technical assistance and dispatched some personnel to Nippon Gangu. The Morimura bisque dolls were distributed by Morimura Brothers in the American market.

However, the First World War drew to a close in 1918 and the European producers returned to the American market. Although the quality of Morimura bisque dolls was on a par with that of European products, Morimura Brothers was forced to withdraw from the American market as they were unable to compete on price with the devaluation of European currencies. Nippon Gangu closed its door in 1921.

The business activities of Morimura Brothers in the United States continued for 65 years until 1941, the beginning of World War II.

As we have learned from the above information provided by Mr. Fukunaga, Morimura Brothers' venture into the manufacture of dolls was relatively short lived. Even though Morimura Brothers bisque-head dolls are marked "Japan," they were all produced during the Nippon era which ended in September 1921.

While the above information concentrated on the production of dolls, we know that Morimura Brothers also exported toys made from other materials, including celluloid and wood. One of their first advertisements in *Playthings* (June 1915) proudly announces that they are "in a position to supply the American trade with original, quaint, well made, and profitable merchandise from Japan." This ad goes on to say that Morimura Brothers has expanded their toy department "to accommodate the enormous demand for these goods." As late as 1921 they were still advertising toys and novelties. It is likely that Morimura Brothers did not make these items themselves but instead was the broker for other Japanese toy and novelty firms.

However, they are best known for the dolls that they did produce, and during their most productive five years 1917 through 1921, they manufactured a variety of all-bisque and bisque-head dolls.

Character babies included their famous Baby Ella. Baby Ella was one of the first dolls produced by Morimura Brothers and was still in production in 1921; therefore, it is one of

the more common Morimura Brothers' dolls found today. It bears the mold number 2 and was produced in sizes 4/0 (7" tall) to 12 (23" tall). Baby Ella can be found with both sleeping glass eyes and painted eyes. It was also the mold Morimura Brothers used for their "Crying Doll" which they advertised in 1919.

They also produced a solid dome head doll named My Darling. Collectors should be aware that the solid dome head baby does not have the typical Morimura Brothers mark on the back of the head. Instead it has only the mold number 3 followed by a dash and then the size number. Because of this marking, collectors may mistake these dolls for German dolls. Since Morimura Brothers advertised their solid dome head dolls from 1917 through 1921, there are quite a few available. However, the only way to be sure it is a Morimura Brothers My Darling is to obtain one with its original box or tag.

Another Morimura Brothers doll commonly found is their "Full Jointed Doll" which is their line of girl dolls with ball jointed bodies. These dolls are mold number 1 and again, were produced in sizes 4/0 (approximately 8" tall) through 11" (approximately 28" tall). In 1920 they would boast "Our Full Jointed Doll is the finest finished Doll made. It cannot be surpassed." These dolls had glass eyes and came with either mohair or human hair wigs.

The other type of bisque-head doll produced by Morimura Brothers was their "Kidolyn" dolls that were "Hip Jointed. Jointed Arms. Hips and Knee Jointed." As the name suggests, these dolls have shoulderplates with imitation kid bodies. They have a rather typical dolly-face, glass eyes, and are mold number 5. They were not produced in the variety of sizes as the "Full Jointed Doll" but were produced from 1917 through 1921.

In addition to bisque-head dolls, Morimura Brothers also produced all-bisque dolls in "a complete line in staple and fancy designs." Some of their well-known all-bisque dolls include Queue San Baby, Baby Darling, Baby Belle, and Dolly.

It is still possible to find some of these dolls with their original stickers which is really the only way to be sure that the doll was produced by Morimura Brothers. In addition to the original sticker, some (but not all) Morimura Brothers' dolls are also marked "Nippon" as the country of origin.

Morimura Brothers owned the rights to Queue San Baby which was patented in February 1916 by Hikozo Araki and Dolly which was patented in October 1917 by Frederick Langfelder. Queue San Baby was produced in a number of different molds and several different sizes. Today the rarest are perhaps the fully jointed and kneeling Queue San Babies. Collectors should be aware that after Morimura Brothers stopped producing dolls, German companies also produced Queue San Baby. The way to tell the difference between the two is by the sticker that is often found on the front of the doll. Dolls produced by Morimura Brothers indicate that they are "Reg U.S. Pat Off;" the German versions do not have this. Also, it is possible to find some Queue San Babies marked "Nippon," a sure sign that they were produced in Japan.

Dolly was also produced in a number of different sizes and also in a celluloid version. What is interesting about Dolly is that the celluloid version matches the patent drawing exactly, with the legs together and the head looking straight. The all-bisque version has the legs apart and the head turned to the side. Both the all-bisque and celluloid version can be found marked "Nippon." Collectors should be careful, however, because there are a number of Nippon dolls that look similar to Dolly but are not. The way to be sure is to buy one with the original label still intact.

During the years Morimura Brothers advertised many types of dolls including "Standing character dolls with Buster Brown and Sailor suits assorted," china limb dolls that repeated "our excellent line of 1919," and celluloid dolls that included "straight limb and celluloid character babies in all sizes" and a "New novelty doll in fancy costume." Today, most of these dolls are hard to identify since Morimura Brothers did not always mark or tag their dolls and, of course, on those dolls that did have tags, the tags have often been removed.

In 1918 – 1919 Morimura Brothers took over the entire output of the American 'Bester' doll factory. These dolls are composition dolls and, as the ad notes, were made in six different sizes with both mohair and natural hair wigs. It is not known why they took over the 'Bester' doll factory's complete output except that Morimura Brothers' own line of dolls was extremely successful, and they had problems filling orders for Morimura Brothers dolls. As was noted in a September 1919 ad, Morimura Brothers had sold out their entire line of

B E S T
AMERICAN MADE DOLL
"THE BESTER DOLL"

FULL BALL JOINTED

EXTREMELY LIGHT   VERY DURABLE
WITH AND WITHOUT EYELASHES
MOHAIR AND NATURAL HAIR WIGS
Made in 16-18-20-22-24-26 Inch Sizes

MORIMURA BROS.

53-55-57 West 23d Street   NEW YORK

dolls for three years running: "Since the advent of this line (three years ago) the entire factory output has been sold, usually the year previous to delivery date, so that we have been obliged to disappoint many of our customers who have not placed early. We have increased our capacity yearly, but same has not been able to keep up with the increased demand."

But even as varied and popular as the Morimura Brothers' dolls were, by 1920 there were growing problems in the production of dolls. Japan was facing increasing competition from the return of German dolls to the market as well as from the United States in the form of composition dolls. Additionally, Morimura Brothers was having problems in meeting manufacturing goals "which are due to the constant increase in wage scales as well as almost prohibitive prices of raw materials." Morimura Brothers stopped producing dolls in 1921 when it closed Nippon Gangu (Japan Toy) and sold its Miscellaneous Import department to Langfelder, Homma, and Hayward, Inc.

Froebel-Kan's Contribution

Froebel-Kan (Froebel House in English) has been in business since 1907 when 'Shiro-maru-Ya' was established by Mr. Jiro Takaichi in Toyko as makers of children's educational materials. In 1909 the company name was changed to Froebel-Kan, taking the name of Dr. Friedrich Froebel (Germany, 1782 – 1852) who was a leader in the establishment of children's education. Today Froebel-Kan is one of the leading publishers of children's books in Japan and a key distributor of children's educational pre-school materials.

When Morimura Brothers began their production of bisque-head dolls, Froebel-Kan provided personnel and technical assistance to them. We are not sure about the types of technical assistance that were provided but, based on correspondence with Froebel-Kan, we do know that Froebel-Kan played a role in the development of a sleeping doll (with patented glass eyes) which was successful after many trials. According to Froebel-Kan, this work was undertaken in 1914. In September 1915 Hikozou Araki (probably of Morimura Brothers since he also patented the Morimura Brothers doll Queue San Baby) submitted a patent application for synthetic (glass) eyes that could be used on dolls. Japanese patent number 32723 was issued in May 1917 and these patented eyes were used on Morimura Brothers dolls. We don't know for sure but it is likely that the technical assistance provided by Froebel-Kan was used in the development of these glass doll eyes. Based on this information it would appear that the Japanese did not receive help from Germany in the manufacture of bisque head dolls. Had they received German assistance they would not have struggled with the development of sleeping glass eyes since Germany had expertise in this area.

According to Froebel-Kan, Morimura Brothers also manufactured dolls for them with a Froebel-Kan mark. We have no information as to the types or numbers of dolls made or whether all of the Froebel-Kan dolls were made for export to the United States. Today, dolls with the Froebel-Kan mark are rare here in the United States. The doll pictured on page 54 is 18" tall on a ball-jointed composition body. The bisque is very thin with wonderful coloring and no flaws. She has solid black eyes and a human hair wig.

Patent No. 32723   Class 134
filed   Sep. 7, 1915
patented May 24, 1917
122 Noritake, Nakamura-aza, Aichi-gun, Aichi-ken
Applicant (also inventor) Hikozou Araki

Specification
Title: Synthetic glass eye

Character and the aim of the invention
This invention is to make the synthetic glass eye. Firstly, make a curved concavity on the top surface of the eye boll and stick a real-like iris in this concavity. Then, make a cavity in the middle of said iris, put the pupil on said cavity, and cover said concavity with a convex lens. The aim is to make the eye light real so that the appearance would look quite the same as the human's eye and to produce this said eye in a simple way.

Brief description of figures
Fig. 1 shows only the main part. Fig. 2 - 4 shows the sectional length, and is drawn in order of the manufacturing method. The same symbols appearing in the figures show the same parts.

Detailed explanation of the invention
This invention is to make the synthetic glass eye with an eye boll (1) that is in a suitable size which can be either hollow or filled inside. Make a curved concavity (2) on the top surface of the eye boll and stick a real-iris (3) in this concavity. Then, make a cavity in the middle of said iris, put the pupil (4) on said cavity, and cover said concavity with a convex lens. (5). The bottom part of said lens should fit in the shape of the top part of the iris. As for the iris, radiated lines should be made in a suitable way. Actual process of production is first to stick the colored glass (A), which is supposed to be the iris, on the top surface of the burnt eye boll (1) as shown in Fig. 2. Then, heat the end of a thin glass stick (3) and make a round shape, put another glass, which is to be a pupil (4), on the surface of the round-shaped glass. Let this stand in the middle of glass (A) and push it slightly. When doing this work, it should be done all on fire. Eventually, the top part of the eye boll will sink, and make a concavity (2) as shown in Fig. 3. At the same time, the natural phenomenon of the melting-colored-glass will make natural radiated lines and round circumference for the iris. Then, cut the part (C) of the thin glass stick

on the top part of the round-shaped glass, heat the left thin stick to melt so as to cover the empty part as shown in Fig. 4. This cover would become a convex lens (5).   The producing method may have some changes in this invention, the pupil is put in the bottom part of the concavity made on the top surface of the eye boll as described before. When the light goes through the lens, it produces a focus around the pupil which makes the eye light look real, and eventually makes the appearance look the same as the real human's eye. The curve of the concavity also makes the eye light real when they are looked at from sides. Moreover, the radiated lines make it look natural, too. The glass eye that had been made before this invention was produced ingeniously, but still did not look real. In this invention, the appearance of the glass eye looks similar to the human's eye, and not only can it be used for human beings, but also for portraits of dolls to make them look real. In short, this invention is to make a curved concavity on the top surface of the eye boll, place a pupil in this center, and cover it with a convex lens which makes it achieve its aim, and as a whole, has a complete effect.

Claims
1.In order to achieve the aim as written before, the method of this synthetic glass eye is to make a curved concavity on the top surface of the eye boll, stick a real-like iris in this concavity, make a cavity in the middle of said iris, put the pupil on said cavity, and cover said concavity with a convex lens which is explained in detail in the text, together with figures in the attached sheet

2.In order to achieve the aim as written before, this synthetic glass eye has the iris with radiated lines and round circumference that was created by the natural phenomenon of the melting-colored-glass which is explained in detail in the text, together with figures in the attached sheet.

3.In order to achieve the aim as written before, this synthetic glass eye has a convex lens that was made by melting the glass. Stick an iris on the top part of the eye boll, let a transparent glass with a bit of black glass, which is supposed to be the pupil, stand in the middle of said iris, push it slightly and make the convex lens which is explained in detail in the text, together with figures in the attached sheet.

Attached: Fig. 1-4

Fig. 1

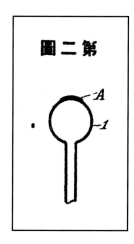

Fig. 2

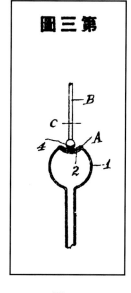

Fig. 3

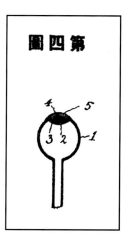

Fig. 4

Froebel-Kan doll.

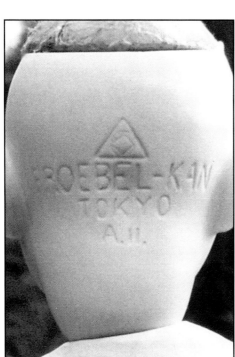

The Kewpie Infringement

The Kewpie doll is one of the most popular dolls ever made. Kewpie began as decoration for the magazine stories Rose O'Neill illustrated in the early 1900s. Rose's memories of a beloved baby brother were her inspiration. Rowena Godding Ruggles in *The One Rose* quotes Rose's own writing: "His starfish hands stretched out to reach your heart...He was a shy little cherub with wings just sprouting."

Rose told her editor, "I have for a long time called these persons Kewpies, diminutive for Cupid, and it seems to me that the name, spelled so, might be amusing to children." The first Kewpie pages appeared in 1909 in the *Ladies' Home Journal* and subsequently in the *Woman's Home Companion, Good Housekeeping*, and *The Delineator*.

Since Kewpie had been popular in print, New York toymakers thought they saw the making of a popular doll. One of them (probably George Borgfeldt) suggested this to Rose O'Neill, and a contract was drawn up and signed for the manufacture of a bisque Kewpie. In 1912 when the first consignment of bisque Kewpies arrived, they were not well received by some toy dealers. However, those dealers who had wives and children that were already Kewpie fans knew better. Women quickly embraced the bisque doll and took him home to their children.

Before the end of 1913, the bisque Kewpie, modeled by Rose O'Neill, was already being produced by more than 20 German factories. According to Rose they were made "as fast as they could pull them out of the ovens." A year later, two more factories began producing Kewpie in celluloid and six months later another factory began producing composition Kewpies. There were 12 sizes produced in bisque and five sizes in celluloid and composition. (Note: These early Kewpies are not Nippon dolls.)

The Kewpie trademark was registered on July 15, 1913, under the name Rose O'Neill Wilson. In the trademark application she claimed that it had been in use since 1912 (the year the doll first appeared). On December 17, 1912, Rose O'Neill Wilson applied for a patent on the doll itself and received a design patent on March 4, 1913 (see Kewpie patent on page 57).

(Note: A design patent is for the actual modeling or look of the doll. In the case of Kewpie, the blue wings, the topnotch, the impish grin, and the starfish hands are all distinctive characteristics of the doll and, therefore, can be patented. A trademark protects the use of the name and/or any distinguishing symbols.)

Advertisements in *Playthings* indicate that George Borgfeldt and Co. was the sole licensee of the Kewpie doll. This means that his company had exclusive rights to market the doll.

When World War I halted German production, George Borgfeldt turned to the Japanese to produce Kewpie dolls in both bisque and celluloid. These dolls often still have a heart-shaped sticker on their tummy and a round sticker on the bottom on their feet indicating that the doll was trademarked and patented. Many people feel that these dolls are also fraudulent copies; however, if that were true, Rose O'Neill and George Borgfeldt would have sued the maker of those dolls. They didn't. In fact they used a photo of a Kewpie with the heart-shaped sticker in their advertisement regarding the Haber Brothers infringement suit. Also, we know that George Borgfeldt was importing dolls from Japan during World War I, and there is no reason to believe that George Borgfeldt would want to stop producing a proven bestseller. Given this, it seems highly unlikely that all Nippon Kewpies are fraudulent copies.

The Nippon Kewpies were produced in a variety of sizes. There are at least three different sizes in the bisque version with the 4½" and 6" Kewpies being the most common. An 8" bisque Kewpie was also made, but it's more difficult to find in this size. The Nippon celluloid Kewpies came in a wide range of sizes from 2" to 22" tall. The 22" Kewpie is quite impressive (see photos on page 58).

Other doll importers took advantage of the doll industry chaos, caused by World War I, to manufacture dolls of a similar style and look to Kewpie. This is where the infringement began. In March 1917 Rose O'Neill took out her first notice in *Playthings* noting that "Kewpie dolls of which I am the Originator and Owner, are being imitated in Japan and elsewhere, and sold in this country contrary to Law and without my Authority." She goes on to say that she will take legal action against those infringing on her patent, trademark, or copyrights (see copy of notice on page 59).

Apparently this didn't stop anyone from marketing Kewpie look alikes. In December 1917 a second notice warns of infringement of Kewpie dolls and statuettes including "a Statuette in the style of a naked soldier with a gun and sword, and wearing a red cap...." The notice states that "These infringements are chiefly, though not entirely, of Japanese origin." (See copy of notice on page 60.)

These notices were apparently not just idle threats. Borgfeldt and O'Neill were successful in several patent infringement suits, the most famous being their 1919 suit against Haber Brothers' Best Baby, a doll made in Japan and shipped from Yokohama. Best Baby was refused entry into the U.S. by the Customs Office on the grounds that the dolls looked too much like Kewpie. There is no mention of whether Best Baby was ever made of bisque; however, a Nippon celluloid Best Baby was produced and a number did make their way into the U.S. (see pages 61 – 63).

Even this victory against Haber Brothers, however, could not keep out all of the Kewpie look alikes and today, it's possible to find a number of Nippon dolls, especially celluloid ones, that either bear a resemblance to or blatantly copy the popular Kewpie doll (see page 63).

UNITED STATES PATENT OFFICE.

ROSE O'NEILL WILSON, OF DAY, MISSOURI.

DESIGN FOR A DOLL.

43,680.   Specification for Design.   Patented Mar. 4, 1913

Application filed December 17, 1912.   Serial No. 737,311.   Term of patent 14 years.

To all whom it may concern:
    Be it known that I, ROSE O'NEILL WIL-SON, a citizen of the United States, residing at Day P. O., in the county of Taney and State of Missouri, have invented a new, original, and ornamental Design for Dolls, of which the following is a specification, reference being had to the accompanying drawing, forming part thereof.
    Figure 1 is a front elevation of a doll

showing my new design; and Fig. 2 is a rear elevation of a doll showing my new design.
    I claim:
    The ornamental design for a doll as shown
        ROSE O'NEILL WILSON
Witnesses:
    EDWARD HENESEY,
    OTIS F. WOOD.

Copies of this patent may be obtained for five cents each, by addressing the "Commissioner of Patents Washington, D. C."

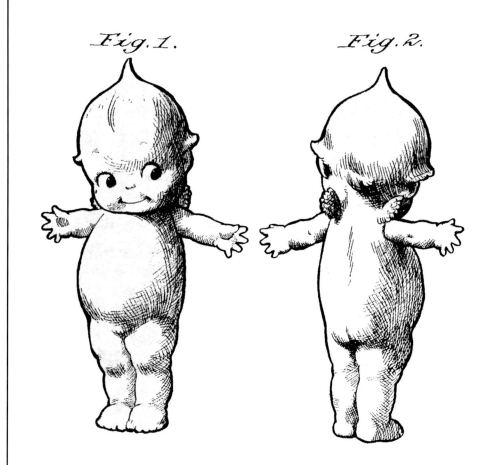

DESIGN.

R. O'N. WILSON.
DOLL.
APPLICATION FILED DEC. 17, 1912.

43,680.

Patented Mar. 4, 1913.

Fig.1.

Fig.2.

WITNESSES

Everary B. Marshall
J. P. Davis

INVENTOR
Rose O'Neill Wilson
BY *Mmmles*

ATTORNEYS

COLUMBIA PLANOGRAPH CO., WASHINGTON, D. C.

The Kewpie Infringement

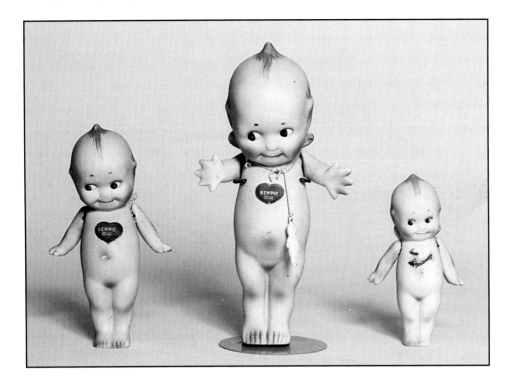

All-bisque Kewpies,
4½" – 8" tall.

Celluloid Kewpies,
3½" – 22" tall.

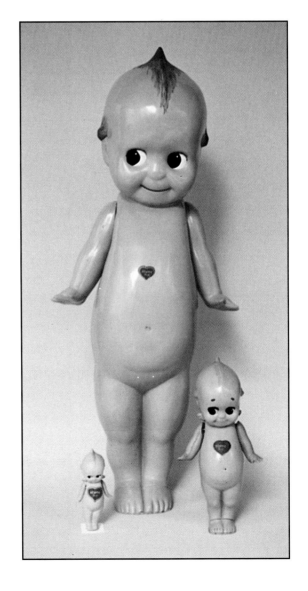

ROSE O'NEILL WILSON

WARNING

New York, March, 1917

Gentlemen:

It has come to my knowledge that

THE KEWPIE DOLLS

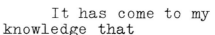

REG. U. S. PAT. OFF.   Des. Pat. 43680

of which I am the Originator and Owner, are being IMITATED in Japan and elsewhere, and SOLD in this country contrary to Law and without my Authority.

Therefore, to put an end to such ILLEGAL INFRINGE-MENTS of my Rights in K E W P I E S, and of the Design Patents, Copyrights and Trade Marks protecting them, I hereby give notice that those rights will be defended to the full extent of the Law, with demand for Accounting and Payment of Damages Sustained.

SOLE LICENSEES

GEO. BORGFELDT & CO.

NEW YORK - TORONTO - MONTREAL

March, 1917 notice in Playthings.

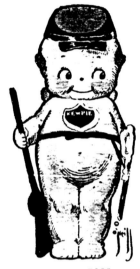

WARNING

New York, December, 1917.

TO THE TRADE:

I call your attention to certain infringements of my

KEWPIE DOLLS and STATUETTES

ATTENTION

Copyright, 1910
Reg. U. S. Pat. Off.
Des. Pat. 43,680

The pirated goods occur in various forms; they are generally of poor quality and are made mainly of bisque and pyroxylin. Besides the familiar KEWPIE DOLL, the most frequent infringement is a Statuette in the style of a naked soldier with a gun and sword, and wearing a red cap, which is taken from my book "THE KEWPIES AND DOTTY DARLING," copyrighted in 1910, and looks like the illustration above.

These infringements are chiefly, though not entirely, of Japanese origin.

Numerous reputable merchants, who were found selling such infringing KEWPIES have made a fair settlement and an agreement to cease infringing, as soon as this matter was called to their attention. I presume no further notice than this will be necessary for other concerns of the same good standing. Where this warning is not heeded, I shall take legal steps to enforce my rights; and I wish to particularly warn all Toy Buyers, both in the wholesale and retail trade, to beware of purchasing IMITATION KEWPIES of any kind, as I shall demand payment of all the profits, damages and penalties provided by the law.

Rose O'Neill Wilson

SOLE LICENSEES

GEO. BORGFELDT & CO.

NEW YORK   BOSTON   DALLAS   TORONTO
CHICAGO   SAN FRANCISCO   LOS ANGELES   MONTREAL

December, 1917 notice in Playthings.

All-bisque imitation Kewpie statuette.

November, 1920 notice in Playthings.

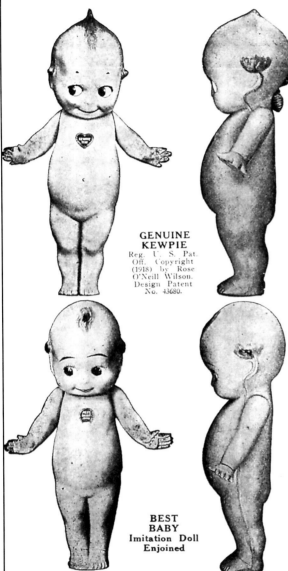
June, 1921 notice in Playthings.

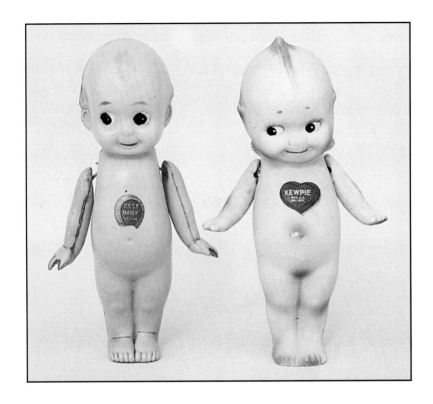

*6" Celluloid Best Baby and
all-bisque Kewpie.*

Celluloid Kewpie look alikes.

The Mystery Doll

No matter what you collect, occasionally something comes your way that is totally different from anything else in your collection. Often times this item's origin is unexplainable as well. That is the case with this doll.

There's nothing really unusual about the doll's mold; it's an FY 503 which is a fairly common mold for Nippon dolls. What sets it apart is that this doll is black. We know that the Japanese produced all-bisque black dolls and there's even a black doll with a cloth body. However, a Nippon black bisque-head doll is rare. We have no record of the Japanese producing black bisque-head dolls although since they made other black dolls, it would not be a complete impossibility.

However, there is one distinct difference between this doll and the other black Nippon dolls. The coloring on this doll does not look at all like the coloring on the other dolls. It has a warm, shiny finish to it, not the dull brown as seen on the all-bisques. It does have painted black hair that is similar to the all-bisques but not like the Caucasian FY 503 that has brushstroke hair. There's practically no lip color (it appears to have worn off) whereas the all-bisques have slightly red lips. Also, the Caucasian FY 503 has painted teeth; this doll does not. The eyebrows and eyelashes are not like the other FY 503 dolls. The dark brown eyes do not sleep and appear to be plastic.

It is the same size as other FY 503 dolls so the head is not a reproduction. (A reproduction head is always smaller than the original head that the mold was taken from.) Also, other than

The mystery doll.

being black, the body is the same type of bent limb composition body found on many Nippon dolls. The color, however, is very even with no chips or flaws, so it is very likely that it has been repainted.

Given that information, what is the origin of this doll? Was it produced by the Japanese on a special order basis? Or, did the Japanese send over "in the white" doll heads that were then decorated here? Black dolls in general are not common so was someone ingenious or devious enough to take a Caucasian doll, repaint it, and turn it

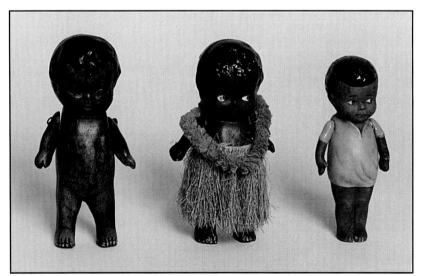

Nippon black all-bisque dolls

into a black doll? According to doll makers that is not impossible to do. In fact, that is the most likely scenario. It appears that some years ago this doll was repainted to be black probably because black dolls are hard to find. The type of paint used on the doll is not the type used today in doll making nor are the eyes the same kind as used today. So the repainting is not of recent vintage; however, it is probably not the same age as the doll either.

It's doubtful that we will ever really know the complete background of this doll or why it was repainted, but this mold does make a cute black doll and he is a charming addition to any Nippon doll collection.

Caucasian FY 503 and mystery doll.

Nippon Makes
a Fashion Statement

We dress to keep warm and comfortable, for protection, and also to make a kind of statement about ourselves. It can let others know our position in society and perhaps our power or wealth.

Before World War I the quantity of fabric in a woman's complete outfit could be as much as 19 yards. Women and children were expected to adhere to a strict set of rules regarding what outfits were appropriate to wear and when it was appropriate to wear them. The introduction of women into the work place and the fact that women wanted less constrained clothing meant that clothing styles had to change. War rationing also made skirts more practical and by the mid 1920s the amount of material in a woman's outfit was reduced to seven yards.

When the war ended, women had become accustomed to more practical clothing. The war had accelerated social and fashion changes. Dresses were at their shortest in history and would continue to get even shorter. Ohio and Utah responded by passing laws that required hemlines to be no more than 7" from the floor!

Children's fashions were changing too. Adults realized that children needed less restrictive clothing in order to be comfortable and to play. Adults began to place less emphasis on children always looking prim and proper. Children were still expected to dress properly, but there were now less layers of clothing, shorter dresses, and no tight fitting styles. Before the turn of the century female children started to wear corsets about the time they were 11 or 12 years old. By the time of World War I, children's corsets were completely out of style. Loose fitting dresses were popular for girls while creepers and rompers were in vogue for younger children.

Hats have always been a part of history, and in 1877 Charles Blanc wrote that bonnets are placed on the head not to protect it but so that they may be seen better. He said that its great use was to be charming. By the turn of the century hats were a dominating feature in both women's and children's fashions, and before World War I it was unthinkable for a woman, or a child for that matter, to be out on the street without a hat or bonnet.

By the late teens and early '20s the modern woman was wearing a cloche hat over her bobbed hair (another new fashion trend). This head-hugging hat was adorned with flowers, beading, embroidery, and/or lace. The cloche looked like a brimless helmet which was worn almost down to the eyebrows. Women's and children's wear catalogs of the time period show that other fashionable hat styles included the mushroom, the beret or tam, the Dutch-inspired toque, and the tasseled stocking cap.

To be "in fashion" has been going on for years and the molded clothes and hats found on Nippon all-bisque dolls reflect the prevailing styles of that time period. We find molded tuxedos, baby clothes, dresses, bathing suits, overalls, union suits, rompers, etc., and even belts, socks, and shoes. Of course, there are molded hats of all types.

Some of the original cloth outfits (not molded) can still be found on Nippon dolls — beautiful dresses, knitted outfits, Red Cross nurse uniforms, Oriental outfits, even hula skirts and leis. Most have not survived over the years and have been replaced with newer clothing; but it is the original outfits that tell us the most about this time in history. Children then as today, wanted their dolls to wear the same fashionable styles that everyone else was wearing. It's amazing how much our Nippon dolls can teach us about World War I era fashion trends.

5½" in original clothes.

5" twins in coordinating crocheted outfits.

Nippon Makes a Fashion Statement

Old Butler Bros. catalog ad
for World War I era hats.

All-bisque dolls with molded
World War I era outfits.

All-bisque dolls modeling
stylish hats.

*Dolls with original handmade clothes.
Note doll on right has "bobbed" hair.*

Original crocheted dresses.

*Original handmade
lace outfit.*

*All-bisque doll with home-
made gown.*

Figural dolls in typical World War I era clothing.

Doll with cloche hat and home-made dress.

5" tall; original Buster Brown-type outfit.

Boy in home-made romper.

A Morimura Brothers all-bisque doll with an exceptional array of home-made clothing including dresses, a nightgown, underclothes, a sweater, and even two hats. Truly a rare find.

Wedding Belles

Queen Victoria wed Prince Albert, and the white wedding gown began to be popular in the 1840s and 1850s as many brides followed suit. At this time, brides did have a choice of colors, and some picked practical colors for their wedding dress so that it could be worn again. However, the very wealthy usually selected white gowns.

Wedding gowns were decorated with orange blossoms or roses which were the favorite trimming. The flowers were either natural or made of cloth. The gowns were made of white satin, silk, brocade, merino, crepe de chine, georgette or even muslin. The veils were lace, tulle or illusion, but it was recommended that they be long and full. The bridal wreath and bouquet were usually made of orange blossoms, either artificial or natural, or other white flowers.

6" all-bisque bride and groom, incised Nippon. Used on an 1893 wedding cake.

4½" tall, incised Nippon.

During the late teens and early twenties cloche type headpieces with long, cathedral length veils were popular. The bandeau, which is a headband, was also used.

Today Nippon dolls can be still be found dressed in clothing from the time period when they were manufactured, and many times they are found dressed in their original wedding attire. The majority of these bride and groom sets were used to top wedding cakes, to deco-

All-bisque bridal party. Unusual because one figure is a minister.

5" tall, incised Nippon.

3½" tall, mark not visible.

rate wedding shower centerpieces, or as wedding party favors.

Most Nippon brides and grooms have clothes made of cloth or crepe paper although there are a couple of dolls that have molded wedding attire. The Nippon bride and groom dolls are usually fairly common all-bisque dolls which could be purchased for just a few cents and then decorated as a bride and groom by the purchaser. The clothes range from fairly simple costumes to elaborate styles outfitted with pearls, lace veils, and flowers. Some grooms even have their own top hats! It isn't only the bride and groom that can be found. It's possible to find wedding parties that include a minister or bridesmaids.

Wedding party. All dolls dressed in crepe paper outfits. Dolls were used at a wedding shower in the early 1920s.

4" tall #6 celluloid Kewpie, marked Nippon.

5" couple, bride only incised Nippon. A rare couple.

Wedding Belles

Women's publications like *Good Housekeeping* and *Ladies' Home Journal* published directions for making wedding party centerpieces and favors, and some, like the 1917 wedding party directions in *Good Housekeeping*, sold dolls that were already dressed in wedding attire. Many crepe paper companies also provided directions for dressing dolls as brides and grooms and for using these brides and grooms as a wedding or shower centerpiece or as party favors. Crepe paper was especially popular because it was easy to work with — it could be cut without fraying and glued in place easily. Crepe paper was also inexpensive, readily available, and came in a wide variety of colors.

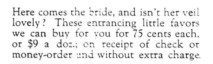

Here comes the bride, and isn't her veil lovely? These entrancing little favors we can buy for you for 75 cents each, or $9 a doz.; on receipt of check or money-order and without extra charge.

Lucky fellow, the bridegroom, you say? Lucky you, if you get him for a favor. He is priced 75 cents each, or $9 a doz., and Good Housekeeping Shopping Service will buy him for you promptly.

Wedding dolls sold in 1917 Good Housekeeping *magazine.*

The majority of the Nippon bride and groom sets are from the late teens and early twenties, but one set came with information that it had been used on an 1893 wedding cake.

5" groom and 5¼" bride. Incised Nippon, original crepe paper clothes.

4" tall, incised Nippon. Original crepe paper outfit.

Another pair was found displayed in a glass-domed case. The following note was attached on the bottom:

The wedding cake ornaments (bride and groom) were first used at the marriage of Rose Beggi (age 27) and Ralph Baird (age 26) on June 16, 1920. They are the maternal grandparents of Robin Smith. The handkerchief covering the base belonged to Olive Parker, wife of William Jackson Parker. They are the maternal great-grandparents of William I. Davis V. The handkerchief was carried by Nora Parker Davis at her marriage to William T. Davis IV on July 26, 1952. It is a delight that the two items can together adorn the cake table at the marriage of Robin to Bill on August 19, 1973.

Bride and groom from glass dome with 4¾" tall attendants.

5" bride and groom in glass dome.

Most Nippon dolls do not come with this type of history. It's always a little sad to think that these items are not still in the families of the original owners, but it's wonderful for the new owner to know of its past.

19" bisque head doll dressed as Victorian era bride. Marked "FY Nippon 403."

Nippon Bathing Beauties

Up until the 1850s the once-a-year bath was the custom for many people. Thankfully, around that time people were encouraged to start taking a Saturday night bath which became popular throughout the country. By the 1860s doctors began promoting bathing in lakes and oceans as an aid to good health, and this now made bathing attire a necessity.

Women wore trousers or bloomers under a dress that reached to their knees. The outfit was usually made of wool or heavy flannel and was layered so her figure was concealed. Stockings, bathing slippers, bathing caps, and probably even a corset completed her outfit. Imagine trying to swim wearing clothes consisting of six yards of wool or more! No wonder they were considered death traps by some.

In the teens, bathing suits became more risqué and, in fact, they became so daring that in 1922 flappers wearing the new California-style suits were carried off the beaches for indecent exposure!

Women's suits had a V-neck tunic with matching shorts and sash. The trunks were attached at the waist and the outfits were made of such materials as wool, broadcloth, taffeta, and satin. Beach caps were worn and were also known as aviator style bathing caps or diving caps. The first bathing suit contest was held at Madison Square Garden in 1916 where these daring costumes were displayed.

By 1920 men's two-piece woolen bathing suits were also replaced by the new California-style one-piece suit. During this time bathing trunks were also introduced for men.

A number of Nippon marked dolls can be found wearing bathing suits that were popular in this era. All have molded clothes and to date more boy dolls have been found than girl dolls. Light blue seems to be the color of choice for these Nippon suits, but research indicates that in actuality the most common colors for men's suits were purple, yellow, red, pale blue, or a combination of black and orange.

The Dolly doll is found wearing a bathing suit from this era. He was patented October 16, 1917, by Frederick Langfelder of New York City, assignor to Morimura Brothers. Dolly is probably the best known of all the bathing suit dolls. He is found in different sizes, both in porcelain and celluloid, and the porcelain version often still has a sticker attached bearing his name. He originally sold for 12 cents to 35 cents depending on size.

Clothes are a reflection of the times in which we live. In fact they have been called the mirror of history, and the Nippon dolls are doing just that. One nice thing about these suits, though, is that they're guaranteed never to shrink in the water!

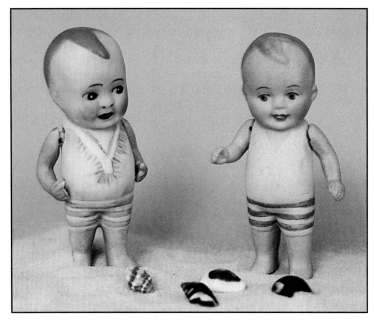

Nippon Bathing Beauties

Doll dressed in the same style
as the bathing beauties on the postcard at right.

Vintage postcard with bathing beauties
of this time period.

23" bisque-head doll
dressed in Edwardian
era bathing outfit.

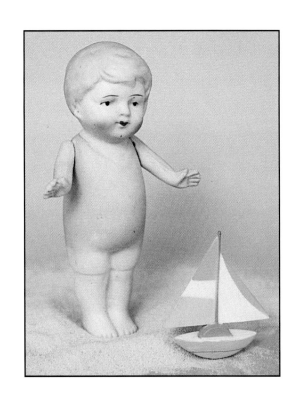

Dressing Your Bisque-Head Dolls

As was noted in a previous chapter, "Nippon Makes a Fashion Statement", the World War I era saw changes in the way women and children as well as Nippon dolls were dressed. Many Nippon bisque head dolls were sold wearing only a chemise made of inexpensive material similar to gauze or cheesecloth. It was then up to the family to dress the doll with either home-made or store bought clothing.

Morimura Brothers did sell some dressed dolls. In fact, a 1918 *Playthings* advertisement for Mrs. K. A. Rauser, designer of doll outfits, noted that Mrs. Rauser was the designer of doll outfits to the "World's Most Famous Dolls" including Morimura Brothers. No doubt other Japanese doll importers dressed some of their dolls to appeal to the American market. Most of these dolls were probably dressed in the United States, not Japan. During that time period it was also not unusual for department stores to dress dolls before selling them.

Bent limb character babies during this time period were often dressed in long baby dresses or gowns that went past the feet. Most of these gowns were made of a white cotton material such as lawn and were often trimmed with lace and ribbons. Many came with matching white cotton bonnets.

Other bent limb babies would be dressed in short doll dresses of lightweight wool or materials such as lawns, dimities, dotted swiss, voiles, and silks. These dresses would have been trimmed with small buttons, lace, and ribbons. Both the long and short baby dresses might have had knit or crochet sweaters and bonnets with them. Bent limb dolls that were intended to be boys were dressed in cotton rompers (gingham and prints were popular) or knit suits. Again, many of

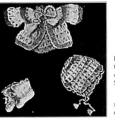

Ad in Playthings, *December, 1918.*

Ad in Playthings, *January, 1918.*

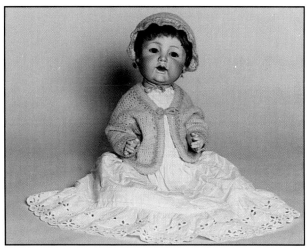

Boys dressed in vintage rompers.

these outfits would have had matching hats, especially knit hats. Baby doll footwear would have been either knit booties or shoes and socks.

The majority of child dolls were dressed as girls. The styles were often simple due to war rationing of materials; skirts and sleeves were made shorter and less full. Lace, embroidery, ribbons, and contrasting fabrics were used as trims. Waists had gotten shorter although dropped waist dresses were still used. Dresses with yokes were popular as were dresses with aprons or jumpers over them. Sometimes bloomers were used under short dresses.

Most outfits were made of materials such as lightweight wools, all types of cottons, and silks. Knitted and crocheted outfits were popu-

All original clothes: drawers, camisole, slip, dress, garters, shoes, socks, knit hat and cape. Clothes marked "Margaret Graves."

Top for sewing kit.

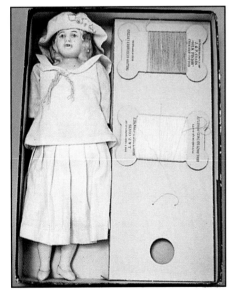

*J.P. Coats sewing kit with a 10½"
Nippon red cloth body doll. Marked
PATENT NO. 30441 NIPPON.
Very rare.*

lar as well. Dolls were occasionally dressed in suits that included a short jacket, skirt and cotton blouse. Hat styles for girl dolls were the same as for children — berets or tams, toques, cloches, mushrooms, and sailor hats. Underwear usually consisted of cotton slips and drawers trimmed in lace. Most doll shoes were made of imitation leather with low or flat heels and would either button or tie across the ankle. Cotton socks would be worn either mid-calf or to the knee.

The few dolls dressed as boys were often put into rompers, suits with short trousers or knickers, or overalls with long legs. Checked or striped shirts would be worn under the overalls. The suits would often have belted jackets and, like the girl dolls, could sometimes be found with a cotton shirt. Sailor suits had been popular for a number of years and continued to be popular for boy dolls. Hats for boy dolls were often berets and knit caps.

During the war years there was a decrease in home-made doll clothes. Part of the reason for this was a decreased emphasis on girls' learning to sew by making doll dresses. Even so most women's publications continued to publish directions for making dolls outfits. However, designing and making doll clothes had become big business in the United States and during the war era, *Playthings* had many advertisements for companies making all types of doll clothes including fur coats and fur sets that included a hat, wrap, and muff.

Knit and crochet outfits and accessories gained in popularity during the war years. This was due to women and girls knitting and crocheting garments for soldiers. Books were published that gave directions for making all types of doll outfits and accessories. One such book, *The Mary Frances Knitting and Crocheting Book*, published in 1918, gave instructions for making doll outfits, coats, all types of hats, bed jackets, a breakfast shawl, booties, and slippers. Knit and crochet accessories included mittens, a muff, a cape, leggings, garters, and purses.

Nippon bisque-head dolls can be found with either painted hair or wigs. Wigs during this era were usually either human hair or mohair (a fine glossy hair from Angora or Tibetan goats). Occasionally animal skins were also used as

Nippon doll dressed in typical World War I era boy clothing.

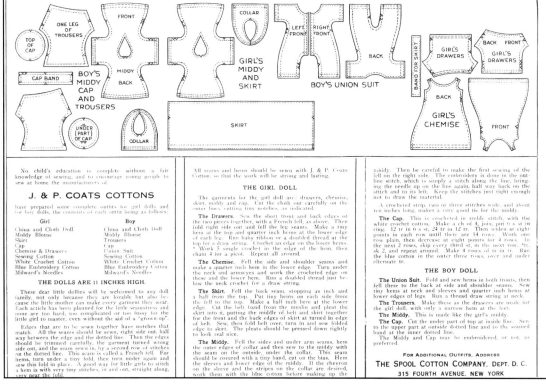

wigs, especially for boy dolls. During the war there were shortages of mohair, and sometimes mohair was mixed with other materials such as wool. The styles that were used on Nippon dolls include long or shoulder-length curls with bangs, long or shoulder-length curls with a center part, the bob and a similar style called "Buster Brown." Short bowl-shaped wigs were used for boys and babies. The popular wig colors were blonde, brown, auburn, and tosca (a brown with golden overtones). Tosca first became popular as a hair

color in 1908, and it was explained that the popularity was due to the similarity to the hair color of so many children. Whether this is true is unclear, but several of the original doll boxes in this book indicate that the hair color of the doll is tosca. Wigs were often adorned with ribbons and large hair bows that matched the doll's outfit.

Unfortunately for Nippon doll collectors, it is difficult to find Nippon dolls with their original or contemporary clothing. By original we mean clothing that was made for the doll at the time the doll was made. Contemporary is clothing made about the same time as the doll but not necessarily for the doll. These dolls were children's toys and, as such, clothing was often dirtied or destroyed during play. Once clothes were damaged, there was no reason for the owner to keep them. Also, many dolls were stored in damp basements or hot attics where they were subject to not only damaging elements but also to insects such as moths. Clothing made of silk is especially prone to deterioration, and little can be done to repair it. Knitted and crocheted items, as well as wool, are often found with moth damage.

If you are lucky enough to find dolls with their original or contemporary clothing still intact, it's best to

1918 wig ad.

Dressing Your Bisque-Head Dolls

Morimura Brothers doll with human hair wig.

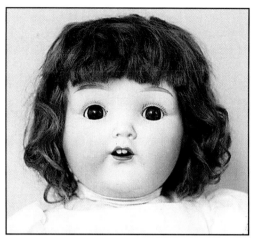

Horsman doll with mohair wig.

keep that clothing on the doll. If you choose to re-dress, tag and store the clothing so that it can be passed on to the next owner of the doll. Sometimes clothing is in such a state of disrepair that it doesn't seem worth keeping. However, documenting the history of a doll helps to retain the value, and the original clothes are part of a doll's history.

If clothing is dirty, most of the cotton materials can be hand washed in a mild soap such as Woolite. Wash by soaking and rinsing, not scrubbing or wringing. Avoid washing clothes in harsh detergents or using bleach although small amounts of bleach can be used on all-white cottons. If you want to whiten clothes, try drying them outside in the sun. Wool and silk clothes can sometimes be dry cleaned. Silk clothing needs to be strong enough to stand the stress however.

Nippon dolls that need to be re-dressed should be dressed in materials and styles that are appropriate to the era. Do not use today's synthetic materials or styles meant for dolls of other eras. Dolls that are dressed correctly retain their value. Antique doll clothing can be found at flea markets, doll and toy shows, and antique malls. Sometimes this clothing can be very expensive but bargains are available, especially for the simpler styles that the Nippon dolls were dressed in. Old baby clothes and bonnets can also be used to dress your Nippon dolls. If

Doll dressed in old clothes including necklace.

Doll in wonderful old plaid dress and brown leather shoes.

Large Morimura Brothers doll dressed in antique baby coat and cape with bonnet.

you sew, knit, or crochet, you can make your own doll clothes with patterns that are available for antique doll clothes. It's also possible to find seamstresses that make doll clothing.

Antique doll shoes.

Doll dressed in fur trimmed coat and hat.

One of the common problems with doll clothing is missing shoes. Antique doll shoes are expensive unless you can find them at a flea market or yard sale. As with the clothes, it is possible to buy new doll shoes and, if you do this, you should choose styles and materials that would have been found on the dolls. It's also possible to buy patterns for making dolls' shoes.

Wigs are another problem area for collectors. Many original wigs have been damaged, discarded,

and then replaced with a new wig of a synthetic material and in an inappropriate style. If the old wig remains on the doll, try to salvage it. One technique is to use a hat or hair bow to camouflage any damage; another is to restyle or add some additional hair to the wig. Human hair wigs can be washed with a mild shampoo and then re-set in an appropriate style. Mohair, however, is difficult to work with. Because of the way mohair wigs were

made, they cannot be easily combed or washed. They often fall apart in washing, and washing should probably not be attempted unless there is no alternative. New human hair and mohair wigs can be purchased in the styles that were popular during the Nippon era.

It is rare to find a Nippon doll dressed in ethnic or clothing of other countries.

Care and Handling of Your Dolls

Cleaning

One question all doll collectors have is "how do I clean my dolls?", and it's often asked with good reason. Many times dolls are found with 80 years worth of dirt on them, and this dirt certainly detracts from the doll. Most all-bisque dolls and all bisque-head dolls can be cleaned with a good soap and water cleaning. Cleaning will not injure bisque-head dolls since the colors are fired in and are part of the bisque. Be careful, however, to not get water into the eyes or mouth areas. Water can loosen the plaster holding in the eyes, teeth, and molded tongues. Serious dirt can be removed with spray cleaners such as Fantastic or 409. It's amazing how much dirt these spray cleaners will remove and how good a doll will look after cleaning.

A word of caution is required however. Some all-bisque dolls, especially those made of stone bisque, have not had a second firing to permanently set the paint. This means that the paint will wash off even with soap and water. Before cleaning your all-bisque dolls, make sure that you check for this.

When cleaning all-bisque dolls, be careful not to remove original stickers or ink marks. It is possible to clean around these areas with a cotton swab.

Composition and imitation kid bodies can be wiped with a slightly damp cloth. These bodies should *never* be washed with a wet cloth or immersed in water. When exposed to water, composition will lose its finish and begin to disintegrate. Some recommend using Jubilee Kitchen Wax to clean and protect composition. Again, use sparingly so that composition does not become overly wet.

Celluloid toys and dolls can be cleaned with mild soap and water or vegetable oil. Be careful when cleaning celluloid items; old celluloid can become brittle and too much pressure can damage the doll. Celluloid experts recommend that household cleaners *not* be used to clean celluloid. Also, do not allow celluloid to soak in water because the celluloid will absorb the water and break down.

Repairing

Repairs to bisque-head dolls are best left to professional doll repairers or hospitals. Breaks and cracks in bisque heads can be repaired, but the work is expensive to have done. Unless the doll is a rare one, such as a pouty or googly, or has sentimental value, the cost of the repair may exceed the value of the doll. Just as with porcelain, repairs to the bisque head tend to reduce the value of the doll. Each collector will have to make the determination for themselves whether or not to undertake major repairs to bisque heads. There are some bisque repairs that are less expensive to have done, and any good repairer will provide you with an estimate of the cost *before* undertaking any repairs. Doll magazines often have advertisements for people who do bisque repairs. Make sure that if you are going to have a repair undertaken that you deal with a reputable doll hospital or repairer. Any doll hospital or repairer should be able to provide references.

Bisque-head dolls may require other types of repairs that have nothing to do with damage to the bisque. Common problems that require attention are the re-setting of loose eyes, restringing of composition bodies, and repair of peeling or broken composition bodies. These repairs can be done at home, and there are several books out on doll repair and restoration that will show you step by step how to do things and also the supplies you will need to do them. Always experiment first with a lesser quality doll and, if unsure, leave the repair to someone experienced in doing these types of repairs. You don't want to do further damage to the doll or do something that will devalue the doll.

A good doll repairer or hospital can do most of these repairs and perform other types of doll repair as well (such as cleaning and re-setting old wigs). They often can provide replacement parts, wigs, shoes, clothing, and other types of doll accessories.

Note that any repair or restoration to a bisque-head doll may affect the value. *Always use a conservative approach in making repairs and replacing parts (including old clothing).* Most collectors would rather have a less than perfect doll than one that has had everything removed, replaced, or repaired.

One of the most common problems with all-bisque dolls is loosening or breakage of the elastic that attaches the arms and legs. This repair can definitely be done by the collector although care needs to be taken. See the end of this chapter for step-by-step instructions.

Another common problem with all-bisque dolls is small chips in the bisque around the armpits. Bisque repairs can be made, but the cost may be prohibitive. It is sometimes possible to camouflage the chip with a little bit of water-soluble paint (never use any paint that can't be removed). These chips do devalue the doll, so take that into consideration before buying all-bisque dolls with any type of chip.

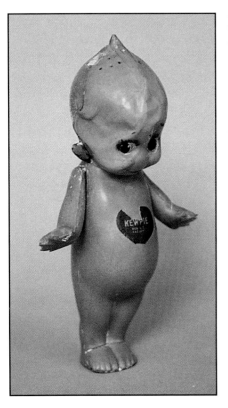

Dented celluloid doll. Repairs to celluoid are difficult if not impossible to make.

Repairs to celluloid toys are difficult but not impossible. Perhaps the most common problem is dents to the blown-mold celluloid toys. These items are hollow so it was easy for children to dent them. There is only one way to repair a badly dented celluloid toy: carefully split the seam, soften the damaged area in hot water, and gently push out the dented area from the inside. After this is done, use a small amount of glue to rejoin the seam. Keep in mind that old celluloid becomes brittle and this process may not work; the dented area may break or split, and surface paint may be removed or marred.

Old loosened elastic is another issue for celluloid collectors. This, too, can be repaired, but it's difficult to do since celluloid dolls don't have arm and leg loops for stringing. Do not pull out the old knot but cut the elastic close to the limb and push the old knot into the limb. With celluloid dolls you have to be able to insert a knotted piece of elastic into the arm or leg hole so that the knot once inside the hole holds the arm or leg on. This of course means that the knot has to be larger than the hole, and it will require some manipulation to get the knot through the hole without damaging the celluloid. With a lot of patience this can be done successfully. As with any other repair, practice on a lesser quality doll before doing this.

Storing

From time to time you might need to store your dolls and playthings. There are ways to safely do this.

1. Store in either acid-free tissue paper or washed, unbleached muslin. Do not use plastic bags and make sure that if you are storing the dolls in cardboard boxes that the dolls' clothes do not come in contact with the cardboard. Cardboard contains an acid that speeds the deterioration of fabric. Unfortunately, silk clothing often deteriorates over time no matter how carefully it is stored or protected. Old silk was made with a solution that has-

tens its demise.

When storing celluloid toys, make sure that they are not stored in tightly closed containers. This may accelerate deterioration and the formation of harmful vapors that can be flammable. Celluloid toys should also be wrapped in acid-free tissue paper.

2. Pack dolls loosely so as not to crush the dress materials or dolls' wigs. If the doll has a hat you should take it off (if possible) and wrap it separately but with the doll so it doesn't get misplaced. Depending on the style of dress or hat, you may want to stuff it with acid-free tissue paper so that it will retain its shape.

3. Pack dolls with sleep eyes face down. This keeps the sleep eyes from rocking back in the head while in storage. Eyes that rock back sometimes break because of the continuous weight on the eye mechanism and the plaster that holds the eyes in. Note: If you are shipping dolls, you should take the pate and wig off (if possible) and stuff the head with paper so that the eyes were held firmly in place. Shippers don't necessarily take care in keeping boxes upright. Stuffing the head will eliminate the possibility of eyes becoming dislodged or getting broken, and also the head being broken.

4. Be careful where dolls are stored. Don't put them in a hot attic or a damp basement. This is not only bad for the clothes but can damage composition bodies, plaster holding in the eyes, and wigs as well. To ward off insects, put a few moth balls into the box but make sure that they do not touch the dolls. Don't store where mice or other animals can get to them.

Displaying

Glass-door cabinets are ideal for displaying all types of dolls. They provide protection from dust as well as keep them out of harm's way. You can also display your dolls under glass domes, or there are specially made acrylic and plastic boxes and covers that you can use to protect dolls from dust. Always keep your dolls out of direct sunlight to prevent fading.

If you do have your dolls in display cabinets, make sure they are spaced so that clothing can hang loose and air can circulate around them. Take dolls out occasionally and fluff up dresses so that set-in creases don't develop. Also, rearrange dolls so that ones that have been sitting can stand for a while.

Collectors also like to display their dolls with antique furniture and accessories. Dolls look cute when displayed in antique highchairs, carriages, and wagons, or with other antique toys. Dolls also tend to look good when displayed in play groups.

Celluloid items should also be kept out of direct sunlight, kept away from excessive heat or flames, and displayed in areas with good air circulation.

Reattaching Arms and Legs on All-Bisque Dolls

These instructions are for those all-bisque dolls where the arm or leg has a stringing loop molded to the top of the arm or the top inside of the leg. These loops fit into the shoulder and thigh holes in the doll body.

To do this you will need only a few items: smaller sizes of elastic which are usually available at fabric stores; sharp scissors in a small, pointed size; toothpicks or large-size sewing needles; and fine wire to pull the elastic through the body and loops although this is usually not necessary.

Make sure that you have a padded surface to work on and good lighting. If there is old elastic stuck in the loops, it can usually be removed by poking it out with either a toothpick or sewing needle. You are now ready to re-attach the arm or leg with these four steps:

1. Once the old elastic is out of the loops, take a piece of the new elastic and thread it through a loop.

2. You will then need to take both ends of the new elastic and thread through the doll body. This is usually not too hard because most all-bisque bodies are not very wide. If you do have trouble threading the two elastic ends through the body, secure a length of wire around the two ends and then thread the wire through the body.

3. Once the elastic is through the body, take one end of elastic and thread it through the other loop. Pull the elastic as tight as possible to ensure a secure fit and then tie a hard knot.

4. At this point the knot and the loose ends of elastic will be on the outside of the doll body. Cut the loose ends to a reasonably short length. Pull the limb slightly away from the body and with a toothpick, poke the knot and the elastic ends into the body of the doll.

Make sure that arms and legs are strung and tied separately, not strung through all four loops and then tied with one knot. This will prohibit the legs from moving correctly.

With a little practice you will soon find that re-stringing bisque doll arms and legs only takes a few minutes.

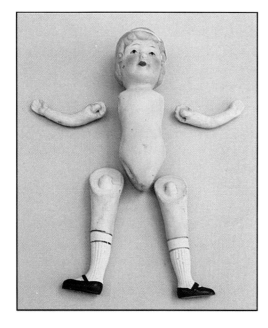 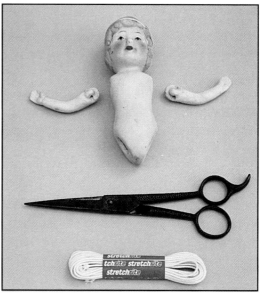

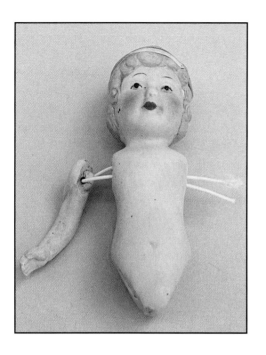

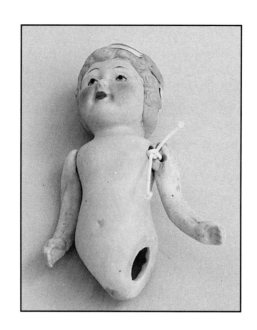

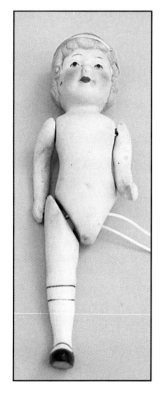

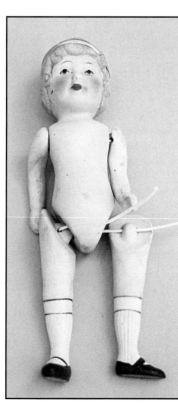

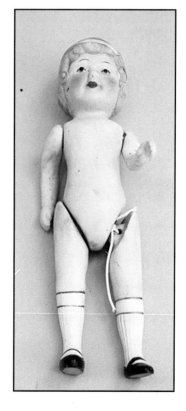

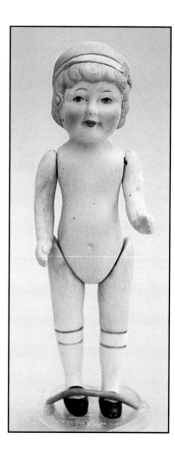

Nippon Doll Names

Provided in this chapter is a list of documented dolls produced and distributed by those companies advertising Japanese dolls during the height of the Nippon doll era (1915 – 1921). Some of these names have been found on actual dolls, i.e., stickers and tags. Other names have been identified through the advertisements and catalogs of doll manufacturers and distributors. In several instances, such as Baby Bud and Kewpie, the same doll was made by German firms before and after World War I and by American companies.

It was prevalent for popular dolls to be blatantly copied and distributed by companies other than those that owned the distribution rights or originally produced the doll. In those instances where the design of the doll was not protected by a patent or where the name was not protected by a trademark, there was no protection from pirating. Even in those instances where the doll was patented or trademarked, it was rare for a company to successfully sue for infringement.

This is by no means inclusive of all the Nippon dolls produced, as no doubt many "named" dolls have lost their original stickers and tags. Also, many Nippon dolls were not given names and were sold as generic baby dolls, child dolls, bathtub babies, penny dolls, etc.

As much information as possible has been given about the dolls, including manufacturer and the approximate date of production, patent and trademark information, and original cost.

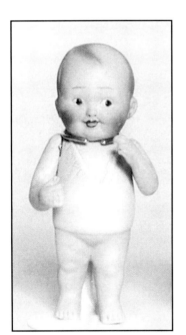

"BABY BUD" CHUBBY BISQUE DOLL

F9807—Fine flesh tinted bisque, painted features, rougish eyes, exposed tongue, short shirt, movable position arms which give different expressions at each pose, each in box. ¼ doz. in pkg....Doz. $1.90

1918 Butler Brothers catalog ad.

BABY BUD: *In 1915 the Baby Bud trademark was registered in Germany by Butler Brothers. These dolls closely resemble Dolly (designed by Langfelder for Morimura Brothers) except for the clothes. The all-bisque Nippon version is incised with "Baby Bud" across the back. It was made in several different sizes.*

BABY BELLE: *Trade name used by Morimura Brothers for an all-bisque doll. This doll is shown in a 1917 Morimura Brothers ad. It was made in at least two different sizes.*

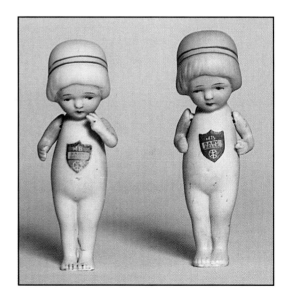

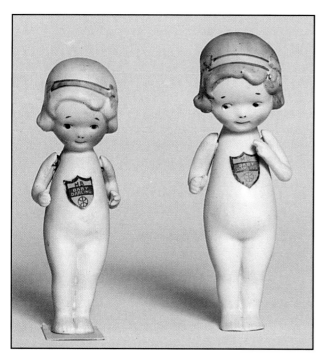

BABY DARLING: *Trade name used by Morimura Brothers for an all-bisque doll. This doll was obviously very popular as it is one of the more frequently available Nippon dolls and it is the same mold as Louis Wolf & Company's "Sweetie" doll. It was made in at least four different sizes.*

Bisque Head Doll. Mohair Wig.

Sleeping Eyes

It is quite natural to fall in love with this charming baby. It would be just like a ray of sunshine to have her in your little arms, nestled, Oh, so close. Composition body, jointed at neck, shoulders and hips. Painted shoes and stockings. Ht., 8¾ in. Ship. wt., 1½ lbs.
49E2622— Price............**98c**

1919 Montgomery Ward ad for Baby Doll.

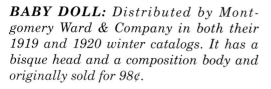
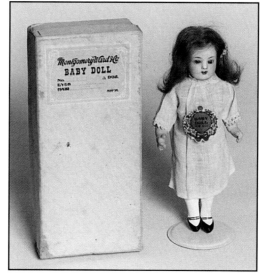

BABY DOLL: *Distributed by Montgomery Ward & Company in both their 1919 and 1920 winter catalogs. It has a bisque head and a composition body and originally sold for 98¢.*

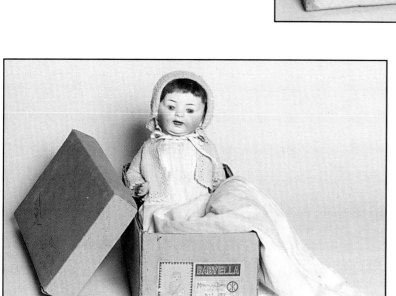

BABY ELLA: *Produced by Morimura Brothers, Baby Ella has a bisque head and a composition baby body. This doll was produced in a variety of sizes; the 8" size sold for 75¢, the 13" size, $3.00, and the 16" size, $4.70.*

BABY KING: *A composition doll produced by the same company that produced bisque head dolls with the "RE in Diamond" mark. The doll is made of oyster shell composition and is 11½" tall. Jointed at the neck, shoulders, and hips, it has molded brown hair and an open/closed mouth. The eyes are painted a vivid blue.*

Photos not available
BABY O'MINE: *Produced by Morimura Brothers circa 1920.*

BABY ROSE: *Produced by Morimura Brothers circa 1919 – 1920.*

BABY LUCY: *Produced by the Tajimi Co. (1918) and the Taiyo Trading Co. (1919 – 1921). It is a bisque-head character baby and came in sizes 10", 12", 14", 16", and 18".*

BEST BABY: *A celluloid doll made for Haber Brothers. It is unknown if it was also made in bisque. An injunction to stop importation was issued on November 11, 1920, because the doll looked too much like a Kewpie. This doll was made in several sizes.*

Rose O'Neill's Kewpies Win Again

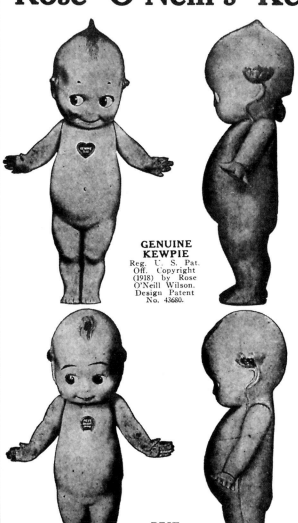

GENUINE KEWPIE
Reg. U. S. Pat. Off. Copyright (1918) by Rose O'Neill Wilson. Design Patent No. 43680.

BEST BABY
Imitation Doll Enjoined

The United States Circuit Court of Appeals has affirmed, with costs, the Decree entered in the District Court for the Southern District of New York in November, 1920, awarding Injunction and Accounting to Rose O'Neill Wilson and Geo. Borgfeldt & Co. against Haber Bros., Inc., Importers at New York, for their infringement of the Kewpie rights.

The Brief submitted by counsel in behalf of the Kewpies contains the accompanying pictures which speak for themselves. The Court effectively refers to them as follows:

. . . "it is sufficient to say that there is an even stronger external resemblance between Plaintiff's Kewpie and Defendant's 'Best Baby' than is exhibited by the drawings inserted in the opinion in Borgfeldt vs. Weiss.

"Decree affirmed with costs."

This case of Borgfeldt vs. Weiss was likewise won in the Court of Appeals, and concerned another Novelty marketed by Geo. Borgfeldt & Co. which had been grossly imitated.

WARNING TO THE TRADE
Beware of Illegal Imitations of Kewpies
NO MATTER UNDER WHAT NAME THEY ARE OFFERED
TO AVOID RISK OF PROSECUTION
DESTROY OR RETURN IMITATION GOODS

We will exact the full penalty allowed by the Law

Rose O'Neill Wilson
GEO. BORGFELDT & CO.
NEW YORK

Kewpie Label

Kewpie Label

June 1921 Playthings *ad showing both Kewpie and Best Baby.*

BLUE RIBBON BABY: A trade name used for a bisque-head doll imported by Carl Silverman. He advertised this doll in 1917 and indicated that it was made in five sizes to retail from $1.00 to $6.00.

BLUE RIBBON BABY

Jointed Character Doll

We have them and can deliver them.

Fine Bisc Head with light and dark hair. Moving eyes.

Five Sizes to Retail from $1.00 to $6.00

The Best Value of the Season.

Come and see them before the output is sold as our sales so far have exceeded our expectations.

We have many other good things

for the shrewd Toy Buyer

CARL SILVERMAN

48 & 50 East 13th St.   NEW YORK

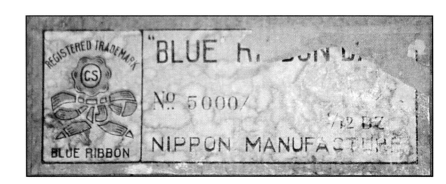

CHO-CHO SAN: *An all-bisque doll distributed by Morimura Brothers. It is jointed at the shoulders with painted clothes and features. It was made in three different versions — standing, kneeling, and sitting.*

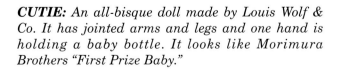

CRINOLINE: *An all-bisque figural doll dressed in blue dress with a full skirt. Her shoes are quite large, probably to keep her upright and balanced.*

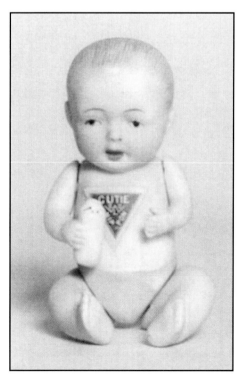

CUTIE: *An all-bisque doll made by Louis Wolf & Co. It has jointed arms and legs and one hand is holding a baby bottle. It looks like Morimura Brothers "First Prize Baby."*

Louis Wolf & Co. are showing a larger and more varied line of character dolls than ever before in the history of the house. One of their latest novelties is the Chubby Doll, which has a number of new features. The arms are movable and the doll is provided

This Doll Wears a Union Suit.

with a close-fitting union suit which gives it a very rakish look. The union suit is warranted to be washed without shrinking, as it is a part of the doll itself and is made of bisque.

CHUBBY: In 1915 a trademark was registered in the U.S. by Louis Wolf & Co. for this doll. They advertised an all-bisque doll with moving arms wearing a union suit. In 1915 and 1916 it was advertised in sizes 4", 5", and 6" priced at 25¢, 39¢, and 49¢.

DESIGN.

T. E. STUTSON.

DOLL.

APPLICATION FILED AUG. 6, 1914.

46,515.

Patented Oct. 6, 1914.

Witnesses
A. I. Siegel
Carl W. Bliss

Inventor:
Thomas E. Stutson,
By his Attorney, W. J. Brown

UNITED STATES PATENT OFFICE.

THOMAS E. STUTSON, OF NEWTON, MASSACHUSETTS.

DESIGN FOR A DOLL.

46,515.

Specification for Design.

Patented Oct. 6, 1914.

Application filed August 6, 1914.   Serial No. 855,518.   Term of patent 3½ years.

To all whom it may concern:

Be it known that I, Thomas E. Stutson, a citizen of the United States, residing at Newton, in the county of Middlesex and State of Massachusetts, have invented a new, original, and ornamental Design for Dolls, of which the following is a specification, reference being had to the accompanying drawing, forming part thereof.

Figure 1 is a rear elevation of a doll, showing my new design. Fig. 2 is a side elevation, partially turned, of a doll, showing my new design.

I claim:

The ornamental design for a doll, as shown.

THOMAS E. STUTSON.

Witnesses:

A. I. Siegel,

Carl W. Bliss.

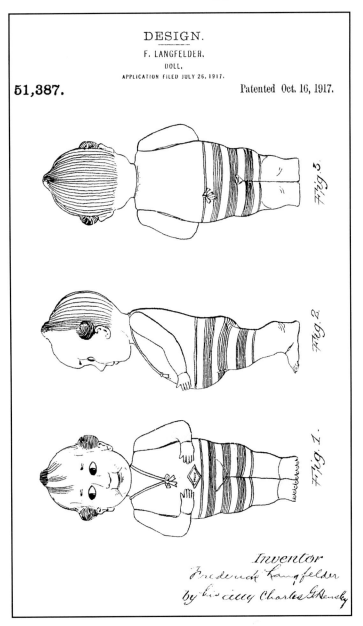

DESIGN.

F. LANGFELDER.
DOLL.
APPLICATION FILED JULY 26, 1917.

51,387.

Patented Oct. 16, 1917.

Fig. 3

Fig. 2

Fig. 1

Inventor
Frederick Langfelder
by his atty Charles G Hensby

DOLLY: *A trade name used by Morimura Brothers for both an all-bisque and a celluloid doll. In 1917 a design patent for Dolly was secured by Frederick Langfelder (of Langfelder, Homma, and Hayward) and assigned to Morimura Brothers. The doll pictured in the patent is the celluloid version, and there is a paper sticker on the back of the celluloid doll indicating the design patent number. The all-bisque version, with its legs apart and the head turned to the side, is different from the celluloid version. Both versions are in a molded blue and white bathing suit. Both dolls were made in several sizes.*

UNITED STATES PATENT OFFICE.

FREDERICK LANGFELDER, OF NEW YORK, N. Y., ASSIGNOR TO MORIMURA BROS., OF NEW YORK, N. Y., A FIRM COMPOSED OF ICHIZAEMON MORIMURA, ESTATE OF TOYO MORIMURA, SANEYOSKI HIROSE, SENEMITSU HIROSE, AND YUSAKATA MURAI.

DESIGN FOR A DOLL.

51,387.

Specification for Design.

Patented Oct. 16, 1917.

Application filed July 26, 1917. Serial No. 182,987. Term of patent 7 years.

To all whom it may concern:
Be it known that I, FREDERICK LANG-FELDER, a citizen of the United States, residing in the city, county, and State of New York, have invented a new, original, and ornamental Design for Dolls, of which the following is a specification, reference being had to the accompanying drawing, forming part thereof.

Figure 1 is a front elevation of a doll, showing my new design, Fig. 2 is a side elevation thereof and Fig. 3 is a rear elevation thereof.

I claim:
The ornamental design for a doll, as shown.

FREDERICK LANGFELDER.

Copies of this patent may be obtained for five cents each, by addressing the "Commissioner of Patents, Washington, D. C."

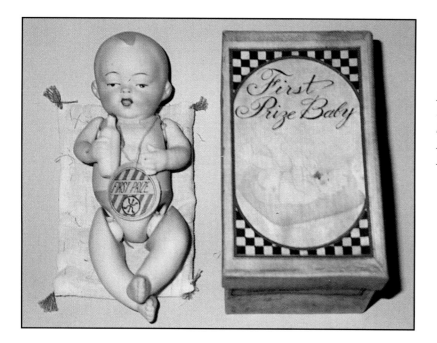

FIRST PRIZE BABY: *Trade name for an all-bisque doll produced by Morimura Brothers. It looks like the Louis Wolf & Co. "Cutie" doll. Morimura Brothers advertised "First Prize Baby" for two years – 1919 and 1920.*

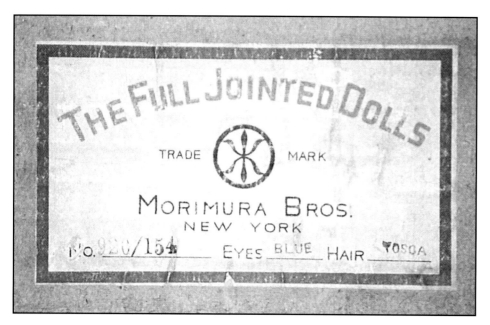

Side of box.

Photo not available
GEISHA: *Advertised by the Taiyo Trading Company in 1920, this doll was dressed as a Japanese Geisha Girl. It is unknown if this doll was bisque or composition, but it was advertised as a "Natural Walking Doll."*

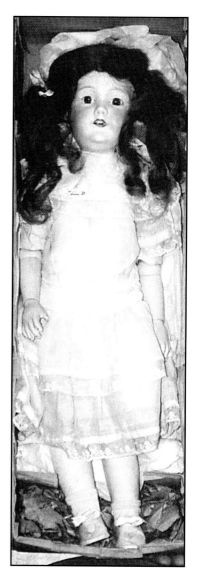

FULL JOINTED DOLL: *A line of bisque-head dolls produced by Morimura Brothers from 1915 – 1921. The doll was made in a variety of sizes and is found with a jointed composition body.*

HAPPIFATS: *This name was registered as a trademark by George Borgfeldt in the U.S. and Germany in 1914. These two dolls (male and female) are based on the Kate Jordan drawings which appeared in* John Martin's Book. *They are all-bisque with jointed arms and molded clothes.*

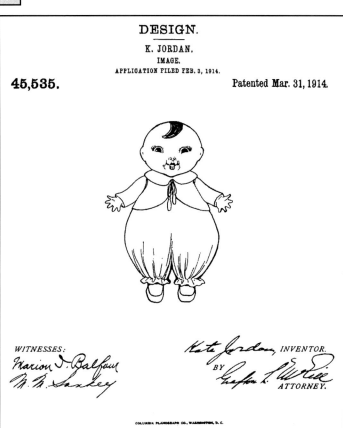

DESIGN.

K. JORDAN.
IMAGE.
APPLICATION FILED FEB. 3, 1914.

45,535. Patented Mar. 31, 1914.

WITNESSES:
Marion I. Balfour
W. B. Saxbey

Kate Jordan, INVENTOR.
BY *Grafton L. McGill*
ATTORNEY.

COLUMBIA PLANOGRAPH CO., WASHINGTON, D. C.

UNITED STATES PATENT OFFICE.

KATE JORDAN, OF NEW YORK, N. Y.

DESIGN FOR AN IMAGE.

45,535. Specification for Design. **Patented Mar. 31, 1914.**

Application filed February 3, 1914. Serial No. 816,369. Term of patent 3½ years.

To all whom it may concern:

Be it known that I, KATE JORDAN, a citizen of the United States, residing at the city of New York, in the State of New York, have invented a new, original, and ornamental Design for Images, of which the following is a specification, reference being had to the accompanying drawing, forming part thereof.

The figure is a front elevation of an image showing my new design.

I claim:—

The ornamental design for an image, as shown.

KATE JORDAN.

Witnesses:
GRAFTON L. McGILL,
MARION I. BALFOUR.

Copies of this patent may be obtained for five cents each, by addressing the "Commissioner of Patents, Washington, D. C."

DESIGN.

K. JORDAN.
IMAGE.
APPLICATION FILED FEB. 3, 1914.

45,534.

Patented Mar. 31, 1914.

WITNESSES:
Marion I. Balfour.
M. M. Sankey

Kate Jordan, INVENTOR.
BY *Grafton L. McGill*
ATTORNEY.

UNITED STATES PATENT OFFICE.

KATE JORDAN, OF NEW YORK, N. Y.

DESIGN FOR AN IMAGE.

45,534.

Specification for Design.

Patented Mar. 31, 1914.

Application filed February 3, 1914. Serial No. 816,368. Term of patent 3½ years.

To all whom it may concern:

Be it known that I, KATE JORDAN, a citizen of the United States, residing at the city of New York, in the State of New York, have invented a new, original, and ornamental Design for Images, of which the following is a specification, reference being had to the accompanying drawing, forming part thereof.

The figure is a front elevation of an image showing my new design.

I claim:—

The ornamental design for an image, as shown.

KATE JORDAN.

Witnesses:
GRAFTON L. McGILL,
MARION I. BALFOUR.

Copies of this patent may be obtained for five cents each, by addressing the "Commissioner of Patents, Washington, D. C."

JOLLIKID: *All-bisque dolls in both a male and female version. Both the male and female have jointed arms and molded clothes. Their clothes come in two different colors.*

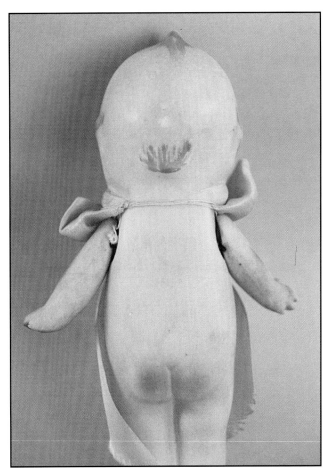

Back view of Kewpie showing blue wings.

KEWPIE: *A popular doll designed by Rose O'Neill for which a design patent was granted in March 1913. She registered Kewpie as a trademark in 1913 and claimed it had been in use since 1912. George Borgfeldt held the production and distribution rights to the doll and granted licenses to other companies.*

In 1915 Montgomery Ward advertised bisque Kewpies 5" and 6⅞" tall for 25¢ and 49¢. Nippon bisque and celluloid Kewpie dolls were made in a number of sizes.

MANIKIN: *An all-bisque doll with jointed arms and molded clothes that look like a tuxedo. His clothes came in two different colors.*

LADYKIN: *An all-bisque doll with jointed arms and a molded dress. Her dress came in two different colors.*

NOTE: HAPPIFATS, JOLLIKID, LADYKIN, AND MANIKIN ALL HAVE THE SAME STYLE STICKERS, HAVE THE SAME TYPE OF INCISED MARK, AND ARE THE SAME TYPE OF DOLL — 3½" TALL, JOINTED ARMS AND MOLDED CLOTHES. IT IS VERY LIKE-LY THEY WERE PRODUCED AND IMPORTED BY THE SAME COMPANY. CRINOLINE ALSO HAS THE SAME TYPE STICKER AND INCISED MARK BUT IS A FIGURAL DOLL.

"MING TOY"

"A Breath of the Orient"

This beautiful little doll from the Far East is typical of the popular character portrayed by Fay Bainter in the big New York theatrical success, "East Is West."

"Ming Toy" is delightfully dressed as a little Chinese kiddie.

Most Doll
Natural on
Walking Earth

Infantile Locomotion Is Absolutely Reproduced

Retails at $5.00

With Excellent Profit
Let us send you a sample doll

"MING TOY" PROMENADES AT THE ASTOR

TAIYO TRADING COMPANY, Inc.

Successors to Takito, Ogawa & Co., *and* The Tajimi Co.
101 Fifth Avenue, NEW YORK   **327 West Madison Street, Chicago**

MING TOY: *A doll representing Fay Bainter in "East is West," it was made by Taiyo Trading Company in 1919. It is unknown if this doll was made of bisque or composition.*

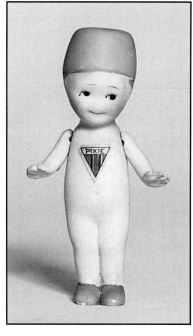

PIXIE: *An all-bisque doll with jointed arms and molded fez-type hat. Doll wears only the blue hat and brown shoes.*

MY DARLING: *A solid dome bisque-head doll produced and distributed by Morimura Brothers from 1915 – 1921. Doll is difficult to identify as it does not have the typical Morimura Brothers mold marks.*

Photo not available
MY SWEETHEART: *Advertised by Morimura Brothers in 1919 and 1920.*

QUEUE SAN BABY: *A line of dolls produced by Morimura Brothers. They used this name as their trademark beginning in October 1915. The trademark was registered in 1916 at which time they stated that the trademark was usually a printed label applied to the boxes or receptacles containing the dolls. Probably later, the label was applied directly to the stomach of the doll. A number of versions have been found. The patent Queue San Baby was designed by Hikozo Araki in 1915 and was patented in 1916 for 3½ years and assigned to Morimura Brothers.*

Dolls that closely resemble this one but are marked "Made in Germany" were either German imitations or perhaps were made in Germany for Langfelder, Homma, and Hayward who acquired Morimura's doll business in 1921.

In 1917 the Baltimore Bargain House advertised all-bisque Queue San Babies 4½" tall for 85¢ a dozen wholesale.

UNITED STATES PATENT OFFICE.

HIKOZO ARAKI, OF BROOKLYN, NEW YORK, ASSIGNOR TO MORIMURA BROS., OF NEW YORK, N. Y., A FIRM COMPOSED OF ITCHIZAEMON MORIMURA, YASUKATA MURAI, AND SANEHIDE HIROSE.

DESIGN FOR A DOLL.

48,625. Specification for Design. **Patented Feb. 29, 1916.**

Application filed November 10, 1915. Serial No. 60,794. Term of patent 3½ years.

To all whom it may concern:

Be it known that I, HIKOZO ARAKI, a subject of the Emperor of Japan, and residing at 417 Monroe street, in the borough of Brooklyn, county of Kings, and State of New York, have invented a new, original, and ornamental Design for a Doll, of which the following is a specification, reference being had to the accompanying drawing, forming part thereof.

Figure 1 is a back view; Fig. 2 a front view and Fig. 3 a side view of the doll showing my new design:

I claim:

The ornamental design for a doll as shown.

HIKOZO ARAKI.

Witnesses:

J. C. LAWRENCE,
C. W. COWLES.

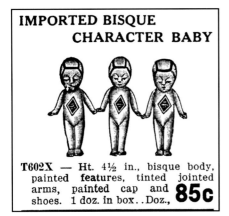

IMPORTED BISQUE CHARACTER BABY

T602X — Ht. 4½ in., bisque body, painted **features**, tinted jointed arms, painted cap and shoes. 1 doz. in box..Doz., **85c**

1917 ad from
Baltimore Bargain House.

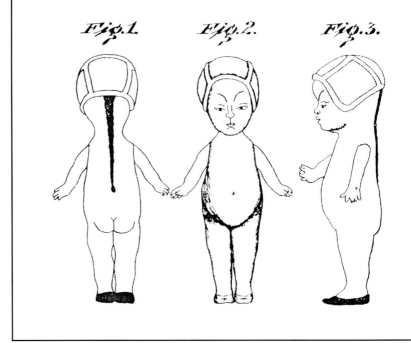

DESIGN.

H. ARAKI.

DOLL.

APPLICATION FILED NOV. 10, 1915.

48,625. Patented Feb. 29, 1916.

Fig. 1. Fig. 2. Fig. 3.

ROSEBUD: A bisque-head doll produced by the E.I. Horsman and Aetna Doll Co. In April 1920 they advertised that "the famous Rosebud Model is now being produced in real bisque...." This doll is apparently a copy of the Horsman Rosebud Baby doll that had a composition head, cloth body, and composition arms and legs.

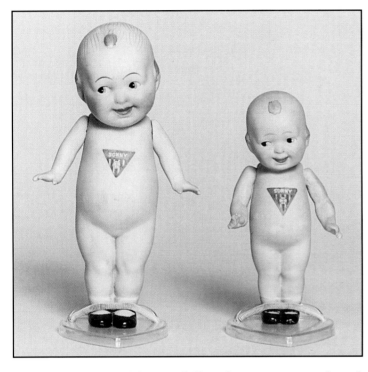

SAMMY: An all-bisque doll with jointed arms that resembles the Louis Wolf & Co. Chubby doll. The sticker with the word "Sammy" looks like a sash around the waist of the doll. "Nippon" is stamped on the bottom of the feet.

SONNY: The Nippon version of the German doll Wide-Awake. A trademark was registered in Germany by Butler Brothers for Wide-Awake, an all-bisque doll with two upper teeth, painted eyes glancing to the side, and painted shoes and socks. Sonny's sticker bears the Morimura Brothers spider symbol.

SUNDAY'S CHILD and other Day of the Week Dolls (Friday's Child, Thursday's Child, etc.): A line of all-bisque dolls produced by Morimura Brothers. They are based on the Charles Twelvetrees drawing and verse "Every Baby Has Its Day" (1915). There is one doll for every day of the week, and each bears a heart-shaped paper label indicating the day of the week and MB for Morimura Brothers.

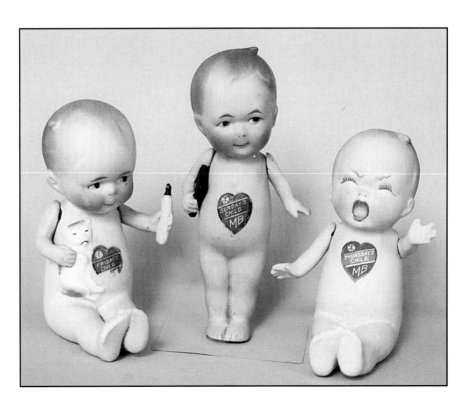

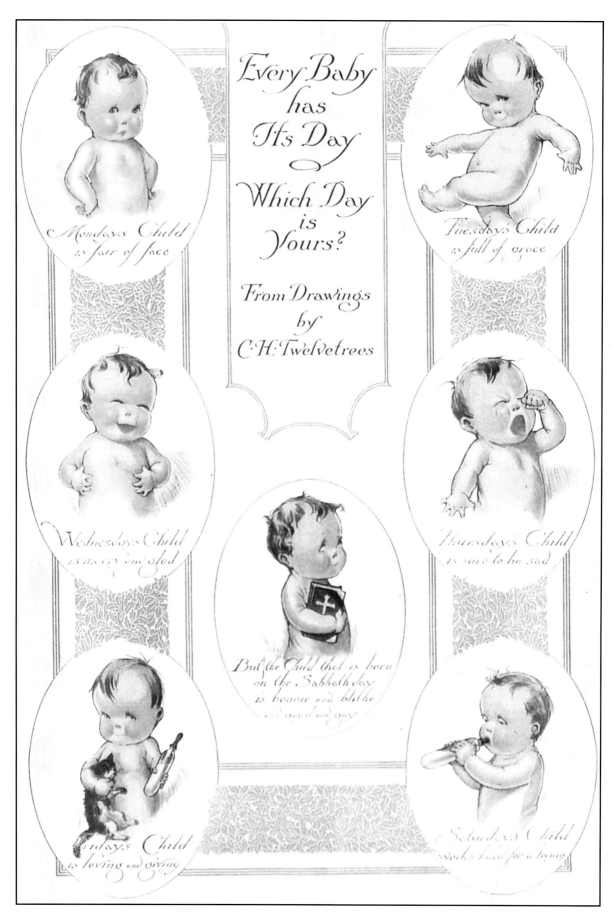

Every Baby has Its Day

Which Day is Yours?

From Drawings by C.H.Twelvetrees

Monday's Child is fair of face

Tuesday's Child is full of grace

Wednesday's Child is merry and glad

Thursday's Child is sure to be sad

But the Child that is born on the Sabbath day is bonnie and blithe and good and gay

Friday's Child is loving and giving

Saturday's Child works hard for a living

Notice how closely the Morimura Brothers dolls (page 107) resemble the illustration.

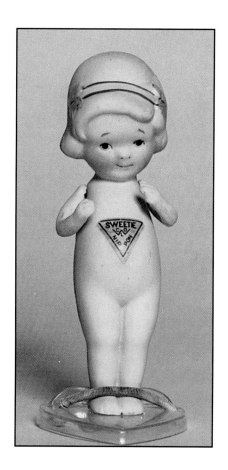

SWEETIE: *Produced by Louis Wolf & Co., this all-bisque doll resembles the Morimura Brothers Baby Darling doll.*

Fake Nippon Dolls

Reproductions of all kinds are flooding the antiques and collectibles market. Nippon is no exception. Nippon porcelain items are currently being manufactured in Japan and China bearing a bogus Nippon backstamp under the glaze.

The McKinley Tariff Act stated that as of March 1, 1891, "all articles of foreign manufacture shall be marked in legible English words so as to indicate the country of their origin." At that time Nippon was the name the Japanese called their country, so it was only natural that they would place this backstamp on their items.

In 1921 lexicographers in the United States determined that the English equivalent of Japan should be used, and the "Nippon" backstamp era came to a halt.

The reproduction manufacturers place a fake Nippon mark usually under the glaze and also place a paper label on the items indicating the actual country of origin, which presently meets U.S. Customs regulations. After purchase, the paper label is easily removed and now we have a so-called Nippon item. That is how the two black figurals shown here came into the U.S. This has been a real problem for many Nippon porcelain collectors, and the black figurals are also troublesome to black Americana collectors. We have included them in this book so that collectors are aware that some figural-type items are being reproduced and may show up at antique shows, flea markets, and auctions.

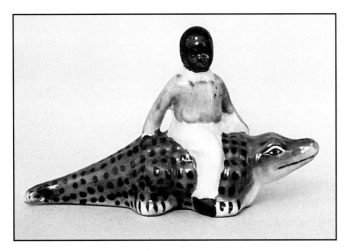

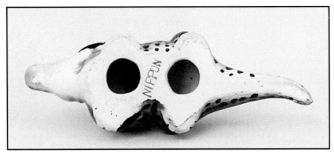

As far as anyone knows, the fake Nippon marked dolls are not being manufactured overseas but right here in the United States. These are small all-bisque dolls and appear to have been made in very small quantities by local doll makers using a Bell Ceramics mold. Some of them are even signed with the name of the doll maker and the date the doll was made (which of course immediately identifies the doll as a fake). These fake Nippon dolls were most likely not made to deceive anyone but made strictly for the use and enjoyment of the doll maker.

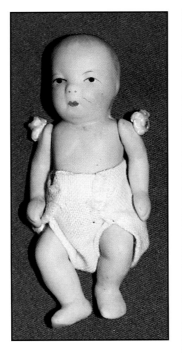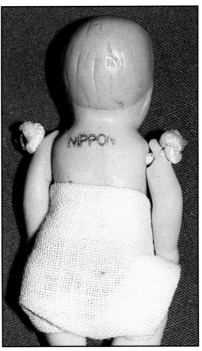

How do you know if an all-bisque doll is a fake or not? There are several clues that the collector should look for:

1) The bisque on the fake dolls is a pre-colored flesh tone. The Japanese, like the French and German doll makers, used only white bisque in the making of dolls and then painted the dolls flesh tone. If you look inside the shoulder joints, you will be able to see this. Also, on Nippon dolls the painting of the flesh tone is often somewhat uneven. This is not true on the fake dolls, which, because of the pre-colored bisque, show no unevenness or imperfections in the flesh tone.

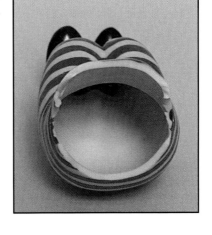

Inside of broken genuine Nippon doll, showing whiteness of bisque.

2) The bisque on the fake dolls has a satiny smoothness whereas the bisque on the Nippon dolls has a slightly rough or grainy feel to it, and one can usually see some imperfections in the bisque. This is because today's liquid slip is made from different materials and is much more refined than the slip used by the Japanese.

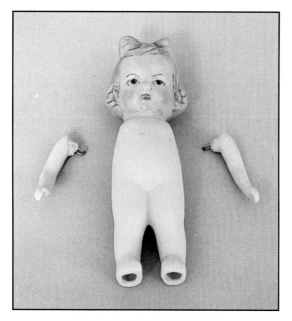

3) Look at the way the arms are attached to the body. On the fake doll shown at left, the stringing "loop" is metal that is embedded into the arm. The Japanese did not use this technique on all-bisque dolls. They either used a bisque loop that was molded as part of the arm or they used a method where there were holes in the arms that were then attached by wire. The other fake shown at the top of page 111 uses elastic that is knotted outside the arm. While this technique is sometimes used to reattach arms on genuine Nippon dolls, it should raise some suspicion on the part of the collector.

4) Look at the bottom of the feet. On some of the fake dolls there are holes in the bottom of the feet. This was not done on Nippon dolls.

5) Lastly, take a close look at the painting of the facial features. Many times, this painting is clearly amateurish and not at all like the facial painting on the Nippon dolls. Today's paint colors are not the same as those used by the Japanese, and most of today's doll makers cannot capture the true "look" of the Nippon dolls.

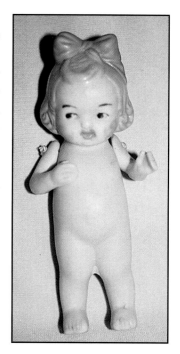

Collectors should handle and examine as many genuine Nippon dolls as possible so that they can know the look and feel of the Japanese bisque, painting, and techniques used to make Nippon dolls. Go to doll and toy shows; look at the dolls and ask the dealers questions about the dolls. Learn as much as you can about what types of dolls were made and how they were made. Also, collectors should buy from reputable dealers and ask for a written guarantee if in doubt.

Fortunately, to date there don't appear to be any fakes of the Nippon bisque-head dolls or children's porcelain items. Of course, new fakes are showing up all the time, so collectors always need to be aware of this.

Reproduction information on the porcelain items can be obtained in the *Collector's Encyclopedia of Nippon Porcelain, Second through Sixth Series,* published by Collector Books.

Remember, knowledge is power. The more you have, the better your collection can be.

Frequently Asked Questions

This Kewpie's arms have been replaced; it should have starfish hands.

The arms on my all-bisque doll are not the same color as the rest of the doll. Have they been replaced?

Not necessarily. Many Nippon dolls have arms and legs that are not quite the same color as the body of the doll. One reason for this is that the arms and legs were likely painted and fired separately from the body of the doll. Since quality control was not important, imperfections were accepted especially since these were inexpensive, mass-produced dolls.

Collectors should pay attention to the types of arms and legs used on Nippon dolls. Some dolls have distinctive types of arms, especially Kewpie that has starfish hands. When buying all-bisque dolls, collectors will have to judge for themselves if the arms and legs look appropriate to the doll.

At doll and toy shows I see that some dealers have the same Nippon doll. Does this mean that those dolls are reproductions?

No, many Nippon dolls were mass-produced, and some of the more popular dolls were sold for a number of years. For example, Morimura Brothers advertised their Baby Ella and Dolly dolls in 1917 and was still advertising them in 1921. A review of trade catalogs indicates that many Nippon dolls had a similar run of popularity. See the chapter on "Fake Nippon Dolls" for those Nippon dolls that have been reproduced.

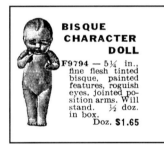

BISQUE CHARACTER DOLL

F9794 — 5¼ in., fine flesh tinted bisque, painted features, roguish eyes, jointed position arms. Will stand. ½ doz. in box.
Doz. **$1.65**

1917 ad.

Morimura Brothers doll with a new composition body.

How can I tell if the composition body on my doll is original and hasn't been replaced by a new body?

Because Nippon dolls were toys and meant to be played with, there is usually some type of damage to the body (unless, of course, the doll has never been played with). The fingers were often the first part of the body to become chipped or broken. Also, unless the body has been restored, the flesh tone of the composition is often discolored in places, there is wear at the joints, and it will look soiled. A new composition body looks new, with even flesh tones, shows no wear, and is very clean.

Two commonly found Nippon all-bisque dolls.

Collectors should remember that not all Nippon bisque head dolls arrived in the U.S. with bodies. Nippon heads were often put together with bodies here and sometimes used as replacement heads for German dolls whose heads had been broken. That is why you may find a Nippon head on the German-marked body.

The composition body on my doll is scuffed and a finger is missing. Does this affect the value?

Overall condition of a doll is always important. When buying bisque head dolls, remember that the most valuable part of the doll is the bisque head, and its condition should be the most important consideration. Most dolls were meant to be played with and some scuffs, soiling, and chips to the body are to be expected. However, generally a doll with a good bisque head and a body in good condition should sell for more than a doll with a good bisque head and a body in poor condition.

Are they reproducing Nippon dolls?

Yes, there are a couple of reproduction all-bisque dolls that have been found but they are not very common. See the chapter on "Fake Nippon Dolls" for more information on those dolls and how to tell a reproduction doll. To date, no reproductions of Nippon bisque-head dolls have been seen.

What is an incised mark?

An incised mark looks like it has been cut into the doll. In fact, these marks were part of the doll mold, which is why some incised marks are very clear, and others are hard to read. If the mold is new, the mark will be deep and very clear; if the mold is old, the mark will be less deep and may even be partly obliterated.

I saw a bisque aviator doll that looks like the Nippon bisque aviator, but it was not marked. Should I buy unmarked dolls?

That is a determination that will have to be made by each collector. This author doesn't recommend it however. Because many dolls were produced in both Japan and Germany (before and after the WWI), it is difficult to be absolutely sure that the doll was actually produced during the Nippon doll era. Don't forget the Japanese copied many German dolls so there is always the possibility that there is a German version of a Nippon doll. Also, marked dolls will maintain their value; an unmarked one may not.

How can I tell if the clothing on my bisque-head doll is original?

It can be very difficult to tell if clothing is original to the doll; most of the time it is not. Original means that clothing was made for that particular doll at the time the doll was made. Unless the doll was packed away, most of the clothing is probably not original. There are a few signs the collector can look for to ascertain if the clothes are original. First, check the general appearance of the doll. Is the wig original and in good condition? Is the body of the doll in good condition with little or no wear, dirt, or damage? If the answer to these two questions is no, then it's likely the doll was played with and the original clothes have been replaced. Study the outfit. Is it the right size or length for the doll? Is it the right style and material for Nippon era dolls? Are the shoes and socks still with the doll? How about the underwear? If the outfit is original, it will most likely have the original shoes, socks, and underwear on the doll. These are all clues that can tell you if the doll's clothing is original.

By the way, just because the clothing may not be original does not mean it's without value. Old or contemporary (made during the same time period as the doll) clothing is just as acceptable for your Nippon dolls.

My doll is wearing its old (original?) clothes but they are dirty and I don't like them. Does replacing them affect the value of my doll?

Yes, it does. Original or contemporary doll clothing should always be kept on the doll whenever possible. If you really don't like the old clothing or if the clothing is in such a state of disrepair as to make the doll less attractive, then remove the clothing, wrap in acid free tissue paper, document the doll it belongs to, and then store it in a plastic bag. Remember to keep shoes, socks, and hats either on the doll or together with the bagged clothes. These items are extremely hard to replace.

Doll re-dressed in vintage clothing.

Did all Nippon bisque-head dolls have sleep eyes?

No, the majority did but there are a few that had set eyes. This

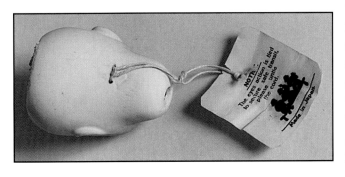

was probably a cost saving measure as it's more time consuming to put sleep eyes in a doll, and it's harder to put sleep eyes in solid dome head dolls. How can you tell if your doll should have sleep eyes? Look at the back head to see if there are two holes near the base of the head. These holes were used to secure the sleep eyes in place during shipment; therefore, if the holes are present, the doll originally had sleep eyes.

My doll's glass eyes don't sleep like they should. Can this be repaired?

Yes, it can be repaired but it may not be easy, depending on what's causing the eyes not to sleep. If you can easily remove the wig and the pate, look inside the head. Sometimes dealers and others put paper in the head to keep the eyes from rocking during packing and shipping, and they forget to take it out when selling the doll. Also, sometimes sleep eyes get stuck. You might be able to get them to move but don't force them. Better to have the original sleep eyes that don't sleep than to break them and have to replace them. The eyes may have also been re-set in plaster so that they no longer sleep. If this is the case, consult a doll repairer. If the old sleep eyes have been removed and replaced with a pair of non-sleep eyes, then you will need to find an old pair of sleep eyes that fit the doll. This is often hard to do, but a doll repairer will be able to advise you on this.

Where's the best place to find and buy dolls?

Nippon dolls can be found at flea markets, antique malls and shows, auctions, and through the Internet. Perhaps the best place to find dolls, however, is the antique doll and toys shows that occur around the country. In addition to finding Nippon dolls at these shows, collectors get the opportunity to see dolls of all types and ask doll dealers questions about doll collecting. If collecting all-bisque or celluloid dolls, make sure you look in the small cases that many dealers have. Those types of dolls are often tucked in with jewelry, linens, and other types of small items.

Do stickers and boxes add to the value of dolls and tea sets?

Yes, definitely. Even partial stickers or broken up boxes can add to the value of an item. Collectors are always looking for dolls and toys in their original boxes. First, these items are usually in very fine condition since they have may never been played with. Secondly,

original boxes, tags, and stickers provide invaluable information as to manufacturers, dates of availability, original prices, doll names, etc.

I've heard that celluloid is very flammable. Is it safe to keep celluloid dolls?

Yes, celluloid is flammable and yes, it is safe to keep celluloid dolls; however, care should be taken to keep them away from excessive heat or flames and they should be displayed in a well-ventilated area.

How do you find Nippon holiday items? Where should I look for them?

As with Nippon dolls and toys, Nippon holiday items can be found at flea markets, antique shows and malls, auctions, and the Internet. If you're really interested in finding Nippon holidays items, there are dealers and shows that specialize in these. Doll and toy shows also usually have some holiday items. However, if buying from a holiday dealer you can expect to pay top dollar for any holiday item. They are a popular cross-collectible.

I saw a cardboard candy container that was marked "Japan." The dealer said it was the same as Nippon. Is it the same?

In this author's opinion, no. While many candy containers made during the Nippon era were probably marked "Japan," this mark was used for many years. There is no way to make sure that you are getting a Nippon candy container unless it's actually marked "Nippon." Remember that items marked "Nippon" specify a certain period of time (1891 – 1921) while items marked "Japan" do not.

My celluloid doll has a dent in the body. Can this be repaired?

Yes, it can, but it's difficult to do and the results are often not satisfactory (see the chapter on "Care and Handling of Your Dolls" for a description of how to do the repair). Take this into consideration when buying celluloid dolls and toys and, if the item is badly dented, you should expect a major reduction in price. If the dents are not too bad, then this author recommends you leave it as is.

What factors should I consider when buying a bisque-head doll?

There are a number of factors to take into consideration when buying a bisque-head doll. First and foremost is the quality of the bisque head. According to the *Collector's Encyclopedia of Dolls,* "The head has always been one of the most valuable parts of a doll, and its proportionate value increases as it becomes an antique." Collectors should look for heads with good, smooth bisque, no cheek or nose rubs, no black specks (caused by dust in the kiln), and, of course, no chips or cracks. Workmanship is another consideration. How good is the facial painting? Is the facial coloring natural looking or are the colors washed out or too dark (high cheek color for example)? Are the brushmarks that produced the eyebrows, eyelashes, and nostrils done well? Artistic quality and rarity of the mold (a googly for example) are another a consideration. Is it a well-modeled character face? Dolls of this type will always be popular, and their value will usually be higher than that for a dolly faced child doll of the same quality.

Overall condition of the doll is the next most important consideration. Is the doll in mint condition or does it have its original parts, wig, and clothes? These dolls will always command a better price. Is the doll body in reasonable condition? Is it the right type and size of body for the doll? Has the wig been replaced with an appropriate wig or a new synthetic wig? Are the clothes new ones in modern materials or old clothes made during the same time period as the doll? As the *Collector's Encyclopedia of Dolls* notes, "If an old doll has head, body, and clothes all of the same period, it is more valuable than one with modern parts and clothes."

Another thing to consider is the rarity or uniqueness of the doll. For example, Morimura Brothers produced a crying doll that has a bellow in the head to produce a sound when the bellow is activated. They used the same head as for their character baby Baby Ella which is a fairly common doll. However, the crying doll is not common, and collectors should take unique items such as this into consideration.

What should I look at when buying a bisque-head doll?

As noted in the previous question, there are a number of things you should look for when buying a bisque head doll. Pay close attention to the bisque to see if there are chips or hairline cracks, black specks (from dust), color rubs (places where the cheek or nose color has rubbed off showing white marks) or stains. Normally, you should also take the wig and pate off to look inside the head. You will be able to see if the pate is old or a replacement. A replacement pate usually indicates that the wig has been replaced. By looking in the head you can see if the plaster that holds in the eyes is new and if other repairs have been done. Most doll heads will show some dirt on the inside; heads that are very clean on the inside may indicate that repairs have been done. A strong light or black light can help locate cracks or repairs, but the light must shine through the head.

Ask to see the doll undressed. Perhaps the body is damaged under the clothing or has mismatched or replaced parts. Check for wear but remember these dolls were meant for children to play with, so some wear is to be expected. Also check to see if the head and body proportions are appropriate. Look to see if the head is too big or too small for the body.

Sometimes it's impossible, however, to thoroughly go over a doll before buying it. If you can't, at least make sure you ask the dealer about repairs and originality. This is especially true now that many people buy through the Internet. Ask for a return privilege so you can inspect the doll upon receipt; most reputable dealers will be happy to provide one.

What is an oyster shell body?

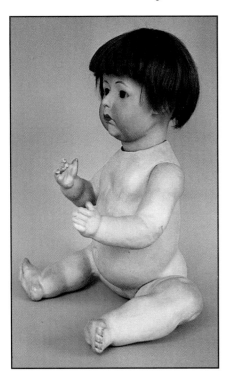

It's a composition-type body (usually a five-piece bent limb baby body) where the main ingredient is ground up oyster shells instead of sawdust. The Japanese had used oyster shells before in doll making and apparently still do. Therefore, using oyster shells for Nippon doll bodies was a natural for them. These bodies tend to be of very fine quality — well-molded, good flesh tone, and a smooth feel. The finish is more lifelike than the regular composition bodies that usually has a shiny finish. The RE in Diamond character babies seem to have oyster shell bodies more often than other Nippon bisque head dolls.

Five-piece oyster shell baby body.

Should dome head dolls be dressed as boys or girls?

Actually, most were originally dressed in long gowns as babies, and you often find them today in the long white baby gowns. Nippon dome head dolls are cute dressed as either a boy or a girl, but many feel that because of their painted hair they make an especially cute boy doll.

Dome head dressed as a baby, very typical.

Dome head dressed as a boy and on a toddler-type body.

I found some Christmas lights that are marked "Nippon Registration." When were these made?

The cardboard house lights were not made during the Nippon era but came much later

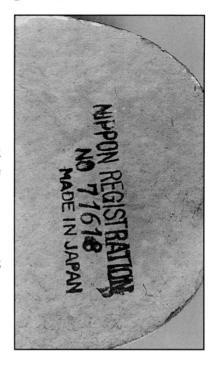

in the 1920s. Many collectors are confused because the mark says "Nippon Registration," but this refers to the fact that the light was registered or patented in Japan.

The starlight-type lights also came much later. The U.S. patent for similar lights is dated 1936.

Did the same doll mold sometimes have different paint or colors?

Two celluloid dolls with different paint schemes.

Two half-dolls with different color schemes.

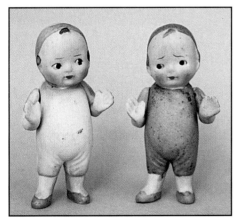

These two all-bisque dolls are the same mold, but note how their facial painting makes them very different.

Definitely, in fact in almost every type of Nippon doll — all-bisque, bisque-head, china glazed half dolls, and celluloid — it's possible to find the same doll with a different paint scheme or coloring.

My doll has both a Nippon and a Made in Japan mark. Why is this?

Beginning on September 1, 1921, the Japanese had to start marking their wares with the word "Japan" not "Nippon" as to the country of origin. These dolls were probably already made with the "Nippon" mark and due to this change also had to be marked "Made in Japan" in order to meet the import regulations. Therefore, dolls marked both "Nippon" and "Made in Japan" probably came into the U.S. during late 1921.

I saw a doll that was marked Nippon in ink across the bottom of the feet. How do I know this is original?

For some reason the Japanese, especially Morimura Brothers, marked many of their all-bisque dolls with ink. We are not sure why they marked them this way, and the ink mark presents a problem for collectors. It's often been washed off or is very hard to see. Also many collectors fail to look for an ink mark which is often on the bottom of the feet.

It's unlikely that most doll dealers would go to the trouble of trying to forge an ink mark. Even with the rising prices for Nippon all-bisque dolls, the German all-bisque dolls are still more expensive and, if the dealer were going to manufacture a mark, it would probably be Germany, not Nippon.

Mark found on a bisque-head doll.

What do the symbols, numbers, and letters on the back of a doll head mean?

Mark found on a celluloid doll.

On all-bisque and the small bisque head dolls, the number that is seen on some of them is a mold number. On celluloid dolls and toys the symbol (if there is one) is usually the trademark of the company that produced the doll or toy.

On bisque-head dolls, the numbers and/or letters usually represent the mold number and size of the doll; the symbol represents the company that produced the doll head. See the section "Deciphering Nippon Bisque-Head Doll Marks," for a more detailed description of the bisque-head doll marks.

I have to store my dolls for a considerable length of time. Is there a safe way to do this?

Yes, there is. See the chapter on "Care and Handling of Your Dolls" for a complete description of how to prepare your dolls for storing.

I was cleaning my dolls and one doll seemed to lose its facial coloring. Why did this happen?

Example of doll where hair color has been washed off.

Because your doll did not have a second firing to set the paint. Many Nippon stone bisque dolls fall into this category. Before cleaning your dolls, take a close look at them. You can usually tell if the paint is fired in. If in doubt, don't clean the doll.

I know that Queue San Baby was made both in Japan and Germany. How can I be sure that I'm buying the Nippon version?

Some are marked Nippon (usually in ink). There are also a fairly large number that have kept their original stickers. Look at the sticker, and on the Nippon dolls you'll see the words "Reg. U.S. Pat. Off." This is because Morimura Brothers held the patent rights to Queue San Baby. The German version does not have those words on the sticker. (Refer to all-bisque doll marks.)

Are Morimura Brothers dolls, which are marked Japan, still considered to be Nippon?

Most doll collectors and dealers do consider them to be Nippon even though they marked their bisque-head dolls "Japan." We know for certain that Morimura Brothers' dolls and toys were made during the Nippon era, and that in 1921 they shut down their doll factory.

Some dolls are made in more than one size. Does size affect the value?

Yes, usually. All-bisque dolls in larger sizes (over 7") are more difficult to find. For example, the 8" Nippon Kewpie is much harder to find than the 6" and 4½" Nippon Kewpies. The same is true for many bisque-head dolls. The larger sizes are often harder to find and, therefore, more expensive. Also, there are Nippon show dolls (over 30"). These are rare, and the price would reflect that rarity.

My doll has what looks like a fur wig. Is this an appropriate wig for the doll?

Yes, it is. Animal skins had been used as material for doll wigs since the 1800s, and with mohair shortages during the war, they continued to be used during the Nippon era. Animal skin wigs definitely give the doll a different look from the traditional human hair and mohair wigs.

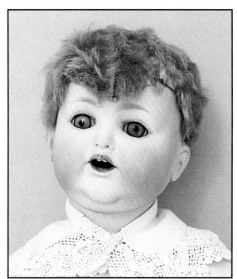

Fur wig in unusual red color. Notice that the wig color matches the eyebrow color.

What pieces can I expect to find in a toy tea set?

A review of old catalogs indicates that Nippon toy tea sets came in a variety of sizes. The smallest set with cups and saucers contained a teapot, sugar and creamer, and 2 cups and saucers. The largest set came with a teapot, sugar and creamer, 6 cups and saucers, and 6 plates. There were even sets with just 3 cups and saucers. We are not sure why they would include just 3 cups and saucers, but old catalog advertisements indicate they did. Many sets came with 4 cups and saucers and/or 4 plates. It was also possible to buy a set with just a teapot, sugar, and creamer. Something to meet every need and for every price range.

1920 Butler Brothers ad.

A dealer told me that the doll I'm interested in is a Nippon Hilda look alike. What is a Hilda look alike and how do I know for sure that this Nippon doll is one?

The German Hilda was a popular character baby introduced by the Kestner firm in 1914. Immediately she became a bestseller and remains extremely popular today with doll collectors. As we know, the Japanese copied many of the popular German dolls and, in fact, in 1919 Louis Wolf &

Mark found on Hilda look alike.

Company advertised Japanese copies of the popular German dolls. Nippon doll collectors and doll dealers tend to agree that the Nippon doll that most closely resembles Hilda is the 'B' mold of the RE in Diamond mark. Therefore, if the doll you are considering buying has that mold mark, then you are getting a Nippon Hilda look alike.

What's the difference between a child's oatmeal set and a breakfast set?

Collectors and dealers tend to use both terms to describe a set consisting of a matching plate, bowl, and small pitcher. However, an ad in a 1920 Montgomery Ward catalog indicates that there was a difference between the two. An oatmeal (or porridge as they called it) set did contain a matching plate, bowl, and pitcher, but the child's breakfast set contained a matching plate, bowl, and small mug.

Child's Porridge Set

Decorated with pretty pictures in four colors. Edged in light blue. Comprises porridge dish, creamer and plate. Diam. of plate, 7¼ in. Ship. wt., 2½ lbs.
I50C772—Price set..**$1.35**

Child's Breakfast Set

Decorated with pictures in four colors. Edged in light blue. Set includes porridge dish, tall cup and plate. Diam. plate, 7¼ in. Ship. wt., 3 lbs.
I50C773—Price set .**$1.25**

I have a large bisque doll head with no body. How can I tell if it should be on a child or baby body? Should I dress it as a boy or a girl?

The shape of the face and neck usually indicates whether it should be on a child ball-jointed body or on a bent limb baby body. If the head has a chubby round face with a short neck, then it was probably originally on a baby body. If it has a longer face and neck, then it was likely on a ball-jointed body. Of course, if it has a shoulderplate, it should be on an imitation kid body or a cloth body and that would make it a child doll. Some doll heads look good on either a baby or ball-jointed body especially if the ball-jointed body is a toddler-type body.

As to whether it should be dressed as a boy or a girl, most dolls were originally dressed as girls or generic babies. However, since many dolls were dressed at home, some were definitely dressed as boys. Many Nippon bisque-head dolls have faces that lend themselves to being dressed as either boys or girls. As you go through this book, you will see dolls that fit this category, and we have several examples of dolls dressed as boys that are in their original clothing.

Doll and Plaything Inventory Sheets

Collectors should always keep a complete inventory of their collections, including both photos and accompanying information. Since dolls and playthings vary from other collectibles, we have devised inventory sheets that should allow you to note all significant information.

Photocopy* these sheets and insert copies in a three-ring binder. Your current collection can be kept in the front part and items that have been sold in the back. Whenever items match pieces in Nippon Dolls and Playthings be sure to make a notation. Reappraise your items every few years and update these prices on your inventory sheet.

*Permission is given by the authors to photocopy the inventory sheet for the PERSONAL use of the collector only.

DOLL INVENTORY SHEET

PLACE PHOTO HERE

Type of Doll _____
     (child, baby, figural, nodder, etc.)

Material _____
    (bisque, celluloid, composition, etc.)

Date Acquired _____

Purchased Date_____

Price Paid $ _____

If exact item in *Nippon Dolls and Playthings:*
    plate # _____
If not exact as shown:
    similar plate # _____

Current Appraisals:
Date_____Value $ _____
Date_____Value $ _____
Date_____Value $ _____
Date_____Value $ _____
Date_____Value $ _____

Markings_____
(Identify all numbers, letters, initials and symbols; document original stickers/labels and boxes)

Description_____
(Include complete description of doll including costume and a description of flaws or repairs)

_____

_____

_____

_____

Date Sold _____

Selling Price $ _____

Sold To_____

PLAYTHING INVENTORY SHEET

PLACE PHOTO HERE

Type of Item _____
          (teaset, candy container, rattle, etc.)

Material _____
         (porcelain, celluloid, cardboard, etc.)

Date Acquired _____

Purchased Date _____

Price Paid $ _____

If exact item in *Nippon Dolls and Playthings:*
    plate # _____
If not exact as shown:
    similar plate # _____

Current Appraisals:
Date_____Value $ _____
Date_____Value $ _____
Date_____Value $ _____
Date_____Value $ _____
Date_____Value $ _____

Markings_____
(Identify all numbers, letters, initials and symbols; document original stickers/labels and boxes)

Description _____
(Include complete description of item including flaws or repairs)

_____

_____

_____

_____

Date Sold _____

Selling Price $ _____

Sold To_____

Pricing

Price guides are always controversial, and we expect the prices listed in this book to be no exception. Collectors and dealers must realize that these prices are merely a starting point in determining a price and are not intended to set them. They are to be used only as a guide.

You will find estimated retail prices listed. Every piece is considered to be in original condition with no chips, cracks, hairlines, dents (in the case of celluloid), excessive wear (some wear is to be expected since these items were intended for children to play with), repairs, or inappropriately replaced parts such as arms/legs, wigs, bodies, or clothes. Any of these conditions will decrease the value of the doll or toy, and this should be reflected in the retail price. On the other hand, dolls and toys with their original stickers and boxes or in mint condition tend to have an increased value.

As we have already discussed in other chapters of this book, the bisque-head dolls are especially hard to price because there are many factors that affect the value of these dolls: the quality of the bisque and the facial painting; the rarity of the doll; the over-all condition and originality of the doll; or the general popularity of a particular doll type (i.e., a character doll). Prices should be decreased for flaws in the bisque such as chips and cracks; poor facial painting such as uneven or unnatural flesh tones; color rubs on the face; composition bodies that are in poor condition; new wigs and clothes in inappropriate styles or materials; or set eyes on dolls that should have sleep eyes. This doesn't mean you shouldn't buy these dolls. It just means that you should expect to see a reduction in the price to compensate for these flaws. Each doll has to be judged on its own merit and workmanship.

Prices for some items are higher because they are cross-collectibles and appeal to more than one group of collectors. Celluloid dolls and toys, children's tea sets, and holiday items are good examples of Nippon playthings that appeal to more than one group of collectors. There are many people who collect these items, and the overall popularity of a collectible drives its price higher.

Prices also reflect collecting fads and the desire of the buyer as well as the size of the pocketbook. Prices vary in different localities and regional tastes differ. Also, some items may be more plentiful in certain areas of the country. The price often is based on the margin of profit the dealer wants. Items may be priced according to what was paid for the piece or a dealer's estimation on what it will bring in a particular market. If a collector wants something badly enough, he/she will probably be willing to pay more than others.

It is hard to tell how, in the future, other factors will affect the price of Nippon playthings. The Internet is now giving people access world wide to Nippon dolls and toys. We already know that many in Japan are starting to take an interest in these items. The Internet also provides doll collectors with a means of finding dolls that they may never have been able to find at a local antique shop or show. Will this generate more interest and cause prices to go higher? Or because there are now more sellers and more selection, will it cause prices to stabilize or go lower?

Collectors should buy what appeals to them regardless of what the collecting trends are at the moment. Fads come and go. What is in favor today may not command as high a price a few years from now. Other items may skyrocket. So buy what you love!

The more you shop for Nippon dolls and playthings, the more you'll be able to disregard the price guides and rely on your own knowledge as to what is the correct price. Five collectors can give an estimated price for what we may think is a $200.00 item, and the five prices will often be all across the board. This does not make any of them wrong; it just proves what an impossible task pricing can be.

Study this book and you'll get an idea of what are more expensive and what are everyday items. Don't pay a premium price for an ordinary or lower quality item. But whatever you do, enjoy your collecting. Whoever said that money can't buy happiness doesn't know where to shop for Nippon dolls and playthings!

Doll is in original, unplayed with condition and would command a higher price.

This doll, while pretty, has several problems that would lower the value. It has a modern synthetic wig, the eyes have been set, and several fingers are broken.

All-Bisque Dolls

All-bisque dolls made by the Germans and French have been popular since the 1880s, and there's evidence that the Japanese imported all-bisque dolls into the U.S. as early as the 1890s. A review of statistical information provided by *Playthings* indicates that the Japanese were definitely supplying dolls to the American market in the early 1900s, but it is unclear what type of dolls were imported into the U.S. All-bisque dolls became especially popular with the introduction of Kewpie, the now famous doll designed by Rose O'Neill. The first Kewpie illustrations appeared in 1909 in the *Ladies' Home Journal* and subsequently in *Woman's Home Companion, Good Housekeeping*, and *The Delineator*. By 1913 a bisque Kewpie doll, modeled by Rose O'Neill, was already being produced by more than 20 German factories. The majority of Nippon all-bisque dolls were made in the years following the introduction of Kewpie. When Germany became involved in World War I, the Japanese quickly filled the void.

World War I era all-bisque dolls usually sold for under 50 cents each. In 1915 Montgomery Ward advertised bisque Kewpies 5" and 6⅞" tall for 25 and 49 cents. These dolls could be purchased at five & ten cent stores, candy stores, craft stores, and novelty stores as well as ordered from a variety of mail order catalogs. Although they certainly appealed to children and were sold to children, many were not originally intended as toys but were meant for the adult market to be used as party favors, centerpieces, cake decorations, candy boxes, pincushions, and knick-knacks. Women often dressed them in crepe paper, ribbon, and other materials for use on top of wedding cakes, as holiday decorations, and as gifts. Both women's magazines and books published by crepe paper companies such as Dennison's provided instructions for decorating the dolls and using them in novel ways. Dressed all-bisque dolls were also commercially made to sell as holiday decorations and pincushions. Collectors should not remove these clothes because they add to the charm and value of the doll. Dolls decorated for holidays tend to be more expensive since they appeal to holiday collectors as well as doll collectors.

The popularity of all-bisque dolls carried through the end of the Nippon era and there are numerous examples of Nippon-marked all-bisque dolls. The Japanese copied all of the popular German dolls — Kewpie, Baby Bud, Chubby, Happifats, Wide-Awake (although the Japanese named him Sonny), and the Kewpie soldier. Morimura Brothers produced many original designs including Queue San Baby, Baby Darling, Baby Belle, and Dolly. Queue San Baby was so popular that after

Ad from booklet "How to Make Party Favors and Table Decorations" by Dennison Manufacturing Co.

Morimura Brothers stopped producing dolls, German companies took over production. Competition was fierce among doll distributors and they often copied each other's dolls. Baby Darling, produced by Morimura Brothers, and Sweetie, produced by Louis Wolf & Co., are good examples of this.

Most Nippon all-bisque dolls are three to seven inches tall. Larger ones are rarer and therefore command higher prices. The majority of Nippon all-bisque dolls have shoulder joints or are jointed at both the shoulder and hip. Those that are not jointed at all are called figurals or statuette dolls. There is one unusual Nippon all-bisque doll that is jointed only at the hips. It is often hard to tell if jointed arms and legs are original to the doll. This is especially true since arms and legs were usually produced and painted separately from the body of the doll and then assembled later. This means that the arms and legs are often not the same flesh tone as the rest of the doll. Collectors should pay attention to the types of arms that were used on the dolls. Some dolls such as Kewpie or Queue San Baby use an arm with what is called starfish hands. It is very obvious if the arms are replaced on these dolls. Because the Japanese performed little, if any, quality control on the dolls, there may be imperfections in the arms, legs, and even the doll itself. The Japanese did not always use the same style arms or legs on the same style doll; they used whatever they had in stock at the time. Collectors will need to judge for themselves if arms and legs look appropriate to the doll or if minor imperfections bother them. Replaced arms and legs may reduce the value of the doll if they don't fit the doll or appear inappropriate.

On Nippon all-bisque dolls, the arms and legs are strung (attached to the doll) with either elastic or wire. On the elastic strung dolls, the arms or legs have stringing loops molded in the bisque to the top inside of the arm or leg. These stringing loops fit into the shoulder or thigh holes in the torso. Over the years the original elastic tends to deteriorate which causes the arms or legs to become loose or fall off. Therefore, it's often necessary to replace the old elastic (see chapter on "Care and Handling of Your Dolls"). Replacing the elastic does not affect the value, and in fact, it improves the appearance and keeps the arms and legs safely on the doll.

Wire strung dolls have a length of wire that goes through a hole in the arm or leg and through the torso. The wire is then looped and bent over the outer side of the arm or leg. Wire doesn't deteriorate like elastic, but it may rust and break when the arms or legs are moved. Again, replacing the wire does not affect the value of the doll.

Another thing for collectors to look for is whether the doll received a second firing in the kiln to permanently set the facial and clothing paint. The majority of all-bisque dolls did receive this second firing, but on some dolls, especially those made of a stone bisque, the doll was painted but not fired again (obviously a cost saving measure). This means that the paint can flake, rub or wash off. Nippon bathtub babies are one example of this type of doll. Collectors need to be very careful when handling and cleaning this type of doll and if in doubt, don't clean the doll. There's almost nothing worse than getting a nice doll and then having all the facial features wash off.

While the majority of Nippon all-bisque dolls are incised with the word "NIPPON" on their back, collectors should also look for marks in ink on the back or bottom of the feet. Many figural dolls are marked in ink on the bottom of their feet. Sometimes the ink mark is very worn and often hard to see. Care should be taken when cleaning ink-marked dolls so that the mark is not further obliterated. Original stickers are also found on some all-bisque dolls and should not be removed. If you're lucky enough to find a doll with its original box, the box should be kept intact and if at all possible, with the doll. Original stickers and boxes add to the value of the doll.

Dolls with molded clothes, figurals (including bathtub babies), dolls dressed in their original clothes, and unusual dolls such as piano babies are most popular with collectors.

All-Bisque Dolls

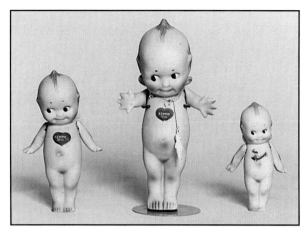

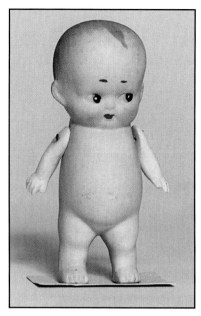

Plate 2
Doll, 4½" tall, mark AB-1, $90.00 – $140.00.

Plate 1
Kewpie doll, 6" tall, mark AB-1, original sticker on stomach and feet, $155.00 – $205.00.
Kewpie doll, 8" tall, mark AB-1, original sticker on stomach and feet, tiny composition Kewpie tied with string around neck may be original, rare size, $350.00 – $400.00.
Kewpie doll, 4½" tall, mark AB-1, partial sticker on stomach and feet, $140.00 – $180.00.

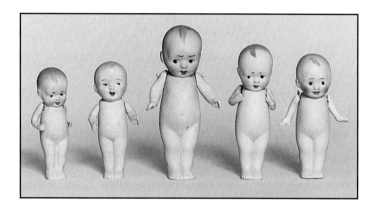

Plate 4
Doll, 4½" tall, mark AB-1, old clothes, $100.00 – $135.00 (as dressed)

Plate 3
Doll, 4½" tall, mark AB-3, $80.00 – $110.00.
Doll, 4¾" tall, mark AB-27, $80.00 – $110.00.
Doll, 6¼" tall, mark AB-1 in ink on bottom of feet, $80.00 – $110.00.
Doll, 5⅝" tall, mark AB-1, also stamped "Japan" on bottom of feet, $80.00 – $110.00.
Doll, 5⅛" tall, mark AB-3, $80.00 – $110.00.

Plate 5
Sonny doll, 6½" tall, mark AB-1, original sticker, $150.00 – $200.00.
Sonny doll, 4¾" tall, mark AB-1, original sticker, $135.00 – $175.00.
Sonny doll, 4¼" tall, mark AB-1, original sticker, $125.00 – $150.00.
Made by Morimura Brothers, some dolls are found with the sticker but are not incised "Nippon."

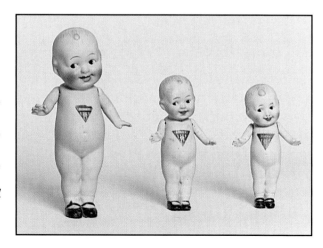

Plate 6
Doll, 4¾" tall, mark AB-1, $90.00 – $100.00.

Plate 7
Same doll as Plate 6; all have original home-made clothes; $135.00 – $165.00 each.

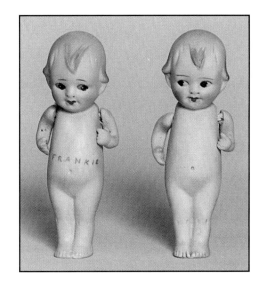

Plate 9
Dolls, 5¾" tall, mark AB-1, doll on left also has "Japan" stamped on bottom of feet, $80.00 – $110.00.

Plate 8
Doll, 5½" tall, mark AB-3, $90.00 – $120.00.
Doll, 4⅜" tall, mark AB-1, $80.00 – $115.00.
Doll, 5½" tall, mark AB-1, original clothes, $90.00 – $120.00.
Note the upside down bows in a different color on each doll.

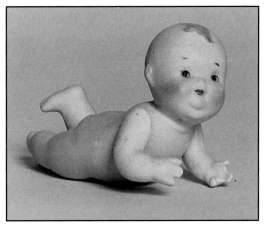

Plate 10
Piano Baby, 4¼" long, mark AB-1, unusual, $145.00 – $195.00.

131

All-Bisque Dolls

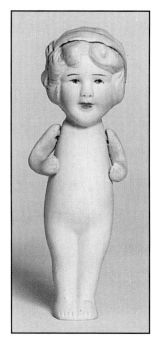

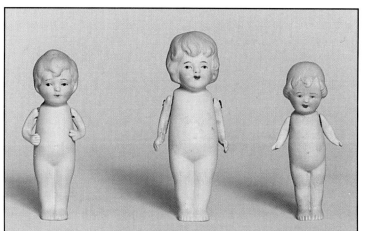

Plate 12
Doll, 4½" tall, mark AB-1, $80.00 – $110.00.
Doll, 5" tall, mark AB-1, $80.00 – $110.00.
Doll, 4¼" tall, mark AB-1, $80.00 – $110.00.

Plate 11
Doll, 5" tall, mark AB-1, $110.00 – $140.00.

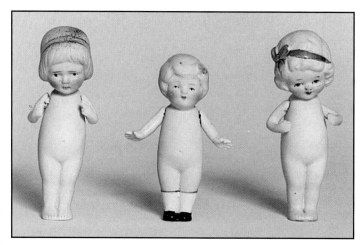

Plate 14
Doll, 4½" tall, mark AB-1, $80.00 – $110.00.
Doll, 4" tall, mark AB-1, $80.00 – $110.00.
Doll, 4½" tall, mark AB-1, $80.00 – $110.00.

Plate 13
Doll, 4⅞" tall, mark AB-1, $80.00 – $110.00.
Doll, 4¾" tall, mark AB-1, $80.00 – $110.00.
These dolls are similar to Baby Darling and Baby Belle but are slightly different; probably copies by another company.

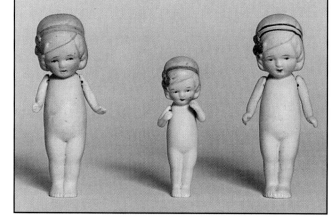

Plate 15
Doll, 5" tall, mark AB-1, $100.00 – $130.00.
Doll, 4½" tall, mark AB-1, $80.00 – $110.00.

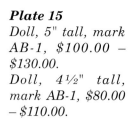

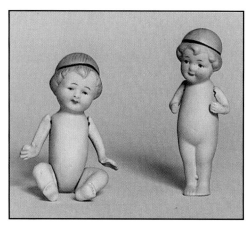

Plate 16
Doll, 5¼" tall, mark AB-1, $80.00 – $110.00.
Doll, 4" tall, mark AB-1, $80.00 – $110.00.
Doll, 5¼" tall, mark AB-1, $80.00 – $110.00.

132

Plate 17
Sunday's Child (by Morimura Brothers), 5" tall, original sticker, rare, $225.00 – $275.00.

Plate 18
Thursday's Child (by Morimura Brothers), 3¾" tall, 2¼" long, mark AB-1 in ink on bottom doll, original sticker and box, rare, $275.00 – $325.00.

Plate 19
Side view of Sunday's Child (Plate 17) showing the gold cross on the Bible.

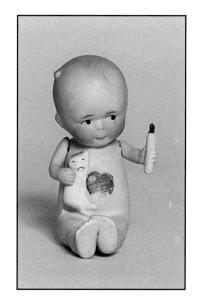

Plate 20
Friday's Child (by Morimura Brothers), 4" tall, 2¼" long, original sticker, rare, $225.00 – $275.00.

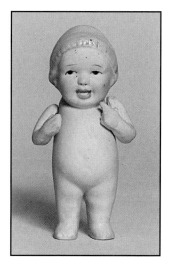

Plate 21
Doll, 4⅜" tall, mark AB-1, $100.00 – $130.00.

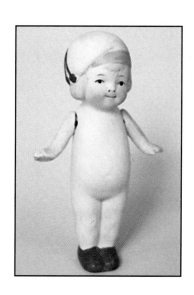

Plate 22
Doll, 4⅞" tall, mark AB-7, $110.00 – $140.00.

Plate 23
*Sweetie (by Louis Wolf &
Co.), 6" tall, mark AB-1,
$135.00 – $165.00.*

Plate 24
*Baby Darling (by Morimura Brothers), 4¾" tall,
original sticker, $115.00 – $140.00.
Baby Darling (by Morimura Brothers), 6½" tall,
original sticker, unusual size, $145.00 – $175.00.
Baby Darling (by Morimura Brothers), 5¼" tall,
mark AB-1 stamped in blue ink on back, original
sticker, $125.00 – $150.00.*

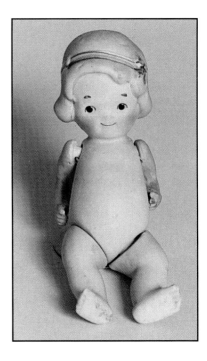

Plate 25
*Doll, 5¾" tall, mark AB-1,
$135.00 – $165.00.*

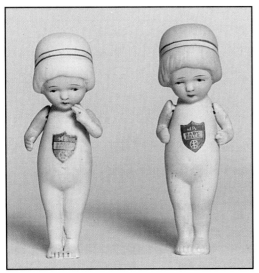

Plate 26
*Baby Belle (by Morimura Brothers), 4½"
tall, original sticker, $115.00 – $140.00.
Baby Belle (by Morimura Brothers), 4¾"
tall, mark AB-1, original sticker, $115.00
– $140.00.*

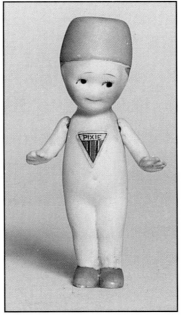

Plate 27
*Pixie, 4" tall, mark AB-1,
original sticker, $110.00 –
$140.00.*

Plate 28
*Dolls, 4½" tall, mark AB-1, $90.00 –
$120.00 each.*

Plate 31
Doll, 4¾" tall, mark AB-1, $90.00 – $120.00.

Plate 29
Doll, 5½" tall, mark AB-1, $135.00 – $165.00.

Plate 30
Doll, 4¼" tall, mark AB-1, $80.00 – $110.00.

Plate 33
Doll, 4½" tall, mark AB-1, $90.00 – $135.00. Doll, 4" tall, mark AB-1, $80.00 – $125.00.

Plate 32
Doll, 4½" tall, mark AB-1, $90.00 – $120.00.
Doll, 4¼" tall, mark AB-3, $90.00 – $120.00.

Plate 34
Doll, 4" tall, mark AB-1, $90.00 – $120.00.
Doll, 4" tall, mark AB-3, $90.00 – $120.00.

135

All-Bisque Dolls

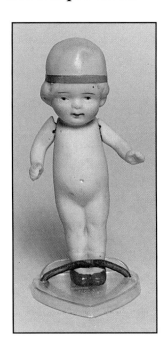

Plate 36
Dolls, 5" tall, mark AB-20, $100.00 – $140.00 (each); note these dolls are the same except that the hats are painted differently.

Plate 35
Doll, 5" tall, mark AB-18, $100.00 – $140.00.

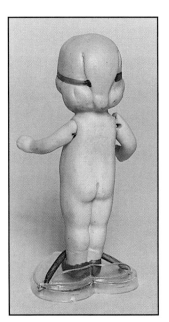

Plate 37
Doll, 4¾" tall, mark AB-1, $100.00 – $140.00.
Doll, 4⅝" tall, mark AB-1, old crocheted clothes, $100.00 – $140.00.
Doll, 4⅝" tall, mark AB-1, $100.00 – $140.00.

Plate 38
Back view of Plate 35.

Plate 39
Doll, 5" tall, mark AB-18, $100.00 – $140.00.
Doll, 5¼" tall, mark AB-1, $100.00 – $140.00.
Doll, 5" tall, mark AB-21, $100.00 – $140.00.

Plate 41
Doll, 5¼" tall, mark AB-13, old crocheted outfit, $100.00 – $140.00 as dressed.

Plate 40
Dolls, 5" tall, mark AB-1, original crocheted outfits, $100.00 – $140.00 each, as dressed.

Plate 43
Doll, 5½", mark AB-1, unusual in that the head is turned to the side, old dress, $110.00 – $140.00.

Plate 42
Doll, 5" tall, mark AB-19, old clothes, $100.00 – $135.00 as dressed.
Doll, 4⅞" tall, mark AB-14, $80.00 – $110.00.

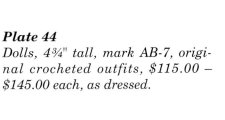

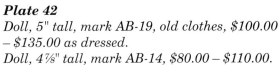

Plate 44
Dolls, 4¾" tall, mark AB-7, original crocheted outfits, $115.00 – $145.00 each, as dressed.

Plate 45
Doll, 4⅞" tall, mark AB-1, painted-on shoes are not original to the doll, $100.00 – $135.00.

137

All-Bisque Dolls

Plate 48
Doll, 5½" tall, jointed arms and legs, mark AB-1, original knitted outfit, $110.00 – $145.00.

Plate 46
Doll, 5⅜" tall, mark AB-20, lamb's wool clothes have been glued on, $100.00 – $140.00.

Plate 47
Doll, 5½" tall, mark AB-22, original home-made clothes, $100.00 – $140.00.

Plate 50
Doll, 5" tall, mark AB-1, old clothes, $100.00 – $130.00.

Plate 49
Doll, 8" tall, mark AB-11, rare large size, $145.00 – $185.00.
Doll, 6½" tall, mark AB-11, old clothes, $120.00 – $150.00.

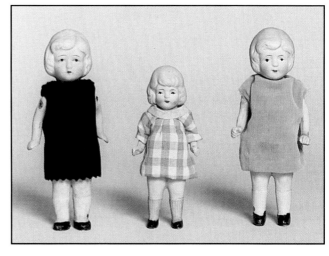

Plate 51
Doll, 5" tall, jointed arms only, mark AB-1, original Buster Brown outfit, $125.00 – $150.00.

Plate 52
Doll, 6⅛" tall, jointed arms only, mark AB-26, $100.00 – $140.00.
Doll, 5" tall, jointed arms only, AB-1, $90.00 – $125.00.
Doll, 6⅛" tall, jointed arms only, AB-1, $100.00 – $140.00.

Plate 53

Doll, 4¾" tall, mark AB-1 stamped in ink across lower back, new clothes, $90.00 – $125.00.
Doll, 4¾" tall, mark AB-1, $90.00 – $125.00.
Doll, 4¾" tall, mark AB-1, old clothes, $90.00 – $125.00.

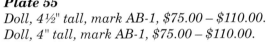

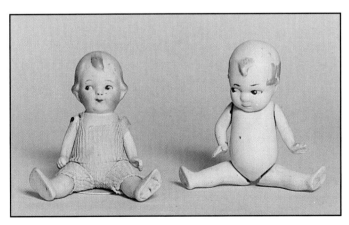

Plate 55

Doll, 4½" tall, mark AB-1, $75.00 – $110.00.
Doll, 4" tall, mark AB-1, $75.00 – $110.00.

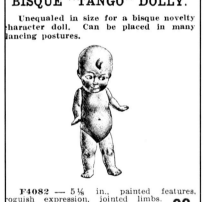

Plate 54

Doll, 4⅞" tall, mark AB-1, new clothes, $75.00 – $110.00.

Plate 56

Old ad for Tango dolly.

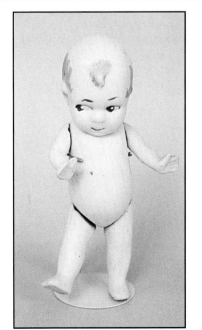

Plate 58

Same doll as pictured in Plate 57 (right) only in standing tango position. See ad in Plate 56. The tango was a popular dance during this era, and no doubt the doll was named in response to this popularity.

Plate 57

Doll, 5¼" tall, mark AB-1, $85.00 – $130.00.
Doll, 5⅜" tall, mark AB-1, poor quality bisque, $70.00 – $100.00.

All-Bisque Dolls

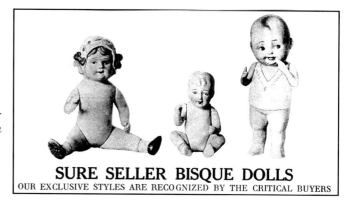
Plate 60
Doll, 6¼" tall, mark AB-4, old dress, $80.00 – $125.00.
Doll, 5⅝" tall, mark AB-4, original dress, $90.00 – $140.00.
Based on their hairstyle and the way the hands are positioned, it is likely that these dolls predate World War I.

Plate 59
Doll, 3¾" tall, mark AB-l, paint worn, old dress, $60.00 – $90.00 if in good condition.

Plate 61
1920 Playthings ad for the Taiyo Trading Company showing three all-bisque dolls. The doll in the middle is shown in Plate 62. The doll on the right is Baby Bud (Plate 97).

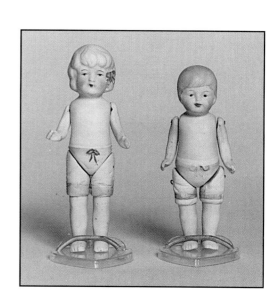

Plate 62
Doll, 3½" tall, mark AB-3, new clothes, $60.00 – $90.00.

Plate 63
Doll, 6½" tall, mark AB-1, $110.00 – $140.00.

Plate 64
Doll, 5¾" tall, mark AB-1, unusual, $130.00 – $160.00.
Doll, 5¼" tall, mark AB-1, $120.00 – $150.00.

140

Plate 65

Doll, 4⅝" tall, mark AB-1, new clothes, $70.00 – $100.00

Doll, 5½" tall, mark AB-10, new clothes, stone bisque, $70.00 – $100.00.

Doll, 4⅝" tall, mark AB-1, new clothes, stone bisque, $70.00 – $100.00.

Those dolls in stone bisque do not have a second firing and the color is likely to wear or wash off. Worn color will devalue the doll.

Plate 66

Doll, 5⅞" tall, mark AB-1, old clothes, $110.00 – $140.00.

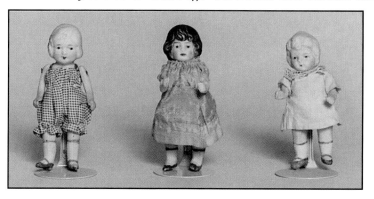

Plate 67

Doll, 4" tall, mark AB-1, old clothes, $70.00 – $100.00.

Doll, 4" all, mark AB-1, unusual brown hair, stone bisque, $70.00 – $100.00.

Doll, 3¾" tall, mark AB-1 with a "7" incised on chest, $70.00 – $100.00.

Plate 68

Doll, 6" tall, mark AB-1, original dress which is longer than the doll, $130.00 – $160.00.

Plate 69

Doll, 6¼" tall, mark AB-1, old dress, $125.00 – $150.00.

Doll, 6½" tall, mark AB-1, $125.00 – $150.00.

Doll, 7" tall, mark AB-1, original dress and underwear, $130.00 – $160.00.

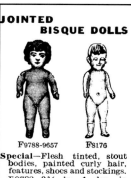

Plate 70

Old Butler Brothers ad.

All-Bisque Dolls

Plate 73
Old Butler Brothers ad.

Plate 72
Doll, 6½" tall, mark AB-1, $125.00 – $150.00.
Doll, 6½" tall, mark AB-1, $125.00 – $150.00.

Plate 71
Doll, 6⅞" tall, mark AB-1, original cro-cheted dress, $135.00 – $165.00.

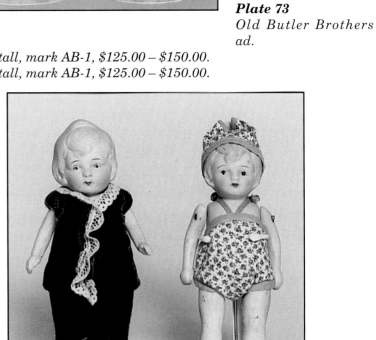

Plate 75
Doll, 6⅞" tall, mark AB-1, $125.00 – $150.00.
Doll, 6¾" tall, mark AB-1, $125.00 – $150.00.

Plate 74
Doll, 7" tall, mark AB-9, original dress, $135.00 – $165.00.
Doll, 7¼" tall, mark AB-9, $125.00 – $150.00.

Plate 76
Doll, 5¾" tall, mark AB-1, penciled on back is "20 ct," prob-ably the original price, dress is old but not original to the doll, $115.00 – $140.00.
Doll, 5⅞" tall, mark AB-1, new clothes, $100.00 – $130.00.

142

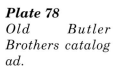
Plate 78
Old   Butler Brothers catalog ad.

Plate 77
Doll, 3⅞" tall, mark AB-1, original mohair wig, $75.00 – $110.00.
Doll, 4¾" tall, mark AB-1, original mohair wig, $85.00 – $120.00.
Doll, 5" tall, mark AB-1, original human hair wig, $85.00 – $120.00.
Doll, 5¼" tall, mark AB-1, original mohair wig, $85.00 – $120.00.
All of these dolls have replaced clothing.

Plate 80
Doll, 7" tall, mark AB-1, original human hair wig, original dress, $135.00 – $165.00.

Plate 79
Doll, 6⅞" tall, mark AB-1, original mohair wig, old home-made dress, $135.00 – $165.00.
Doll, 7" tall, mark AB-1, original human hair wig, old dress, $135.00 – $165.00.
Note that both dolls have had their wigs cut in the then popular bob style.

Plate 81
Doll, 3½" tall, mark AB-7, replaced wig and dress, $40.00 – $60.00.
Doll, 5¼" tall, mark AB-1, original mohair wig, replaced clothes, $75.00 – $110.00.

Plate 82
Doll, 5¾" tall, mark AB-1, original human hair wig, original ethnic clothes, unusual, $130.00 – $165.00.

143

All-Bisque Dolls

Plate 85

Doll, 8½" tall, mark AB-11, glass sleep eyes, mohair wig, old clothes, Nippon all-bisque dolls with glass eyes are rare, $225.00 – $275.00.

Plate 84

Doll, 7" tall, mark AB-1, original mohair wig, old Red Cross dress, $135.00 – $165.00.

Plate 83

Doll, 6⅜" tall, mark AB-1, original mohair wig, original clothes probably made by a child, $120.00 – $150.00.

Plate 87

Doll, 4½" tall, mark AB-1, unusual flocked wig, original clothes, $100.00 – $125.00.

Plate 88

Doll, 6½" tall, mark AB-1, unusual large size, $130.00 – $160.00.

Plate 86

*Doll, 5" tall, mark AB-1, $90.00 – $135.00
Doll, 5¾" tall, mark AB-1, had "15" penciled on the back which may be the original price, $110.00 – $145.00.*

Plate 89

Old Butler Brothers ad.

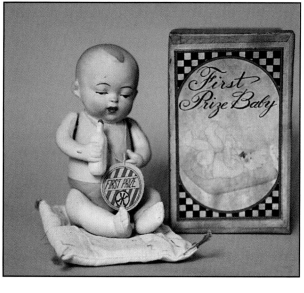

Plate 90
First Prize Baby (by Morimura Brothers), 5½" tall, marked AB-1 on back in purple ink, original tag and box, box marked "652/135 Made In Japan 1 pcs," in unplayed with condition complete with original pillow, rare, $275.00 – $325.00. The doll was made to lie on its back (on the pillow) with its feet in the air and the bottle up to its mouth.

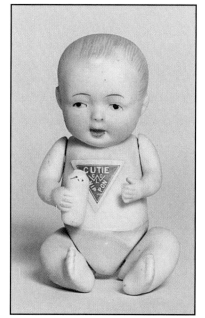

Plate 91
Cutie (by Louis Wolf & Co.), 5¾" tall, mark AB-1, original sticker, nipple of bottle is broken off, $135.00 – $165.00.

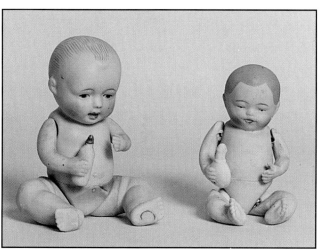

Plate 92
Doll, 5" tall, mark AB-1, $110.00 – $145.00.
Doll, 4½" tall, mark AB-1, note the old style bottle, $100.00 – $135.00.

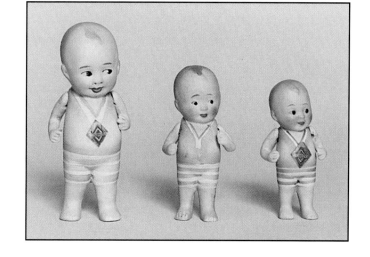

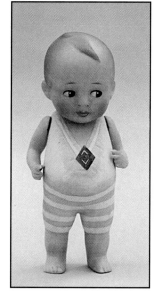

Plate 94
Dolly (by Morimura Brothers), 5" tall, mark AB-1, original sticker, $125.00 – $150.00.
Dolly (by Morimura Brothers), 3⅝" tall, mark AB-1, no sticker, $90.00 – $120.00.
Dolly (by Morimura Brothers), 3¼" tall, mark AB-1, original sticker, $100.00 – $125.00.

Plate 93
Doll, 4" tall, mark AB-8, $90.00 – $125.00.

Plate 95
Dolly (by Morimura Brothers), 7" tall, mark AB-1 in ink on bottom of feet, original sticker, unusual large size, $245.00 – $275.00.

All-Bisque Dolls

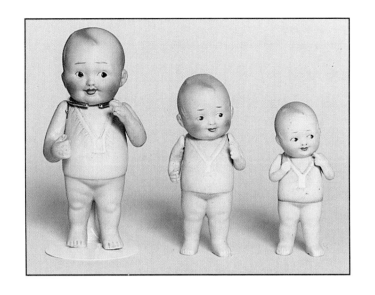

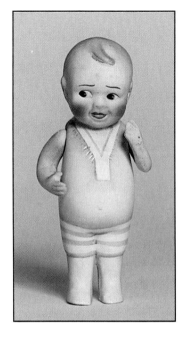

Plate 96
Old Butler Brothers ad
for Baby Bud doll.

Plate 97
Baby Bud, 6½" tall, mark AB-12, $150.00 – $190.00.
Baby Bud, 5⅜" tall, mark AB-12, $130.00 – $160.00.
Baby Bud, 4½" tall, mark AB-12, $120.00 – $150.00.

Plate 98
Doll, 4½" tall, mark AB-1,
$110.00 – $145.00.

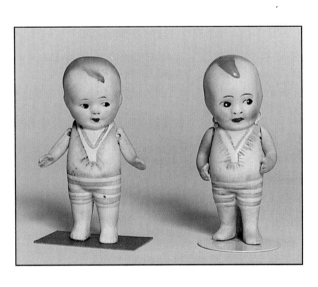

Plate 100
Chubby (by Louis Wolf &
Co.), 6¼" tall, original sticker,
$150.00 – $200.00.

Plate 99
Doll, 3¾" tall, mark AB-1, $100.00 – $135.00.
Doll, 3¾" tall, mark AB-1, unusual green suit,
$100.00 – $135.00.

Plate 101
Doll, 5½" tall, mark AB-1, $135.00 – $160.00.
Doll, 5¾" tall, mark AB-1, $125.00 – $150.00.

146

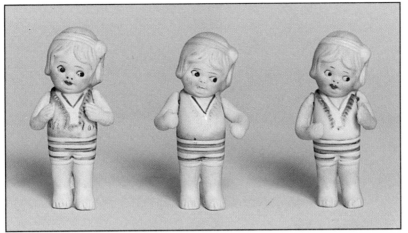

Plate 103

Dolls, 3½" tall, mark AB-1, $100.00 – $135.00 each. Note that each doll is painted differently, and the doll on the left has "Willard" written across its tummy.

Plate 102
Doll, 5" tall, mark AB-1, $135.00 – $160.00.

Plate 104
Doll, 3¾" tall, mark AB-1, $100.00 – $135.00.
Doll, 4¼" tall, mark AB-1, $110.00 – $145.00.

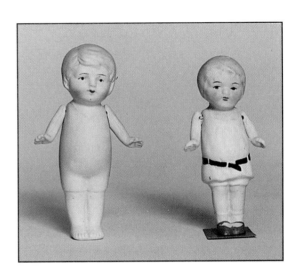

Plate 105
Doll, 4⅝" tall, mark AB-1, $110.00 – $145.00.
Doll, 4¼" tall, mark AB-1, $110.00 – $145.00.

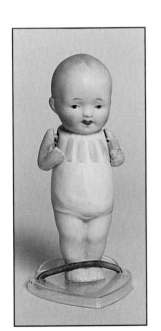

Plate 106
Doll, 4¾" tall, mark AB-1, $110.00 – $145.00.

Plate 108
Sammy, 3½" tall, mark AB-1 in ink on bottom of feet, original sticker, $115.00 – $145.00 with sticker.

Plate 107
Doll, 5" tall, mark AB-1, $140.00 – $170.00.

All-Bisque Dolls

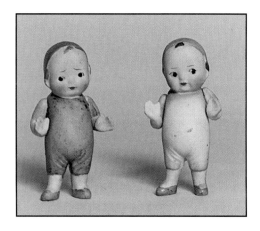

Plate 109
*Dolls, both 3¾" tall, mark AB-1,
$100.00 – $140.00.*

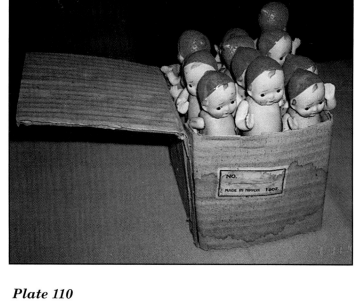

Plate 110
*Twelve dolls in their original shipping box. Note the lack
of packing material in the box; it is likely that many
dolls were damaged during shipment.*

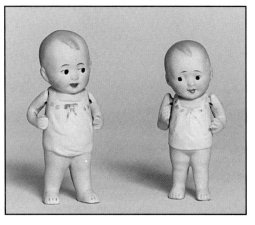

Plate 111
*Doll, 3¾" tall, mark AB-1, $100.00 –
$135.00.
Doll, 3½" tall, mark AB-1, $100.00 –
$135.00.*

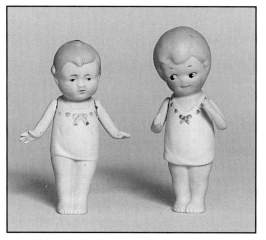

Plate 112
*Doll, 4¼" tall, mark AB-1,
$100.00 – $135.00.
Doll, 4⅝" tall, mark AB-1,
$110.00 – $145.00.*

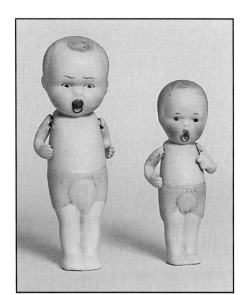

Plate 113
*Doll, 5" tall, mark AB-
1, $110.00 – $145.00.
Doll, 4" tall, mark AB-
1, $100.00 – $135.00.*

Plate 114
*Doll, 4¾" tall, mark AB-1,
$125.00 – $155.00.*

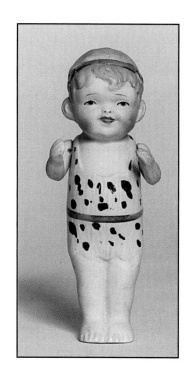

Plate 116
Doll, 4⅞" tall, mark AB-1,
$135.00 – $165.00.

Plate 115
Doll, 5" tall, mark AB-1, heavy stone bisque, modeled like a Baby Bud, rare, $160.00 – $205.00.
Doll, 4⅝" tall, mark AB-1, stone bisque, $140.00 – $180.00.
These dolls did not receive a second firing to set the color so the brown finish will chip and flake off (see toes of doll on right).

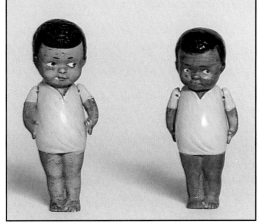

Plate 118
Dolls, 3¾" tall, only boy is marked AB-1 stamped in ink across bottom of feet, $110.00 – $140.00 each.

Plate 117
Doll, 5" tall, mark AB-1, $130.00 – $160.00.
Doll, 4¾" tall, mark AB-1, stamped in ink on bottom of feet, $130.00 – $160.00.

Plate 119
Dolls, 3⅞" tall, mark AB-1, $100.00 – $135.00.

Plate 120
Doll, 5⅝" tall, mark AB-1, $135.00 – $165.00.
Doll, 3⅞" tall, mark AB-1, $115.00 – $140.00.

149

All-Bisque Dolls

Plate 121
Doll, 4¾" tall, mark AB-1, $110.00 – $140.00.
Doll, 4¾" tall, mark AB-1, $110.00 – $140.00.

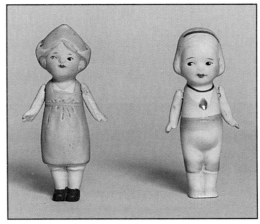

Plate 122
Doll, 4" tall, mark AB-1, $110.00 – $140.00.
Doll, 3⅞" tall, mark AB-1, $100.00 – $135.00.

Plate 123
Doll, 4½" tall, mark AB-1, poor quality bisque, $80.00 – $100.00.

Plate 124
Doll, 5" tall, mark AB-25, $140.00 – $170.00.

Plate 125
Doll, 4⅜" tall, mark AB-1, $140.00 – $170.00.

Plate 126
Piano Baby, 5" long, mark AB-1, made to lie flat on back with legs raised in air, unusual, $175.00 – $225.00.

Plate 127
Doll, 5" tall, mark AB-1, $140.00 – $170.00.

Plate 128
Happifats boy, 3½" tall, mark AB-1, $200.00 – $250.00.
Happifats girl, 3½" tall, mark AB-1, original sticker, $200.00 – $250.00.

Plate 129
Back view of Happifats boy and girl.

Plate 131
Happifats baby, 3¾" tall, mark AB-1, rare, $250.00 – $300.00.

Plate 130
Two Happifats girl dolls of varying quality. The doll on the left is larger and of a much poorer quality than the girl on the right. The quality of the bisque is like pottery or soft paste, and there are flaws in the bisque and painting. Flaws such as this devalue the doll.

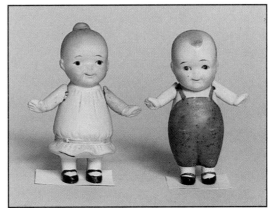

Plate 133
Same as Plate 132, in different colors.

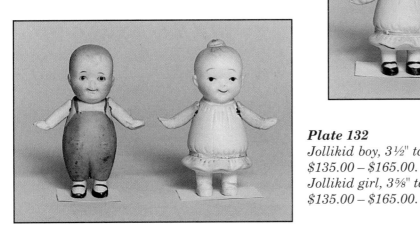

Plate 132
Jollikid boy, 3½" tall, mark AB-6, original sticker, $135.00 – $165.00.
Jollikid girl, 3⅝" tall, mark AB-6, original sticker, $135.00 – $165.00.

All-Bisque Dolls

Plate 135
Manikin, 3½" tall, mark AB-6, original sticker, black jacket, $135.00 – $165.00.

Plate 134
Ladykin, 3½" tall, mark AB-6, original sticker, $135.00 – $165.00.
Manikin, 3½" tall, mark AB-6, original sticker, dark blue jacket, $135.00 – $165.00.

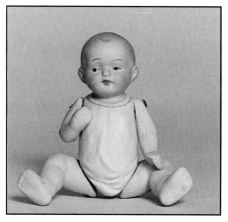

Plate 137
Doll, 5½" tall, mark AB-1, $135.00 – $165.00.

Plate 138
Doll, 6" tall, mark AB-1, $135.00 – $165.00.

Plate 136
Dolls, 3¾" tall; mark AB-6, no sticker but looks like Ladykin, $115.00 – $140.00 each.

Plate 139
Doll, 5¾" tall, mark AB-1, $135.00 – $165.00.

Plate 140
Doll, 3⅛" tall (in sitting position), 4¼" tall (in standing position), mark AB-1, rare, $150.00 – $175.00.

Plate 141
Dolls, 5" tall, mark AB-1, original clothes in excellent condition, $135.00 – $180.00 each, depending on condition of clothes.

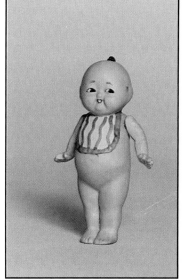

Plate 142
Doll, 5" tall, mark AB-1 in ink on bottom of feet, unusual, $135.00 – $165.00.

Plate 143
Dolls, 5" tall, mark AB-1, original clothes in excellent condition, $135.00 – $180.00 each, depending on condition of clothes.

Plate 145
Dolls, 5" tall, mark AB-1, original clothes and box, rare to find with original box, $200.00 – $250.00. Printed on box in Japanese-like writing is the following:
A baby from the Orient
I bring you greetings true
My smile brings luck
My hues will cheer
May fortune be with you

Plate 144
Doll, 5" tall, mark AB-1, original clothes, composition dog is of same vintage and may be original to the doll, $135.00 – $180.00.

Plate 146
Doll, 5" tall, mark AB-1, original clothes, $125.00 – $165.00.
Doll, 5" tall, mark AB-1, original clothes are marked "Made in Japan," $125.00 – $165.00.

All-Bisque Dolls

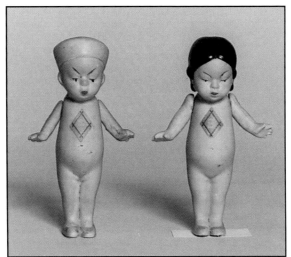

Plate 147
Queue San Baby (by Morimura Brothers), 5" tall, mark AB-1 in ink on bottom of feet, original sticker, ribbons are original, $150.00 – $200.00

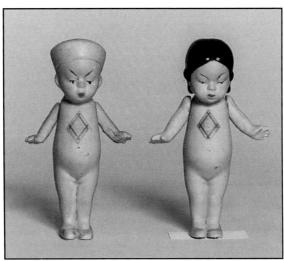

Plate 148
Queue San Baby (by Morimura Brothers), 4¾" tall, original sticker, $135.00 – $185.00
Queue San Baby (by Morimura Brothers), 4¾" tall, original sticker, doll inscribed "Grab Bag Prize E C & P 12/24/18 A. E. Vaillenmot", $145.00 – $185.00

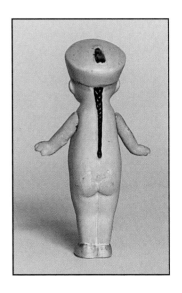

Plate 150
Back view of Queue San Baby showing the braid (queue) going down back.

Plate 149
Queue San Baby (by Morimura Brothers), both 3½" tall, mark AB-1 in ink on bottom, original sticker, $175.00 – $225.00 each.

Plate 152
Queue San Baby (by Morimura Brothers), 5" tall, original sticker, $175.00 – $225.00
Queue San Baby (by Morimura Brothers), 5" tall, original sticker, rare to find with original clothes, $200.00 – $250.00

Plate 151
Queue San Baby (by Morimura Brothers), 4¾" tall, original sticker, on original pincushion, $175.00 – $225.00

154

Plate 155

Doll, 3" tall, mark AB-5, unusual Nippon frozen Charlotte penny doll, stone bisque, poor quality, $25.00 – $40.00.

Plate 153

Cho-Cho San (by Morimura Brothers), 3¾" tall, original sticker, $150.00 – $180.00.

Cho-Cho San (by Morimura Brothers), 4⅝" tall, original sticker, $140.00 – $170.00.

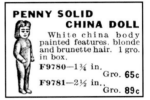

PENNY SOLID CHINA DOLL
White china body painted features, blonde and brunette hair. 1 gro. in box.
F9780—1¾ in. .... Gro. 65c
F9781—2½ in. .... Gro. 89c

Plate 154

Doll, 6" tall, mark AB-1, $125.00 – $160.00.

Plate 156

Old Butler Brothers ad for penny doll.

Plate 157

Bathtub doll, doll 2⅛" tall, tub 3" long, both doll and tub marked AB-1, stone bisque, $110.00 – $140.00.

Bathtub doll, doll 2⅛" tall, tub 2½" long, both doll and tub marked AB-1, stone bisque, $110.00 – $140.00.

These dolls do not have a second firing to set the facial and hair color, and the colors are often worn.

Plate 159

Bathtub doll, doll 1¾" tall, tub 2½" long, only tub marked AB-1, stone bisque, $110.00 – $140.00.

BABY DOLL IN BATH TUB

F9786—1¾ in., sitting detachable baby, painted hair and features, white china 2⅜ in. tub, heavy gilt rim. 1 doz. in box ....Doz. **75c**

Plate 160

Old Butler Brothers ad for bathtub doll pictured in Plate 158.

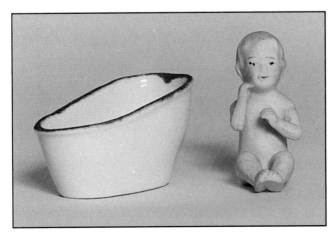

Plate 158

Bathtub doll, doll 2⅜" tall, tub 3⅛" long, both doll and tub marked AB-1, stone bisque, doll's arms are molded separately from the doll, $120.00 – $150.00.

This doll does not have a second firing to set the facial and hair color, and the colors are often worn.

155

All-Bisque Figurals

Plate 161
Figurals, 4" tall, mark AB-1, $225.00 – $300.00.
Note: Figurals are popular with collectors, and this is reflected in the price guide.

Plate 162
Figurals, 4" tall, mark AB-1, $225.00 – $300.00

Plate 163
Figural, 3¼" tall, mark AB-1, unusual "googly" Indian, $175.00 – $225.00.

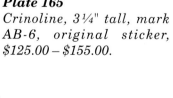

Plate 166
Figural, 4¼" tall, mark AB-1 in ink on bottom of feet, $150.00 – $200.00.

Figural, 4¼" tall, mark AB-1, $150.00 – $200.00.

Plate 164
Figural, 3¾" tall, mark AB-1, $200.00 – $250.00.

Plate 165
Crinoline, 3¼" tall, mark AB-6, original sticker, $125.00 – $155.00.

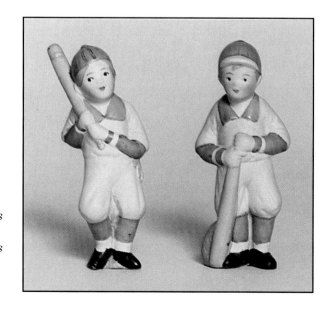

Plate 167
Figural, 4⅛" tall, mark AB-1 in ink across bottom of feet, $200.00 – $250.00.
Figural, 4" tall, mark AB-1 in ink across bottom of feet, $200.00 – $250.00.

Plate 169
Figural, 4½" tall, mark AB-1, $175.00 – $225.00.
Figural, 4¼" tall, mark AB-1, $175.00 – $225.00.

Plate 168
Doll, 4⅜" tall, mark AB-1, jointed arms, harder to find than the figural version, $150.00 – $200.00.
Figural, 4⅜" tall, mark AB-1, $150.00 – $200.00.

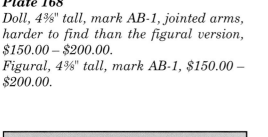

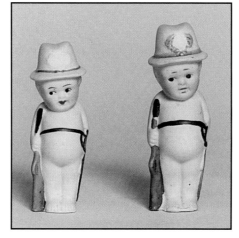

Plate 172
Figural, 4½" tall, mark AB-1 stamped in ink on bottom of feet, $175.00 – $225.00.

Plate 170
Figural, 3⅞" tall, mark AB-1, $125.00 – $155.00.
Figural, 4¼" tall, mark AB-1, $125.00 – $155.00.

Plate 171
Figural, 4⅛" tall, mark AB-1, $125.00 – $155.00.
Figural, 4¼" tall, mark AB-1, stone bisque, $125.00 – $155.00.

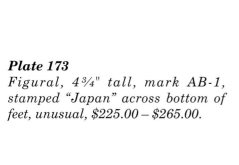

Plate 173
Figural, 4¾" tall, mark AB-1, stamped "Japan" across bottom of feet, unusual, $225.00 – $265.00.

Plate 174
Figural, 4" tall, mark AB-1 in ink across back, $175.00 – $225.00.

All-Bisque Dolls

Plate 175
Figural, 4" tall, mark AB-1 in ink across bottom of feet, $150.00 – $200.00.
Figural, 4¼" tall, mark AB-1 in ink across back, $150.00 – $200.00.
Figural, 4" tall, mark AB-1 in ink across bottom of feet, $150.00 – $200.00.

Plate 176
Figural, 4¼" tall, mark AB-1 in ink on bottom of feet, "25¢" written in pencil on bottom of feet, probably the original price, $175.00 – $225.00.

Plate 177
Figural, 4¼" tall, mark AB-1, $175.00 – $225.00.

Plate 179
Two figural animals, part of a set of six (see also Plates 180 and 181), both unmarked, $700.00 – $800.00 for set of six.

Plate 180
Two figural animals, part of set of six, reclining tiger, marked AB-1 in purple ink on bottom, "10¢" written in pencil on bottom, probably the original price, standing tiger is unmarked. $700.00 – $800.00 set.

Plate 178
Figural, 3¾" tall, mark AB-1, $130.00 – $175.00.

Plate 181
Two figural animals, part of a set of six, both marked AB-1 in purple ink on bottom, "10¢" written in pencil on bottom, probably the original price, elephant is 3¼" tall and 4¼" long. $700.00 – $800.00 set.

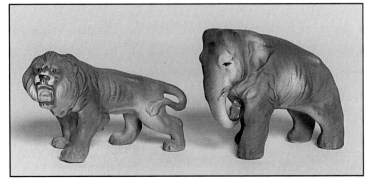

158

Plate 184
1919 Charles William Stores ad for pincushion doll.

Plate 182
Pincushion, 4½" tall, mark AB-1, $110.00 – $135.00.

Plate 183
Pincushion, 4" tall, mark AB-1, jointed arms and legs, mohair wig, $110.00 – $135.00.

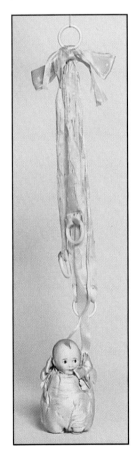

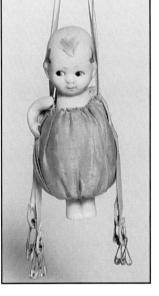

Plate 187
Same as Plate 186, shown in hanging position.

Plate 186
Pincushion, 5¾" tall, mark AB-1, $125.00 – $150.00.

Plate 185
Pincushion, 3¼" tall, mark AB-1 in ink on bottom of feet, probably made to hang from a child's crib, $125.00 – $150.00.

Plate 188
1917 Butler Brothers ad for pincushion doll.

Plate 189
Pincushion, 4" tall (including pincushion), mark AB-1, $135.00 – $165.00.

Dolls Dressed in Crepe Paper Clothes

Plate 190
Doll, 5¼" tall, mark AB-1, crepe paper dress, $100.00 – $125.00.

Plate 191
Doll, 6" tall (including dress), mark AB-1, crepe paper dress, hat, and parasol, $125.00 – $145.00.

Plate 192
Doll, 7" tall (including hat), mark AB-1, crepe paper outfit and painted face, $140.00 – $175.00.

Plate 194
Doll, 4½" tall overall, jointed arms and legs, mark AB-1, crepe paper dress, probably used as a box cover, $110.00 – $135.00.

Plate 193
Wedding party: groom 5¾" tall, mark not visible; bride 5¾" tall, Baby Darling sticker; bridesmaids 4¾" tall, mark AB-1; all dressed in crepe paper, used at a 1920 wedding shower, $500.00 – $600.00 for set.

Plate 195
Doll, 8½" tall over-all (doll is 6½" tall), mark AB-1, multi-layered crepe paper dress supports doll, $125.00 – $145.00.

Plate 196
Doll, 7¾" tall over-all (doll is 4" tall), original Chubby sticker on stomach, multi-layered crepe paper dress supports doll, $155.00 – $185.00 (price based on Chubby doll).

Plate 197
Doll, 9" over-all (doll is 4½" tall), jointed arms and legs, mark AB-1, multi-layered crepe paper dress supports doll, $125.00 – $145.00.

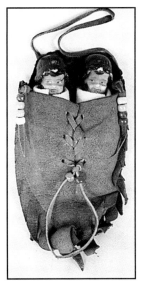

Plate 198
Souvenir item, doll 4½" tall, mark AB-1, doll partially painted to look like an Indian, original felt holder 9½" tall, $125.00 – $150.00.

Plate 199
Souvenir of Niagara Falls, doll 4½" tall, mark AB-1, doll partially painted to look like an Indian, original leather holder 8" tall, marked "Niagara Falls" on front, $145.00 – $175.00.

Plate 200
Doll, painted to look like West Virginia University football player, 5" tall, mark AB-1, inscribed on feet: BY "PRETT" 21, unusual, $125.00 – $145.00

Plate 201
Doll, made into lamp, 14" tall overall, doll 5" tall, mark AB-1, unusual, $135.00 – $175.00.

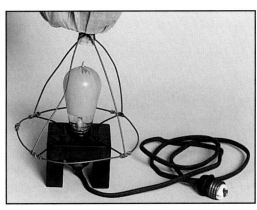

Plate 203
Wire frame for Plate 201, original light bulb and screw-in plug.

Plate 202
Doll, 4½" tall, mark AB-1, original yarn dress, $110.00 – $135.00.

Plate 204
Doll, 7¼" tall over-all, doll 5" tall, mark AB-1, original crepe paper outfit, $110.00 – $125.00.

All-Bisque Doll Marks

This listing of marks provides those marks that to date we have been able to document. There are likely all-bisque Nippon dolls that have different marks and mold numbers on them which we just have not documented yet. The majority of the marks on Nippon all-bisque dolls provide only the country of origin or a mold number. There is often some variation in the way the marks are incised, but in general they fall within the types of marks listed below. The marks on Nippon all-bisque dolls usually do not have any indication as to the maker or importer. The exception to this is the Louis Wolf & Company marks. Please note that some of these marks are hand-drawn and may differ slightly from the actual mark. At the end of the listing of marks we have provided pictures of the stickers found to date on Nippon dolls. A few of these stickers identify Morimura Brothers as the maker of the doll.

Marks: (AB = All-Bisque)

AB-1	**NIPPON**	incised on back or ink stamped on back or feet; ink colors usually purple, black, or blue
AB-2	**MADE IN NIPPON**	incised
AB-3	ИIPPOИ	incised; N's are backwards
AB-4	₦IPPO₦	incised; slightly curved
AB-5	**N I P P O N**	incised vertically down the back
AB-6	*Nippon*	incised in script
AB-7	*Nippon*	incised in script

AB-8   **PATENT**   incised
        NIPPON

AB-9   L W & CO.   incised on Louis Wolf & Co. dolls
        NIPPON

AB-10   L.W. CO   incised on Louis Wolf & Co. dolls
        NIPPON

AB-11   (logo)   incised on Louis Wolf & Co. dolls
        NIPPON

AB-12   **BABY BUD**   incised; notice that "NIPPON"
        Nippon   is in script going down the back
                            of the shirt

AB-13   **NIPPON**   incised
        D

AB-14   **NIPPON**   incised
        84

AB-15   **NIPPON**   incised
        87

AB-16   **93**   incised
        NIPPON

AB-16   **NIPPON**   incised
        96

AB-18   **97**   incised
        NIPPON

AB-19   **98**   incised
        NIPPON

AB-20   **NIPPON**   incised
        101

AB-21	**102** **NIPPON**	incised		AB-25	**144** **NIPPON**	incised	
AB-22	**103** **NIPPON**	incised		AB-26	**221** **NIPPON**	incised	
AB-23	**NIPPON** **113**	incised		AB-27	**222** **NIPPON**	incised	
AB-24	**NIPPON** **122**	incised					

Stickers

Sticker found on the feet of Nippon Kewpies.

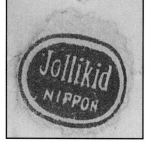

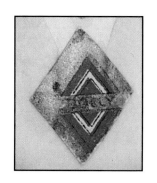

Bisque-Head Dolls

For purposes of this book, we have divided this chapter into two sections — those bisque-head dolls whose mark does not have a symbol identifying either the maker or the importer and those whose mark does have a symbol identifying either the maker, importer, or the company that owned the mold.

The dolls without a symbol are usually smaller dolls (under 10") which display less quality and detailing than those dolls with a symbol. Because there is no symbol on these small dolls, we have no idea who made them or imported them although we know that some were likely made by Morimura Brothers. These dolls are marked "NIPPON" on either the head or shoulderplate and sometimes have a mold number or letter.

Those dolls with a symbol provide some identification as to either the maker, the importer, or the company that owned the mold. Most of these dolls are 8" or larger and are the character babies and dolly-faced child dolls that were so popular during the early 1900s. Generally they are marked with the symbol, mold numbers and/or letters, and the country of origin — Nippon or, in the case of Morimura Brothers dolls, Japan. In some cases, these symbols may have been trademarked.

The bisque-head dolls covered in this chapter have bodies made of cloth, kid or imitation kid, and composition/papier-mache. These dolls were manufactured as children's toys and, therefore, unlike many of the all-bisque dolls, were meant to be played with.

Bisque-Head Dolls with No Symbol

These bisque-head dolls tend to have one of two body types, either cloth or composition/papier-mache.

It appears that the cloth bodied china limb dolls (bisque shoulderplate heads with bisque arms and legs) were some of the earlier Nippon dolls manufactured and imported during the World War I era. This assumption is borne out by the Japanese patent number 30441. This patent is for a cloth-bodied doll with a bisque shoulderplate head and bisque limbs. The doll was designed in 1913 and the patent issued in February 1914. Most striking about the patent is that the doll was designed so the head would not fall off, and this "would make the doll strong enough to be suitable for exporting." Of course, this design is not unique and the French and Germans had been using this design for their china glazed dolls for many years. Today, it's possible to find a variety of Nippon china limb dolls with this Japanese patent number on the back of the shoulderplate.

The Nippon china limb dolls came in a variety of sizes with the smallest being approximately 5" tall and the largest being approximately 18" tall. The sizes are approximate because the size of the doll varies depending on the body. Although many of these small bisque shoulderplate heads were put on replacement or homemade bodies it's still possible to find Nippon china limb dolls with original bodies made of red, pink, or white muslin. Occasionally, one can find these dolls with their original ABC cloth bodies. ABC cloth bodies became popular in the early 1900s for the German china glazed dolls. It was generally thought that this type of body was educational.

The shoulderplate heads can be found both in boy and girl styles. The boys have short molded hair whereas the girls often have hairstyles complimented with molded hair bows or headbands. There are some shoulderplate heads made with a bald head that requires a wig. Finding these dolls with their original wigs intact is hard to do.

Registered Utility Model No. 30441   DOLL

Filing Date: Dec. 26, 1913
Registered Date: Feb. 12, 1914

Applicant (inventor): Kusutaroh Nakamura
Address: 2160 Araijuku, Ooaza, Iriarai-mura, Ebara-gun,
                      Tokyo

DOLL

Claim: Doll having a porcelain-made head-breast, hands, and
            feet attached to its body
Description: The drawing is showing the structure of the claiming doll.
            (1) is a porcelain-made head-breast, (2) is a body made as a normal
doll with said porcelain-made head-breast, attached to said body,
(3) is hands made either by porcelain or by bisque, and (4) is feet made the same as the hands, with hands/feet attached to the body by way of normal process.

Doll used to have its head inserted directly to its body which made the head to fall off easily. This claimed doll has a head-breast as one part which would prevent the head from falling off, and at the same time, would make the doll strong enough to be suitable for exporting.

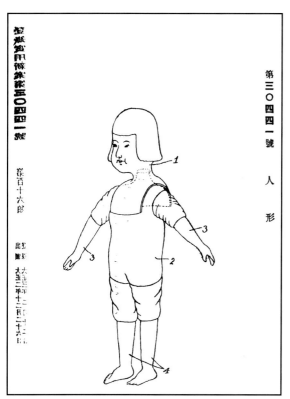

Patent number 30441.

Bisque-Head Dolls

China limb dolls were generally sold undressed so it was up to the buyer to make clothes for the doll. As was pictured in the chapter "Dressing Your Bisque-Head Dolls," the J. & P. Coats Company sold a kit with patterns for dressing both a boy and girl china limb doll. The doll included in this kit is a Nippon china limb doll with a white muslin body. Today it's rare to find such a kit. It is also hard to find the china limb dolls with their original homemade outfits.

Many of these dolls are made of a cheaper bisque called "stone bisque." This bisque is heavier and less translucent than the bisque used on most other Nippon dolls. Usually the limbs are not well executed either in terms of the modeling or the painting. The arms and legs are usually left "in the white" with no flesh coloring added. Sometimes simple shoes are painted on.

Unfortunately for the collector, finding the Nippon china limb dolls with their facial or hair coloring still completely there is sometimes difficult. This is because many of these dolls did not have a second firing to set the facial and hair painting. This means that the coloring comes off easily if a doll is played with or washed. Look closely at the dolls pictured here and you can see those dolls that have had their paint washed off.

Both Butler Brothers and Morimura Brothers advertised china limb dolls, and in 1920 the Charles William Stores catalog advertised a 7½" china doll, with red cloth body for 15 cents. Even though it was advertised as a china doll, the catalog picture shows that it was not a china glazed doll. As indicated by the price, these were inexpensive dolls that were not as popular as the all-bisque or bisque-head dolls with composition bodies. By the late teens and early twenties, china limb dolls were going out of style. Even today these dolls are less popular with collectors than the other types of Nippon dolls.

More popular were the Nippon dolls with bisque heads and bodies made of composition or papier-mache. These Nippon bisque-head dolls are generally small in size with most being less than 10" tall. It is likely that many of these dolls were made by the same companies making the all-bisque dolls. In fact, it's possible to find bisque-head dolls that match all-bisque dolls. Many of these dolls are marked with a mold number or letter in addition to the word "NIPPON." The mold number may also identify the size. For example, B2 is a smaller version of the doll marked B3.

These small bisque heads are socket heads that are strung onto what is usually a crudely made five-piece composition or papier-mache body (see photo on next page). These dolls were modeled in a variety of character faces including those with painted googly eyes; many have molded hair or hats. The majority do have painted eyes, but there are a few with glass eyes. Some also have bald heads that require wigs. It's difficult to find these dolls, especially with their original wigs intact.

Like the other Nippon dolls, Germany was making dolls of this type before World War I. Gebruder Heubach and Armand Marseille were two of the German firms producing these small bisque-head dolls. It is evident that the Japanese copied many of their designs, including the Heubach googly dolls and the Armand Marseille mold number 322. For the Japanese these small bisque-head dolls were probably easier to produce than the larger bisque-head dolls which they originally struggled with making. These small dolls did not require the same technical doll making expertise as the larger ones since the heads were molded and painted in the same manner as the all-bisque dolls.

Montgomery Ward advertised these bisque-head dolls in their 1919 and 1920 catalogs including 6" "bisque head baby dolls" three for 65¢. Dolls of this type were usually sold wearing cheap cheesecloth-like chemises, and the catalog states these were "dolls for dressing." Ward also advertised a 7½" doll with "roguish eyes and smiling face" for 48¢.

168

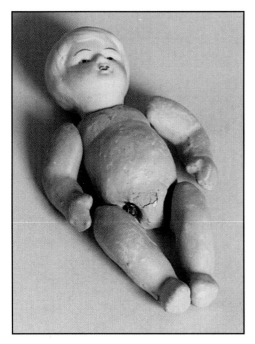

Composition body used on Nippon bisque-head dolls.

This doll wore a cotton slip. It was up to the child or the mother to make clothes for the doll.

Occasionally one can find flange-neck bisque heads on pincushions. These pincushions are hard to find because the silk-like material on them tends to disintegrate over time, and there's little that can be done to stop it. Sticking pins into the silk broke down the material and hastened the disintegration. These flange-neck bisque heads are sometimes modeled after the all-bisque dolls and are marked on the neck. They are popular with pincushion collectors as well as doll collectors.

As with any other doll or toy, always look for good quality dolls with no chips or cracks. Of course, dolls with worn paint are less desirable. The composition or papier-mache bodies on these small dolls were often poorly made, and this lack of quality shows today with many bodies having imperfections. Collectors should expect to see bodies in this condition and unless severely damaged, these imperfections do not affect the value of the doll.

It is sometimes possible to find either the small shoulderplate or bisque heads with the body missing. It is difficult to find old replacement bodies for these dolls, so collectors should keep that in mind before buying these heads. Newly made bodies can be purchased, but replacement of bodies drastically lowers the value of the doll.

Flange-neck heads used on pincushions.

Bisque-Head Dolls

Plate 205
Dolls, 7½" tall, bisque head with flange neck, cloth body with bisque arms and legs, old clothes, mark BH-1, $100.00 – $125.00 each.

Plate 206
Doll, 9½" tall, bisque shoulderplate, red cloth body with bisque arms and legs, mohair wig (probably replaced), replaced clothes, mark BH-1, $75.00 – $100.00.
Doll, 9" tall, bisque shoulderplate, red cloth body with replaced arms and legs, replaced wig, old clothes, mark BH-3, $65.00 – $95.00 if in good condition with no replaced parts.
These two dolls are made of a poor quality bisque and the color has not been fired a second time. As you can see, the facial coloring may wear or wash off.

Plate 207
Doll, 12" tall, bisque shoulderplate, original pink muslin body with bisque arms and legs, of a finer quality bisque with the color fired in, mark BH-11, $135.00 – $165.00.

Plate 209
Doll, 11" tall, bisque shoulder-plate, muslin body with bisque arms and legs, good coloring even though the colors did not receive a second firing, original clothes, mark BH-3, $135.00 – $160.00.

Plate 208
Doll, 18" tall, bisque shoulder-plate, imitation kid body, good quality bisque with the color fired in, unusual large size, clothes appear to be old, mark BH-2, $235.00 – $285.00.

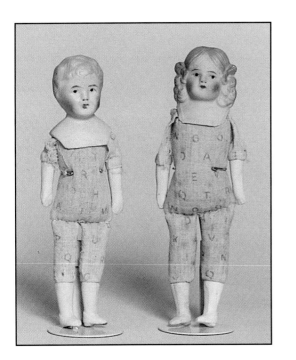

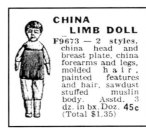

Plate 211
Old Butler Brothers ad.

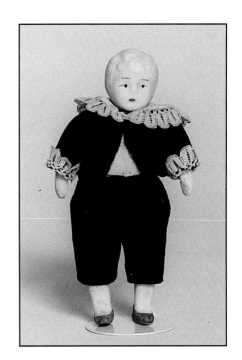

Plate 212
Doll, 5½" tall, bisque shoulderplate, muslin body with bisque arms and legs, facial coloring is worn, outfit may be old, mark BH-3, $70.00 – $90.00 if in good condition with good facial coloring.

Plate 210
Doll, 6½" tall, bisque shoulderplate, ABC cloth body with bisque arms and legs, in unplayed with condition so the coloring is excellent, mark BH-3, $125.00 – $155.00.
Doll, 6½" tall, bisque shoulderplate, ABC cloth body with bisque arms and legs, in unplayed with condition so the coloring is excellent, mark BH-1, $125.00 – $155.00.

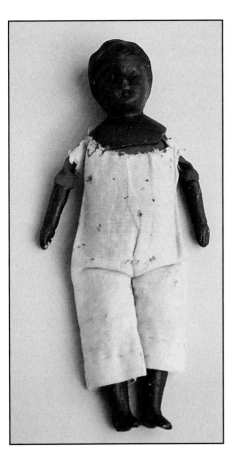

Plate 213
Doll, 7" tall, bisque shoulderplate, red cloth body with bisque arms and legs. It is rare to find a black cloth-bodied Nippon doll, old clothes, mark BH-3, $150.00 – $175.00.

Plate 214
Doll, 13" tall, bisque shoulderplate, red cloth body with bisque arms and legs, hair and facial coloring worn off, old blouse with new skirt, mark BH-1, $140.00 – $165.00 if in good condition with good facial coloring.

Plate 215
Old Butler Brothers ad.

Plate 216
Doll, 10" tall, bisque head on a jointed composition body, old dress, mark BH-11, $165.00 – $200.00.
Wooden lacquer bucket is also marked "Nippon," $20.00 – $40.00.

Plate 218
1919 Montgomery Ward ad for doll in Plate 217. The catalog number in the ad matches stock number printed on the box.

Plate 217
Doll, 9" tall, bisque head on a composition body with painted shoes and socks, blue sleep eyes, mohair wig, open mouth with four upper teeth; original chemise; doll is unmarked but has the original tag and box; made for Montgomery Ward and sold through their catalog in 1919 and 1920, rare, $350.00 – $450.00.

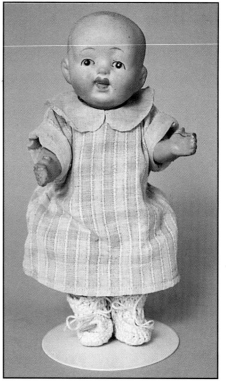

Plate 219
Doll, 8" tall, bisque head with a new composition body, new clothes, mark BH-1, $120.00 – $150.00 if it has original body and old clothes.

Plate 220
Doll, 6½" tall, bisque head with composition body, old clothes, mark BH-7, $125.00 – $150.00.

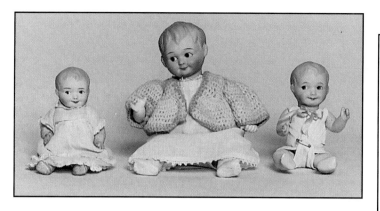

Plate 221
Doll, 6" tall, bisque head with composition body, clothes appear original, mark BH-1, $130.00 – $155.00.
Doll, 9½" tall, bisque head with composition body, old clothes may be original, mark BH-1, $225.00 – $250.00.
Doll, 7⅛" tall, bisque head with composition body, unusual blue eyes, mark BH-1, $140.00 – $165.00.

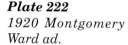

Bisque Head
Big value. A sweet little baby doll who just loves to be good and never cries.
Bisque head. Composition body, jointed at neck, shoulders and hips. Wears white slip, lace trimmed. Height, 9 inches. Ship. wt., ¾ pound.
49C2621 Price........**79c**

Bisque Head
Our cute little baby with roguish eyes and smiling face. Has bisque head. Composition body, jointed at neck, shoulders and hips. Wears white slip. Height, 7¾ inches. Shipping weight, ½ pound.
49C2620 Price........**48c**

Plate 222
1920 Montgomery Ward ad.

Plate 223
Doll, 5½" tall, bisque head with composition body, doll is the same as the dolls pictured in Plate 221 but has had lambskin wig added, original knitted clothes, mark BH-1, $140.00 – $165.00.

Plate 224
Dolls, 5" tall, bisque head with composition body, new clothes, mark BH-1, $115.00 – $140.00 each.

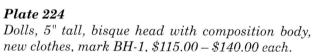

Plate 225
Doll, 10" tall, bisque head with composition body, blue set eyes (never meant to sleep), brushstroke hair, open-closed mouth with painted teeth, old clothes, mark BH-6, $225.00 – $265.00.
Doll, 11½" tall, bisque head with composition body, blue set eyes (never meant to sleep), brushstroke hair, open-closed mouth with painted teeth, old clothes, mark BH-24, $250.00 – $295.00.
Doll, 10" tall, bisque head with composition body, blue set eyes (never meant to sleep), brushstroke hair, open-closed mouth with painted teeth, old clothes, mark BH-6, $225.00 – $265.00.

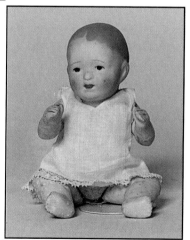

Plate 226
Doll, 5½" tall, bisque head with composition body, hair has been repainted probably to camouflage a crack or break, mark BH-1, $115.00 – $140.00 if in good condition with no breaks or repairs.

173

Bisque-Head Dolls

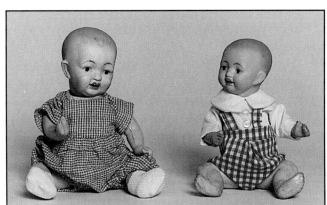

Plate 228

Doll, 9½" tall, bisque head with composition body, open mouth with painted upper teeth, old clothes, mark BH-6, $140.00 – $180.00.

Doll, 8½" tall, bisque head with composition body, open mouth with painted upper teeth, new clothes, mark BH-5, $130.00 – $170.00.

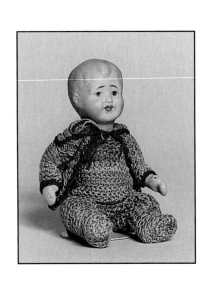

Plate 230

Doll, 8" tall, bisque head with composition body, original crocheted clothes, mark BH-9, $140.00 – $180.00.

Doll, 8½" tall, bisque head with composition body, new clothes, mark BH-12, $140.00 – $180.00.

Plate 227

Doll, 8" tall, bisque head with composition body with painted shoes and socks, old clothes, mark BH-1, $140.00 – $190.00.

Plate 229

Doll, 7¾" tall, bisque head with composition body, replaced clothes, mark BH-1, $130.00 – $170.00.

Plate 231

Doll, 5½" tall, bisque head with composition body, original crocheted clothes, mark BH-1, $120.00 – $150.00.

Plate 232

Doll, 7¾" tall, bisque head with composition body, replaced clothes, mark BH-1, $140.00 – $170.00.

Doll, 7½" tall, bisque head with composition body, body has molded shoes and socks which have been painted over, replaced clothes, mark BH-28, $140.00 – $170.00.

Plate 234

Doll, 7" tall, bisque head with composition body, old clothes, mark BH-4, $140.00 – $180.00.
Doll, 6⅝" tall, bisque head with composition body, old clothes, mark BH-1, $140.00 – $180.00.

Plate 233

Doll, 8" tall, bisque head with composition body, old clothes, mark BH-1, $140.00 – $170.00.

Plate 235

Close-up of writing found on doll in Plate 236.

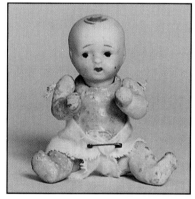

Plate 236

Doll, 7" tall, bisque head with composition body, new clothes, writing on body "Maude's lst baby–1919" adds to value and interest of doll, mark BH-1, $150.00 – $190.00.

Plate 237

Doll, 5" tall, bisque head with composition body, old crocheted dress, mark BH-25, $120.00 – $150.00.

Plate 239

Doll, 4¾" tall, bisque head with composition body, mark BH-14, $110.00 – $135.00.

Plate 238

Doll, 5½" tall, bisque head with composition body, old clothes, mark BH-1, $120.00 – $150.00.
Doll, 6⅛" tall, bisque head with composition body, old crocheted dress, mark BH-18, $120.00 – $150.00.
Doll, 6" tall, bisque head with composition body, old clothes, mark BH-19, $120.00 – $150.00.

175

Bisque-Head Dolls

Plate 242
Doll, 6½" tall, bisque head with composition body, open mouth with painted upper teeth, old clothes, mark BH-29, $120.00 – $150.00.

Plate 241
1919 Montgomery Ward catalog ad.

Plate 240
Doll, 6½" tall, bisque head with composition body, original clothes, mark BH-23, $140.00 – $170.00.
Shown with all-bisque doll in the same mold. Many times doll makers used the same head mold on both all-bisque and bisque-head dolls.

Plate 243
Doll, 5¾" tall, bisque head with composition body, some of the original wig is left, old clothes, mark BH-1, $130.00 – $160.00.
Doll, 7" tall, bisque head with composition body, original wig, old clothes, mark BH-27, $140.00 – $170.00.
It is easier to find the small bisque-head dolls with painted hair than with wigs.

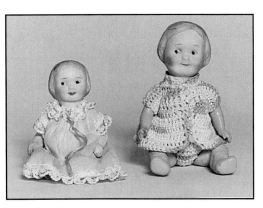

Plate 244
Doll, 4¾" tall, bisque head with composition body, old clothes, mark BH-23, $120.00 – $150.00.
Doll, 6¾" tall, bisque head with composition body, new clothes, mark BH-1, $130.00 – $160.00.

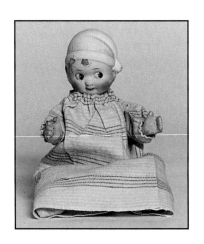

Plate 245
Doll, 7" tall, bisque head with composition body, old clothes, mark BH-1, $140.00 – $170.00.

Plate 246
Doll, 9" tall, bisque head with composition body, old clothes, mark BH-10, $150.00 – $180.00.

Plate 247
Doll, 4⅞" tall, bisque head with composition body, original chemise, $120.00 – $150.00.
As shown in the 1919 Montgomery Ward catalog ad (Plate 241), many of these dolls were sold wearing only a chemise made of a cheap material like cheesecloth.

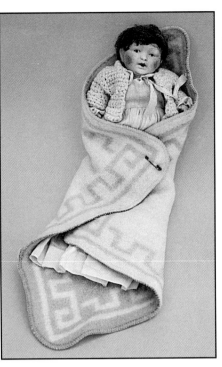

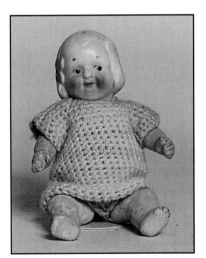

Plate 248
Doll, 7¼" tall, bisque head with composition body, painted shoes, old dress, mark BH-15, $130.00 – $170.00.

Plate 250
Doll, 7" tall, bisque head with composition body, old clothes, mark BH-8, $130.00 – $170.00.

Plate 249
Doll, 7½" tall, bisque head with composition body, original wig, original clothes, mark BH-27, $160.00 – $200.00 with original wig and clothes.

Plate 251
Doll, 6" tall, bisque head with composition body, original crocheted clothes, mark BH-24, $130.00 – $170.00.

Plate 252
Doll, 6" tall, bisque head with composition body, old knitted dress, mark BH-20, $130.00 – $170.00.

Plate 254
Doll, 6¾" tall, bisque head with composition body, old clothes, mark BH-17, $130.00 – $170.00.
Shown with all-bisque doll in the same mold. This is a popular head mold and it is found on a number of different dolls: all-bisque, bisque-head, and bisque-head with flange neck.

Plate 253
Doll, 5½" tall, bisque head with composition body, new clothes, mark BH-13, $120.00 – $150.00.

177

Bisque-Head Dolls

Plate 256
Doll, 8½" tall, bisque head, flange neck, new cloth body, mark BH-1, $60.00 – $90.00.

Novelty Asst—6 styles, aver. 5 to 10 in., doll heads and muff shape, soft stuffed cretonne, sateen and satin, ribbonzene rosettes, checkered and satin ribbon bands, bows and hangers, vari-colored pins and ivory rings with safety pins. Asstd. styles and colors.
N1498—¼ doz. in box.
Doz. **$2.10**

Plate 257
1917 Butler Brothers ad.

Plate 255
Pincushion, 5½" tall, bisque head, flange neck, original silk covered pincushion, mark BH-1, $90.00 – $130.00.
Pincushion, 4½" tall, bisque head, flange neck, original silk covered pincushion, mark BH-1, $90.00 – $130.00.

12 K 8577
Dresden Ribbon Hanging Pin Cushion with doll. Trimmed with bows.
Each, del'd free **49c**

Plate 258
1919 Charles William Stores catalog ad.

Plate 260
Pincushion, 3½" tall, bisque head, flange neck, original silk covered pincushion painted to look like a body, unusual, mark BH-21, $120.00 – $150.00.

Plate 259
Pincushion, 5½" tall, bisque head, flange neck, old cloth pincushion, mark BH-1, $90.00 – $130.00.

Plate 261
Pincushion, 3½" tall, bisque head, flange neck, original silk covered pincushion, mark BH-1, $90.00 – $130.00.

178

Bisque-Head Doll Marks with No Symbols

This listing provides those marks that to date we have been able to document. There are likely Nippon dolls that have different marks and mold numbers on them; we just have not documented them yet. All of these marks provide the country of origin and some provide a mold number. None of the marks have any indication as to the maker or importer.

Letters and/or numbers are often used to indicate the mold type or the size. Many times it is hard to decipher the exact letter or number on the doll because the mark is so worn or because of the way the letters or numbers were formed. For example, a B is sometimes confused with an 8. Given that, we have attempted to be as correct as possible.
Marks: (BH = Bisque Head, no symbol)

BH-1	**NIPPON**	incised on the back of the head or shoulderplate
BH-2	*Nippon*	incised on back of shoulderplate
BH-3	**PATENT NO. 30441 NIPPON**	incised on back of shoulderplate
BH-4	**Ⓗ NIPPON**	incised
BH-5	**2 NIPPON**	incised
BH-6	**3 NIPPON**	incised; found on two different dolls
BH-7	**NIPPON 20**	incised
BH-8	**NIPPON 21**	incised
BH-9	**NIPPON 22**	incised
BH-10	**NIPPON 23**	incised
BH-11	**NIPPON 24**	incised
BH-12	**No. 32 NIPPON**	incised

BH-13	**NIPPON 50**	incised
BH-14	**NIPPON 77**	incised
BH-15	**NIPPON 80**	incised
BH-16	**NIPPON 81**	incised
BH-17	**NIPPON 82**	incised
BH-18	**NIPPON 86**	incised
BH-19	**NIPPON 88**	incised
BH-20	**NIPPON 89**	incised
BH-21	**A 3 NIPPON**	incised
BH-22	**A 13 NIPPON**	incised

BH-23	**NIPPON B1**	incised
BH-24	**NIPPON B5**	incised; found on two different dolls
BH-25	**NIPPON B10**	incised
BH-26	**NIPPON B11**	incised
BH-27	**C 02 NIPPON**	incised
BH-28	**X NIPPON**	incised
BH-29	**NIPPON 0**	incised

Sticker:

Bisque-Head Dolls with Identifying Symbols

Bisque-head dolls were made in France as early as the mid-1800s. These early dolls were usually child dolls with glass eyes and closed mouths. Fashion dolls that looked like adult women with elaborate costumes and wardrobes were also popular. These dolls were most commonly found on wood, composition, or kid bodies. Extremely beautiful with fine bisque, delicate painting, and wonderful clothing, these early French bisque-head dolls today are considered the crème de la crème of dolls.

At that time character dolls and bent limb baby dolls were not produced. It would not be until the early 1900s when the Germans began producing character dolls that many of the bisque-head dolls the Japanese would copy first appeared. The German doll industry, in an effort to compete with the French, began to experiment with producing dolls whose "faces are copied from American baby model...." The German manufacturers went to great trouble to get the right look for their dolls. They hired artists who could copy the face in the different sizes needed to produce dolls noting that "with these baby faces a separate model must be used for each size, as it will not do to enlarge or diminish from the same model to produce larger or smaller heads." Because of the work involved to produce the character head, the prices were high at first. Nevertheless, their popularity swept through the doll market, and by the time Nippon dolls were being produced, character dolls accounted for a large percentage of the dolls sold. It was only natural then that when the Japanese started producing bisque-head dolls they, too, would produce character dolls in addition to dolly face dolls.

World War I changed the doll industry at least for six years. With Germany unable to produce dolls and the rest of Europe severely limited, the Japanese saw this as a prime opportunity to enter the marketplace. Some speculate that since Germany knew they were going to war, they may have provided Japan with the molds, glass eyes, and expertise necessary to begin doll production. This is not likely however. Why would Germany or any other country want to help a competitor? We know that as early as 1914 Froebel-Kan and Morimura Brothers were working on the development of glass eyes for bisque-head dolls and that they had many trials before they were successful. Their 1917 patent for glass eyes would be used on Morimura Brothers dolls. Had the Japanese received help from Germany, they would not have struggled with the development of glass eyes themselves.

A 1917 *Playthings* article does mention that "experts were engaged, who know just what was wanted, and were sent to Japan with instructions to build a factory for the manufacture of dolls." It is likely that American doll importers and distributors provided this expertise. According to a

EXHIBIT OF JAPANESE DOLLS BY FOULDS & FREURE. INC.
Foulds & Freure, Inc. has just received a large shipment of Japanese bisque doll heads, as well as an assortment of complete dolls with bisque heads and jointed bodies, sleeping eyes and hair wigs or air brushed hair. These are mostly character dolls. The display shown above represents actual stock on hand. Of course, in view of present conditions, there is naturally a big demand for these dolls and a great many orders have already been filled.

January 1997 article published in *The Stangl/Fulper Times,* in 1914 there was a mass migration of German doll manufacturers to the United States. Some of these German doll experts went to work for doll importers such as Butler Brothers, George Borgfeldt, and Louis Wolf & Company, so it's possible that German expertise was provided to the Japanese but not through Germany. Morimura Brothers in 1915 announced that Horace Bates, who for 14 years had worked for George Borgfeldt & Co., had become associated with their toy department, and later they employed Fred Langfelder. It was, after all, to the benefit of the American doll importers to provide look alikes of the popular German dolls and thus maintain their market and customer base. Sometimes these importers owned the doll molds, making it easy for them to provide the Japanese with samples.

Even with this expertise, the Japanese experienced problems with their doll production. A 1917 *Playthings* article (published in its entirety at the end of this chapter) documents some of the obstacles they initially encountered:

> One of the most difficult of these was the modeling so as to catch the true European expression. In spite of the fact that the original model was before him, the Japanese artisan, true to the natural instinct of his race, persisted in getting a little of the Asiatic expression in the features. After infinite patience, a characteristic trait in the Japanese, a perfect reproduction was secured.
>
> Then the glass eyes had to be made. Again perseverance triumphed. The proper elastic to connect the joints had to be secured; then the proper material to make the body so that it would be durable.
>
> In spite of all the care that was taken, the first product did not turn out well, and heavy losses were entailed by those backing the enterprise.... The Japanese, however, refused to be discouraged. They went at the problem with renewed vigor. Profiting by past experiences, the first mistakes were eliminated and success rewarded their persistent efforts.

Unfortunately, these early problems led many to believe that all Nippon dolls were of poor quality. This misconception still exists today. However, as a practical matter many Nippon bisque-head dolls are on par with their German counterparts and are, in some cases, better. Even the better German firms produced some dolls of mediocre quality.

Nippon doll manufacturers used the same process as the Germans to produce bisque doll heads. Thick liquid porcelain was poured into two-piece plaster molds. After standing for about ten minutes, the liquid began to harden, and the excess liquid was poured off. After the liquid porcelain hardened sufficiently, the head was removed from the mold by simply separating the two-piece mold. The head was now in a greenware state. At this point the mold seams were cleaned, the eye sockets cut out (this was a problem for the Japanese as they tended to cut the eyes sockets too small giving the doll an Asian look), and the mouth openings cut out. If the doll had pierced nostrils, this was done then too. The heads were then fired in a kiln to a white bisque. The next step was to paint the heads flesh color and when this was dry, cheek, lip, eyelash, and brow color was painted in. The heads were then fired a second time to set in the colors. After this the teeth and sleep eyes were inserted.

Doll head molds could only be used for about 50 heads, so it was necessary to keep making new molds. This explains why some doll heads are less detailed than others. Those heads made first had a sharper detail than the last heads made from a mold. Molds were made from clay models sculpted by expert modelers, and for character dolls it was necessary to have a separate clay model for each doll size made.

The Japanese made both socket and shoulderplate bisque heads with a variety of bisque finishes including some rare "oily" bisque finishes. These oily bisque doll heads have a shiny look to them, like someone has put a coat of baby oil on their faces. This oily finish is not as glossy as the china glazed dolls. They also made both open and closed mouth dolls, dolls with wobble tongues, dolls with glass or painted eyes, dolls with pierced nostrils, and dolls with a crying mechanism in their heads. If the Germans made a certain type of doll, then it's likely the Japanese made a similar type. The one exception appears to be dolls with pierced ears. To date, none have been found on Nippon dolls.

The Japanese copied many of the most popular German dolls. The Kestner Hilda (mold no. 245) introduced in 1914, the Heubach pouty mold no. 6969 (circa 1912), and the Hertel Schwab mold no. 151 are just three examples. In fact, the Morimura Brothers Baby Ella character doll bears a striking resemblance to Kestner's Sammy character doll mold no. 211 (circa 1912). If you look through any of the doll books, you'll notice a distinct similarity between the Nippon dolls and dolls produced by companies such as Armand Marseille, Hertel Schwab, Franz Schmidt, and Kestner.

Morimura Brothers was one of the leading bisque-head doll manufacturers and importers. They advertised bisque-head dolls of every type including bisque-head dolls with French glass eyes with or without eyelashes and with or without mohair or natural hair wigs, dolls with bald heads, and dolls with kidolyn or kidoline (imitation kid) bodies. They also advertised crying dolls and "standing character dolls with Buster Brown and Sailor suits...." Their bisque-head character dolls bear the MB mark and are marked "Japan" even though they were all produced during the Nippon era.

Little information is available about the other companies producing Nippon bisque-head dolls. Much of the information in Japan was destroyed during World War II, and many companies, both Japanese and American, failed to keep good records. Of course, many of these companies are no longer in business, which makes it even tougher to get information. Most of what we know today is through publications like *Playthings* which has some wonderful advertisements for Nippon dolls.

There are a number of different symbols found on Nippon dolls that may represent either the company that made the doll or perhaps the importer. We are not really sure what companies most of the symbols are associated with. In the next section on "Deciphering Nippon Bisque-Head Doll Marks," we will provide as much information as we have about the various symbols and mold numbers found on Nippon bisque-head dolls. We do know that, like the German dolls, the mold numbers usually stand for the type or look of the doll and/or the size, but there are some instances where no mold or size number is marked on the doll. There is also some inconsistency in the markings of the dolls, and therefore, it's possible

Japanese Dolls and Toys on Import

The Famous "Baby Ella" Character Dolls

Bisque Head French Glass Moving Eyes with or without Eyelashes. With and without Wigs (Mohair and Natural Hair), 16 to 57 centimeter.

JOINTED DOLLS. 23 to 54 centimeter with or without Eyelashes. Natural Hair Wigs.

"KIDOLYN" Kid Body Dolls. Hip Jointed. Jointed Arms. Hip and Knee Jointed.

BISQUE BABIES of all descriptions.

FULL LINE OF HEADS FOR JOINTED DOLLS. With or without Wigs. With or without Eyelashes.

MORIMURA BROS.

53-55-57 West 23d Street　　　　　NEW YORK

to find two dissimilar dolls with the same mold number. Also, over the years doll molds were sometimes changed or refined so two dolls with the same mold number may not be the same size or look alike.

Two of the more commonly found symbols are the FY and the Scrolled FY which are believed to be the marks of Yamato Importing. Yamato Importing did not advertise dolls

until 1919, but it's clear from *Playthings* advertisements that Foulds and Freure was importing dolls with the FY and Scrolled FY symbols as early as 1917. The FY and Scrolled FY symbols can be found on dolly-faced child dolls, character babies, shoulderplate child dolls on cloth bodies, and the much sought after pouty character doll. Their dolly-faced child dolls with ball jointed bodies (mold series 400) and the solid domehead character baby (mold series 500) were obviously manufactured and sold in large quantities as they are some of the more commonly found dolls today.

Genuine Bisque Dolls
AND
Doll Heads

A Large Stock on Hand for Immediate Delivery

Only One Genuine Bisque
Doll Manufacturer in Japan

YAMATO IMPORTING CO.
301-309 WEST ADAMS STREET
CHICAGO

New York Office: Edwin E. Besser Co., Inc.
41 Union Square West (Southwest Cor. Broadway and 17th St.)
NEW YORK, N. Y.

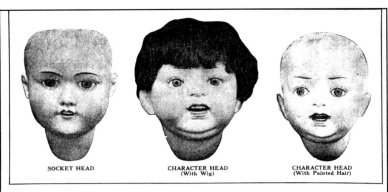

SOCKET HEAD   CHARACTER HEAD   CHARACTER HEAD
                      (With Wig)   (With Painted Hair)

JAPANESE DOLL HEADS

THE above cuts are made from **actual photographs** of bisc doll heads, with sleeping glass eyes, made in Japan. A liberal stock of these has already been landed on the Pacific Coast, and will be ready for shipment from New York within a very short time. Additional stock is both in the course of manufacture and on the way from Japan. We are, therefore, pleased to advise the trade that we will be in a position in the near future to supply the long-felt want of a satisfactory sleeping eye bisc doll head in abundant quantities.

WE already have stock of the complete character dolls, with the heads as illustrated above. These dolls have proven to be wonderful sellers, some of the best buyers being unable to distinguish them from the German goods. We strongly urge buyers to get in their orders on these goods before the proposed additional duty and still greater advances in freight rates go into effect.

OUR GENERAL LINE COMPLETE

WE have stock of practically all styles and sizes of doll wigs, arms, limbs, bodies, slippers and accessories, and are also featuring the following items for immediate shipment:

FLAGS AND PATRIOTIC BADGES
at Sacrifice Prices

Harmonicas, tennis racquets, Cornelian marbles, silk flags for automobiles; cotton flags, mounted, and bunting; better grade bunting flags; masks, games and a general line of toys and novelties. Write for catalog.

IMPORTED KID BODY DOLLS IN STOCK

FOULDS & FREURE, Inc.
83 Chambers Street   NEW YORK

Another common symbol for Nippon dolls is the RE in a Diamond. We do not know who the manufacturer was, but we know that Louis Wolf and Company imported some of the Nippon dolls with this mark. In fact, he used a shoulderplate head with this symbol on his Superba line of imitation kid bodied dolls. Many of the RE in a Diamond dolls are character babies, and this trademark is found on the Nippon look-alike of Kestner's popular Hilda doll. In 1919 Louis Wolf & Company advertised Japanese dolls modeled

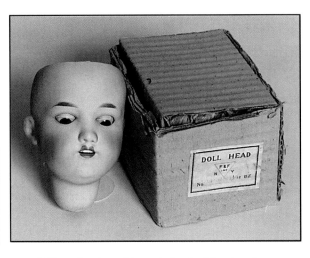

Socket head doll in ad is the same as the one shown in its original shipping box (right).

FY socket head in original shipping box.

after the old German designs, so it's possible they were importing many of these dolls. RE in a Diamond dolls were also sold through the Montgomery Ward catalog.

From 1917 through 1921 the Tajimi Company advertised Baby Lucy, a "perfected character doll with a bisque head, moving eyes, moving limbs, and mohair wig." According to their ad, Baby Lucy was "pronounced by all to be the Best Yet Produced in Japan." It is not known what trademark the Tajimi Company used on Baby Lucy, but these dolls as pictured in their advertisements bear a resemblance to some of the Nippon dolls with the HS in an oval symbol.

Some of the more sought after Nippon dolls are those of the Horsman Company. In 1919 Horsman joined forces with Fulper, an American pottery company, to produce bisque-head dolls. This was a new venture since American companies had traditionally shied away from bisque-head doll production, concentrating instead on composition dolls. According to *The Stangl/Fulper Times* article, Armand Marseille doll heads were used to produce the molds. In June of 1919 the first Fulper bisque doll heads were displayed. These heads, originally selling for $3 and later $2, were used by Horsman on their composition bodies. By the fall of 1919, Horsman and Fulper were having disagreements over the pricing and marketing of the doll heads. This conflict would result in Horsman turning to the Japanese for bisque doll heads. With this information now available to us, we know that the Nippon Horsman heads were made sometime after the fall of 1919. From the Horsman advertisements for the Fulper-made dolls we can tell that the same molds were used for the Nippon made Horsman dolls. In August, September, and October 1920, Horsman placed two-page advertisements in *Playthings* for bisque-head dolls. Since there is no mention in these ads that the dolls were "Made in America," we can assume that these are ads for Nippon Horsman dolls. Because they were produced for such a short period of time, Nippon Horsman dolls are fairly difficult to find. They are popular with both Horsman and Nippon doll collectors.

While most Nippon bisque-head dolls range in size from 8" to 24" tall for the composition bodied child dolls and 8 to 18" for bent limb babies, collectors can find some child dolls as large as 28" tall and some babies as large as 24" tall. These larger dolls are harder to find than some of the mid-size Nippon dolls. In 1918 Foulds and Freure advertised that they had "just received 1,000 import-

ed kid dolls, jointed dolls, character dolls, and dressed dolls, including about 30 large show dolls measuring from 30" to 42" in height."

Many Nippon bisque-head dolls were made in more than one size. For example, Morimura Brothers produced their Full Jointed Doll (a bisque-head child doll) in 16 different sizes, ranging from the smallest at 8½" tall to the largest at 28" tall. The majority of the Nippon doll makers were not so ambitious, and their dolls came in only four or five sizes. Carl Silverman advertised his "Blue Ribbon Baby" was available in five sizes to retail from $1.00 to $6.00. The Tajimi Company advertised that Baby Lucy was available in 10", 12", 14", 16", and 18".

Nippon shoulderplate dolls are usually found on imitation kid or cloth bodies. The kid and cloth bodies have bisque arms from slightly below the elbow on down. The dolly face child dolls (socket head type) are most often found on ball-jointed composition bodies, and the character babies are usually found on composition bent limb baby bodies. Some dolls have bodies that resemble composition but are actually made from crushed oyster shells. For the collector, it is important to remember that not all of the bodies were made in Japan. Many times only the doll heads were imported and then put on bodies that were made elsewhere. Some firms, called jobbers, specialized in putting dolls together, dressing them, and then selling them as a complete doll. Doll hospitals advertised that they could supply replacement heads for any size doll body. Given the anti-German sentiment during and immediately after the war, it is probable that some German heads were replaced with Nippon heads. For many families it was more practical to replace just the head than the entire doll.

The Nippon character dolls are probably more popular with collectors than the dolly-faced child dolls. These character dolls have wonderful expressions ranging from flirty to serious, impish to sweet. The most sought after characters are the pouty and the googly molds, and these dolls are a rare find today. It's unclear why so few of these characters were made. Those dolls with pierced nostrils are also popular with collectors and appear to have been made by only one company as they all bear the FY or Scrolled FY mark. Character dolls are most often found on bent limb baby bodies although some are on toddler bodies.

When buying bisque-head dolls, there are a number of things the collector should consider. First and foremost is the quality of the bisque head. Look for heads with no chips, cracks, or flaws. The flesh tone coloring should be even with no rubs and of a natural color — not washed out or too dark. If the sleep eyes were meant to sleep, then they should not be reset so that they no longer sleep. The wigs should be original or appropriate replacements; the same for the clothes. Bodies should be in reasonably good shape. Remember that these dolls were children's toys and were played. It's rare to find a Nippon bisque-head doll in pristine condition

so collectors should take that into consideration when buying Nippon dolls. Some flaws are to be expected although dolls with major damage should be avoided.

The popularity or rarity of a particular doll is another consideration for collectors. Some dolls were popular at the time they were made and remain popular today. The Kestner Hilda and the Nippon "Hilda look alike" are not uncommon dolls, but they are popular with collectors, and their price reflects that popularity. The Morimura Brothers doll with a crying mechanism is hard to find. They used a mold no. 2 (Baby Ella) to make their crying dolls. This mold is common; however, the addition of the crying mechanism changes that and makes it a more desirable doll (especially if the crying mechanism still works). Dolls with their original boxes or stickers are also popular with collectors. Collectors will need to take all of these things into consideration when buying bisque-head dolls.

JAPAN IN A NEW INDUSTRY

At the outbreak of the European War there was consternation in the ranks of the dealers who had been supplying Miss Young America with her dolls, as Germany had been producing most of the dolls used. America jumped in and showed the world what she could do in doll manufacturing, and then came the surprise when Japan began the manufacture of dolls. A leading Japanese importing house promptly took the matter up. Experts were engaged, who knew just what was wanted, and were sent to Japan with instructions to build a factory for the manufacture of dolls.

This was no easy matter as many natural obstacles had to be overcome. One of the most difficult of these was the modeling so as to catch the true European expression. In spite of the fact that the original model was before him, the Japanese artisan, true to the natural instinct of his race, persisted in getting a little of the Asiatic expression in the features. After infinite patience, a characteristic trait in the Japanese, a perfect reproduction was secured.

Then the glass eyes had to be made. Again perseverance triumphed. The proper elastic to connect the joints had to be secured; then the proper material to make the body so that it would be durable.

In spite of all the care that was taken, the first product did not turn out well, and heavy losses were entailed by those backing the enterprise. All the wiseacres joined in the chorus "We told you so;" "It can't be done," etc. The Japanese, however, refused to be discouraged. They went at the problem with renewed vigor. Profiting by past experiences, the first mistakes were eliminated and success rewarded their persistent efforts. At last a doll was produced which has attracted considerable attention.

That the Japanese have been able to accomplish what they have done in this field of endeavor, is a remarkable tribute to their ingenuity and resourcefulness.

The fact that Japan will in the future furnish Miss Young America with part of her dolls, that plaything that appeals so strongly to our sympathy and affection, founded as it is on the noblest instinct known to mankind, "Mother Love," will go a long way towards cementing the friendship of Japan and America, started when Perry opened the commerce of the world for the Island Empire, a friendship that has weathered every storm raised by jingoism and plotters. Today Japan and America understand each other.

PLAYTHINGS
October, 1917

TOYS FOR GROWN-UPS

Do you play with toys?

This query isn't addressed to the small boy, who, of course, plays with them. It is addressed to the grown man. For if you don't play or have some sort or other of plaything, you are a bit unusual.

Did you ever see a young father spend more time on Christmas day playing with his small son's new electric railway than the small son spent? He was just following the natural instinct of the grown-up to play.

This instinct perhaps accounts for the intense liking for bric-a-brac that many women, otherwise quite staid and reserved, feel. They really love to dust and handle their precious ornaments. They unbend and warm up over their bits of china and metal and wood, carved or cast in whatever shape they may be, as they never unbend and warm up over their friends.

There are many persons, too, who lead lives filled with intense mental work that find great pleasure in little knick-knacks that are really no more nor less than playthings. Ibsen, it is said, always writes with a pen tray full of tiny animals at hand on his desk. A well-known artist has a small woolly lamb that stands before his plate throughout meals. A great French actress has an elaborately dressed doll that is the delight of her leisure hours.

So the liking for playthings by grown-ups can hardly be called a fad. It is rather an instinctive desire to get away from realities occasionally, to relax and play hard.

There are many really lovely things nowadays that can be had as playthings by the grown-ups. The Japanese babies, almost life-size, and bewitchingly lifelike in expression, are among them. Then there are the sleepy cats that, on silk or velvet cushions, doze eternally in most attractive fashion. There are all sorts of other animals, too, from tiny mice to huge parrots in rings to hang in the window. And all of them satisfy the one desire of grown-ups — to play.

If you haven't played since you donned the attire of maturity, by all means begin to play now. You can really lose more worries and gain more cheerfulness in the presence of some charming and inanimate plaything than you can, very often, as a result of the most ardent resolutions to stop worrying and relax.

PLAYTHINGS
March, 1917

Morimura Brothers

Plate 263
Doll, 8" tall, bisque socket head with composition body, blue sleep eyes, open mouth with two upper teeth, replaced wig, new clothes, mark BHS-1, size 4/0, the smallest mold no. 1 doll, $150.00 – $200.00.
Doll, 10¾"
tall, bisque socket head with ball jointed composition body, brown sleep eyes, open mouth with two upper teeth, original human hair wig, dressed in original underclothes, shoes, and socks, home-made gingham wrapper, mark BHS-1, size 2/0, $225.00 – $275.00.
Vase on table is also marked Nippon and was made by the Noritake Company, 3" tall, $50.00 – $75.00.

Plate 262
Group of Morimura Brothers bisque socket head dolls, mold no. 1, showing some of the various sizes. The smaller doll shown in the front is the smallest size made. The large doll in the back is the largest size made. Dolls are described in various photographs in this section.

Plate 264
Label found on box of doll shown in Plate 265.

Plate 265
Full Jointed Doll in original box, 22" tall, bisque socket head on ball jointed composition body, sleep eyes, open mouth with four upper teeth, original human hair wig, original clothes and shoes, unplayed with, mark BHS-1, size 5, rare to find in original box, $650.00 – $750.00.

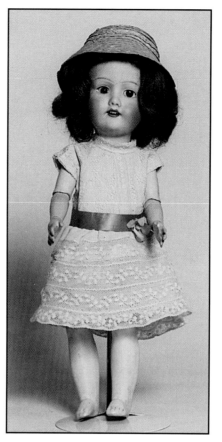

Plate 267

Doll, 14½" tall, bisque socket head on ball jointed composition body, blue sleep eyes, open mouth with four upper teeth, original human hair wig, redressed, BHS-1, size 1, $225.00 – $275.00.

Plate 266

Doll, 12¼" tall, bisque socket head on ball jointed composition body, blue sleep eyes with eyelashes, open mouth with four upper teeth, original wig, original clothes, mark BHS-1, size 0, $250.00 – $300.00 as shown in original condition.
Vase is also Nippon and was made by the Noritake Company, 3" tall, $50.00 – $75.00.

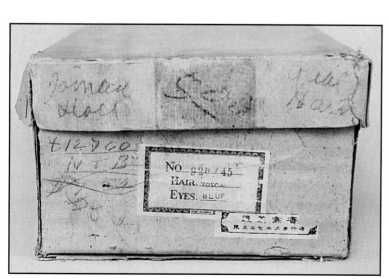

Plate 268
Label found on box of doll shown in Plate 269. Notice the writing on the box which describes the doll as "jointed doll,"
"real hair," *and gives the original price of $5.00. The Japanese writing says "Life-like glass eyes / Patent No. 32723." See the chapter on Froebel-Kan for a copy of this patent. Because of the patent information, we know that this doll was made some-time after May 1917, the issue date of the patent.*

Plate 269
Doll in original box, 18" tall, bisque socket head on ball jointed composition body, blue sleep eyes, open mouth with four upper teeth, original human hair wig, unplayed with, mark BHS-1, size 2, rare to find in original box, $600.00 – $700.00.

Bisque-Head Dolls

Plate 271
Doll, 9½" tall, bisque socket head on jointed composition body, sleep eyes, open mouth with four upper teeth, original wig, old clothes, BHS-1, size 3/0, $200.00 – $250.00.

Plate 270
Doll, 19" tall, bisque socket head on ball jointed composition body, blue sleep eyes, open mouth with four upper teeth, replaced human hair wig, old clothes, BHS-1, size 4, $350.00 – $400.00.

Plate 272
Doll, 23" tall, bisque socket head on ball jointed composition body, blue sleep eyes, open mouth with four upper teeth, original wig, old clothes, BHS-1, size 7, $500.00 – $550.00.

Plate 273
Doll, 27" tall, bisque socket head on ball jointed composition body, blue sleep eyes, open mouth with four upper teeth, new wig, new clothes, BHS-1, size 8, $550.00 – $600.00.

Plate 275
Close-up of 28" doll in Plate 274.

Plate 274
Doll, 28" tall, bisque socket head on ball joint-ed composition body, blue sleep eyes, open mouth with four upper teeth, original human hair wig, new clothes, BHS-1, size 11, proba-bly the largest doll in the mold no. 1 series, $600.00 – $650.00.

Doll, 26½" tall, bisque socket head on ball jointed composition body, blue sleep eyes, open mouth with four upper teeth, replaced mohair wig, new clothes, BHS-1, size 9, $550.00 – $600.00.

Plate 277
Doll, 16" tall, bisque socket head on an unusual "walking" body (when the legs move back and forth, the head turns from side to side), blue sleep eyes, open mouth with four upper teeth, replaced mohair wig, old clothes and shoes, mark BHS-1, size 1, $475.00 – $525.00 price reflects "walking" body.

Doll, 8" tall, bisque sock-et head on a composition baby body, blue sleep eyes with eyelashes, open mouth with two upper teeth, original mohair wig, old clothes, mark BHS-2, size 3/0, $150.00 – $200.00.

Plate 276
Close-up of 26½" doll in Plate 274. Even though the two dolls in Plate 274 are the same Morimura Brothers no. 1 mold, they look somewhat different. Bisque-head dolls of the same mold often look dissimilar because of the way the eyes or mouth was cut or the facial coloring of the doll. Over time, molds too were changed, giving the same mold numbers a different look.

191

Bisque-Head Dolls

Plate 279
Doll, 9" tall, bisque socket head on a composition baby body, blue sleep eyes, open mouth with two upper teeth, replaced mohair wig, old crocheted clothes, mark BHS-2, size 2/0, $200.00 – $250.00.

Plate 278
Group of Morimura Brothers bisque socket head dolls, mold no. 2, showing some of the various sizes. The large doll in the back is the largest size that was made. The dolls are described in various photographs throughout this section.

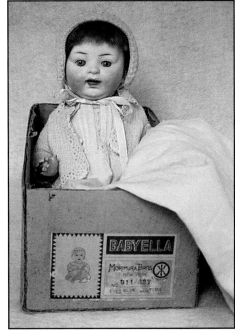

Plate 281
Baby Ella in original box, 13" tall, bisque socket head on a composition baby body, blue sleep eyes, open mouth with two upper teeth, original mohair wig, original clothes, unplayed with, mark BHS-2, size 4, rare to find in original box, $600.00 – $700.00.

Plate 280
Doll, 15" tall, bisque socket head on a composition baby body, blue sleep eyes, open mouth with two upper teeth, original mohair wig, dark brown glossy eyebrows are unusual, old clothes, mark BHS-2, size 5, $350.00 – $400.00.

Plate 282
Doll, 10" tall, bisque socket head on a composition baby body, painted eyes, open mouth with two upper teeth, replaced wig, old clothes, mark BHS-2, size 2/0, $175.00 – $225.00.
Doll, 9" tall, bisque socket head on a composition baby body, painted eyes, open mouth with two upper teeth, original mohair wig, new

clothes, mark BHS-2, size 3/0, $150.00 – $200.00.
Morimura Brothers used painted eyes on some of the smaller sizes of characters babies. Therefore, it's possible to find the same doll with either glass eyes (as in Plate 279) or painted eyes (as in Plate 282).

Plate 284

"Crying" doll, 15" tall, bisque socket head on a composition baby body, has crying bellows in head (see Plate 287 for example), blue sleep eyes, open mouth with two upper teeth, original mohair wig, old clothes, mark BHS-2, size 5, $450.00 – $500.00 with crying mechanism.

Doll, 16½" tall, bisque socket head on a composition baby body, blue sleep eyes, open mouth with four upper teeth, unusual animal skin wig, old clothes, mark BHS-2, size 7, $375.00 – $425.00.

Plate 283

Doll, 9¼" tall, bisque socket head on a jointed composition toddler body with painted shoes and socks, sleep eyes, open mouth with two upper teeth, old wig, original Scottish outfit. It is unusual to find ethnic clothing on a Nippon-era doll; note that the color of the painted socks matches the outfit. Mark BHS-2, size 3/0, $225.00 – $275.00.

Plate 285

Doll, 22½" tall, bisque socket head on a ball jointed composition body, blue sleep eyes, open mouth with two upper teeth, human hair wig, new clothes, mark BHS-2, size 11, $550.00 – $600.00.

Plate 286

"Crying" doll, 13½" tall, bisque socket head on a composition baby body, has crying bellows in head (see Plate 287), blue sleep eyes, replaced mohair wig, new clothes, mark BHS-2, size 4, $400.00 – $450.00 with crying mechanism.

Plate 287

Crying mechanism used in Morimura Brothers "crying" dolls. It is made of wood and paper. When the string is pulled, it produces an "angh" sound. This same type of crying mechanism was used by Armand Marseille in their crying dolls.

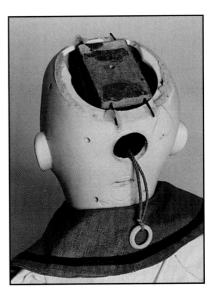

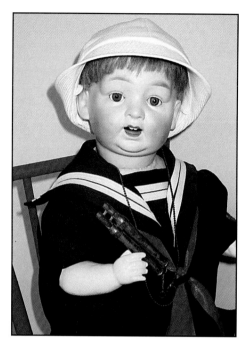

Plate 288
Doll, 23" tall, bisque socket head on a composition baby body, blue sleep eyes, open mouth with two upper teeth, original mohair wig, new clothes, mark BHS-2, size 12, the largest size made in this mold number, $575.00 – $625.00.

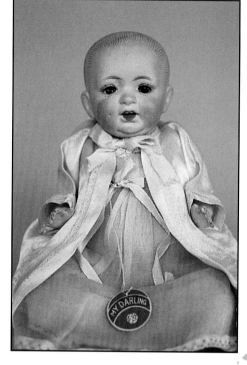

Plate 289
My Darling doll with original tag, 9¼" tall, bisque socket head on composition baby body, blue sleep eyes, open mouth with two painted upper teeth, brushstroke hair, original clothes, mark BHS-3, size 2/0, rare to find with original tag, $300.00 – $350.00 with original tag.

Plate 290
Doll, 11" tall, bisque socket head on a composition baby body, painted eyes, open mouth with two painted upper teeth, brushstroke hair, old clothes, mark BHS-3, size 2, $150.00 – $200.00.
Doll, 8" tall, bisque socket head on a composition baby body, painted eyes, open mouth with two painted upper teeth, brushstroke hair, old clothes, mark BHS-3, size 3/0, $125.00 – $175.00.
The value on these two dolls is decreased because they lack an original tag identifying them as Morimura Brothers dolls. For some reason Morimura Brothers did not incise their symbol on the heads of their line of solid domehead dolls. See "Deciphering Nippon Bisque-Head Doll Marks" for a complete description of the mark and a photo of the My Darling tag.

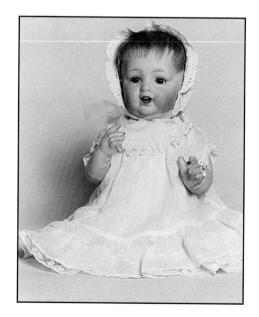

Plate 291
"Crying" doll, 18" tall, bisque socket head on a composition baby body, has crying bellows in head (see Plate 287), blue sleep eyes, original mohair wig, old clothes, mark BHS-2, size 10, $550.00 – $600.00 with crying mechanism.

Plate 292
Doll, 13" tall, bisque socket head on a composition baby body, brown sleep eyes, open mouth with two upper teeth, molded tongue, original mohair wig, original clothes, mark BHS-4, size 2, $275.00 – $325.00.

Plate 293
Doll, 21" tall, bisque socket head on a composition baby body, blue sleep eyes, open mouth with two upper teeth, molded tongue, original human hair wig, new clothes, mark BHS-4, size 11, $600.00 – $650.00.

Plate 294
Doll, 18" tall, bisque socket head on a composition baby body, blue sleep eyes, open mouth with two upper teeth, wobble tongue, replaced mohair wig, old clothes, mark BHS-4, size 10, $500.00 – $550.00.

Plate 295
Close-up of doll in Plate 294 showing the excellent quality of the bisque and a great character face. Dolls of this quality will always be sought by collectors.

Plate 297
Close-up of doll in Plate 296. The face is very much like the face of the Morimura Brothers no. 1 mold. The main difference is that the no. 5 mold is a bisque head shoulderplate on an imitation kid body, and the no. 1 mold is a bisque socket head on a ball jointed composition body.

Plate 296
Group of Morimura Brothers bisque-head shoulderplate dolls (mold no. 5) showing some of the various sizes of the doll. These dolls were originally sold with imitation kid bodies (in their ads, Morimura Brothers called these bodies kidalyn or kidaline). Left to right: Doll, 18½" tall, imitation kid body with bisque arms, sleep eyes, open mouth with four upper teeth, human hair wig, old clothes, mark BHS-5, size 3, $300.00 – $350.00.
Doll, 24" tall, imitation kid body with bisque arms, sleep eyes, open mouth with four upper teeth, old wig, old clothes, mark BHS-5, size 5, $325.00 – $375.00.
Doll, 14" tall, kid body (probably replaced), sleep eyes, open mouth with four upper teeth, replaced wig, replaced clothes, mark BHS-5, size 2, $200.00 – $250.00.
Doll, 20" tall, imitation kid body with bisque arms, sleep eyes, open mouth with four upper teeth, replaced wig, replaced clothes, mark BHS-5, size 4, $300.00 – $350.00.

Plate 298
Doll, 14½" tall, bisque socket head on a composition baby body, dark brown sleep eyes, human hair wig, open mouth with four upper teeth, original clothes, rare Asian Morimura Brothers doll, mark BHS-6, size 1, $550.00 – $650.00.

Plate 299
Doll, 14½" tall, bisque socket head on a composition baby body, dark brown sleep eyes, human hair wig, open mouth with four upper teeth, original clothes, rare Asian Morimura Brothers doll, mark BHS-6, size 1, $550.00 – $650.00.

Plate 301

Close-up of doll in Plate 300. This doll is hard to find and was probably one of the later Morimura Brothers dolls produced.

Plate 300

Doll, 22" tall, bisque socket head on a composition baby body (with unusual jointed wrists and very large hands), blue sleep eyes, open mouth with two upper teeth, molded tongue, original human hair wig, new clothes, unusual Morimura Brothers mold number, mark BHS-7, size 12, $650.00 – $700.00.

Plate 302

Doll, 18" tall, bisque socket head on a composition baby body, blue sleep eyes, open mouth with two upper teeth, replaced wig, dressed in a wonderful 3' long antique christening gown, mark BHS-8, size 11, $475.00 – $525.00.

Doll, 10" tall, bisque socket head on a composition baby body, blue sleep eyes, open mouth with two upper teeth, replaced wig, replaced clothes, mark BHS-8, size 2, $200.00 – $250.00.

Plate 303

Doll, 12" tall, bisque socket head on a new composition baby body, painted eyes, open mouth with two upper teeth, replaced wig, old underclothes, mark BHS-8, size 2, $200.00 – $250.00 if body is original.

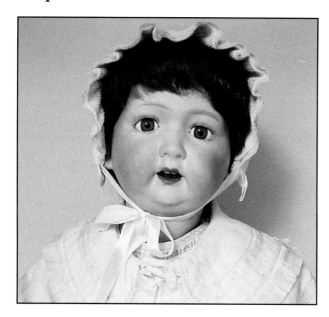

Plate 304
Doll, 22" tall, bisque socket head on a composition baby body, blue sleep eyes, open mouth with two upper teeth, replaced wig, dressed in antique baby's coat/cape combination and bonnet, mark BHS-8, size 12, $550.00 – $600.00.

Plate 305
Doll, 7" tall, bisque socket head on a composition baby body, painted eyes, open mouth with two upper teeth, original mohair wig, new clothes, mark BHS-8, size 4/0, $125.00 – $175.00.

Plate 306
Doll, 12" tall, bisque socket head on a composition baby body, blue sleep eyes with eyelashes, open mouth with two upper teeth, replaced wig, old clothes, unusual Morimura Brothers mold no., mark BHS-9, size 3, $300.00 – $350.00.

Plate 307
Close-up of doll in Plate 306. This doll is hard to find and was probably one of the later Morimura Brothers dolls produced.

Plate 309
Group of FY and Scrolled FY Breather (pierced nostrils) dolls. Even though the marks are different, the molds are the same. Doll, 15" tall, bisque socket head on a composition baby body, blue sleep eyes, open mouth with two upper teeth, brushstroke hair, old clothes, mark BHS-23, size 104, $325.00 – $375.00. Doll, 21" tall,

Plate 308
Doll, 13" tall, bisque socket head on a composition baby body, brown sleep eyes, open mouth with two upper teeth, replaced wig, old clothes, mark BHS-10, $175.00 – $225.00.

bisque socket head on a composition baby body, blue sleep eyes, open mouth with two upper teeth, brushstroke hair, old clothes, mark BHS-11, size 106 (see close-up photo of this doll in the Glossary, page 314), $525.00 – $575.00.
Doll, 13" tall, bisque socket head on a composition baby body, blue sleep eyes, open mouth with two upper teeth, brushstroke hair, old clothes, mark BHS-23, size 103, $275.00 – $325.00.

Plate 310
Doll, 15" tall, bisque socket head on a composition baby body, brown sleep eyes, open mouth with two upper teeth, replaced wig, old clothes, mark BHS-12, size 203, $300.00 – $350.00.

Plate 311
1920 Montgomery Ward catalog ad.

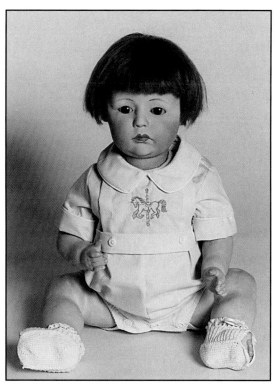

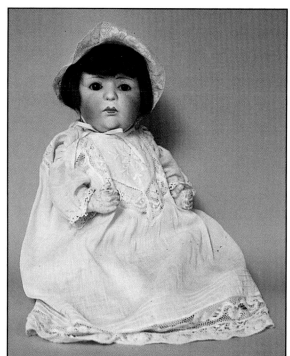

Plate 313
Pouty doll, 13" tall, bisque socket head on a composition baby body, brown sleep eyes, closed pouty mouth, original mohair wig, old clothes, rare, mark BHS-13, size 302, $800.00 – $1,000.00.

Plate 312
Pouty doll, 18" tall, bisque socket head on an oyster shell baby body, brown sleep eyes, closed pouty mouth, original mohair wig, new clothes, rare, mark BHS-13, size 305, $1,100.00 – $1,300.00.

Plate 315
Close-up of middle doll in Plate 314 showing the excellent quality of the bisque and the wonderful pouty expression. These dolls were modeled after the Heubach 6969 mold. Nippon pouty dolls are very much sought after by collectors.

Plate 314
Group of FY 300 series pouty dolls showing three of the probably six different sizes.
Pouty doll, 17" tall, bisque socket head on a composition baby body, brown sleep eyes, closed pouty mouth, original mohair wig, old clothes, rare, mark BHS-13, size 304, $1,000.00 – $1,200.00.
Pouty doll, 14" tall, bisque socket head on a composition baby body, brown sleep eyes, closed pouty mouth, original mohair wig, old clothes, rare, mark BHS-13, size 302, $800.00 – $1,000.00.
Pouty doll, 18" tall, bisque socket head on an oyster shell baby body, brown sleep eyes, closed pouty mouth, original mohair wig, new clothes, rare, mark BHS-13, size 305, $1,100.00 – $1,300.00.

Plate 317
Group of FY 400 series dolls showing three of the six different sizes.
Doll, 20" tall, described in Plate 318.
Doll, 14" tall, described in Plate 319.
Doll, 24" tall, bisque socket head on a ball jointed composition body, brown sleep eyes, open mouth with four upper teeth, replaced wig, old clothes may be original, mark BHS-14, size 405, $475.00 – $525.00.

Plate 316
Doll, 22" tall, bisque socket head on a ball jointed composition body, sleep eyes, open mouth with four upper teeth, original wig, old clothes, mark BHS-14, size 404, $350.00 – $400.00.

Plate 318
Doll, 20" tall, bisque socket head on a replaced kid body, brown sleep eyes, open mouth with four upper teeth, replaced wig, replaced clothes, mark BHS-14, size 402, $325.00 – $375.00 if on a ball jointed composition body.

Plate 319
Doll, 14" tall, bisque socket head on a ball jointed composition body, brown sleep eyes, open mouth with four upper teeth, replaced wig, old dress, mark BHS-14, size 401, $250.00 – $300.00.

Bisque-Head Dolls

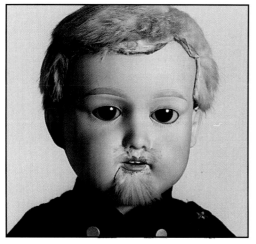

Plate 320
Close-up of doll in Plate 321 showing rabbit fur wig, mustache, and goatee.

Plate 321
Doll, 22" tall, bisque socket head on a ball jointed composition body, brown sleep eyes, open mouth with four upper teeth, unusual rabbit fur wig and facial hair, unusual original clothes. Doll was obviously dressed to portray a certain character unknown to us. Mark BHS-14, size 405, $525.00 – $575.00.

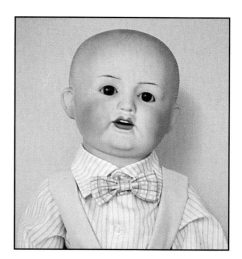

Plate 322
Group of FY and Scrolled FY 500 series solid dome head dolls showing four of the six different sizes. Even though the marks are different the molds are the same.
Doll, 19" tall, bisque socket head on a composition baby body, brown sleep eyes, open mouth with two painted upper teeth, brushstroke hair, new clothes, mark BHS-15, size 505, $400.00 – $450.00.
Doll, 13" tall, bisque socket head on a composition baby body, blue sleep eyes, open mouth with two painted upper teeth, brushstroke hair, replaced clothes, mark BHS-26, size 502, $250.00 – $300.00.
Doll, 10½" tall, bisque socket head on a composition baby body, blue sleep eyes, open mouth with two painted upper teeth, brushstroke hair, new clothes, mark BHS-15, size 501, $175.00 – $225.00.
Doll, 16" tall, bisque socket head on a composition baby body, brown sleep eyes, open mouth with two painted upper teeth, brushstroke hair, new clothes, mark BHS-26, size 504, $325.00 – $375.00.

Plate 323
Close-up of 19" doll in Plate 322.

Plate 324
Doll, 17" tall, bisque socket head on a composition baby body, brown sleep eyes, open mouth with two painted upper teeth, brushstroke hair, new clothes, mark BHS-15, size 504, $350.00 – $400.00.

Plate 325
Doll, 16" tall, bisque socket head on a compo-sition baby body, blue sleep eyes, open mouth with two upper teeth, mohair wig, old clothes, mark BHS-16, size 603, $350.00 – $400.00.

Plate 326
Group of FY 1600 series bisque-head shoulderplate dolls showing three different sizes. Unlike many of the other Nippon shoulder plate dolls that have imitation kid bodies, these dolls are usually found with cloth bodies.
Doll, 18" tall, bisque-head shoulderplate on cloth body with lower bisque arms, blue sleep eyes, open mouth with two upper teeth, replaced human hair wig, old clothes, mark BHS-17, size 1602 $250.00 – $300.00.
Doll, 24" tall, bisque-head shoulderplate on cloth body with lower bisque arms, blue sleep eyes, open mouth with two upper teeth, replaced wig, new clothes, mark BHS-17, size 1604, $325.00 – $375.00.
Doll, 16" tall, bisque-head shoulderplate on cloth body with lower bisque arms, blue sleep eyes, open mouth with two upper teeth, replaced human hair wig, new clothes, mark BHS-17, size 1601, $200.00 – $250.00.

Plate 328
1918 Novem-ber-December Montgomery Ward grocery catalog ad. Notice that the ad talks about the dolls now being available after a "lapse of years."

Plate 327
Close-up of 18" doll in Plate 326.

Bisque-Head Dolls

Scrolled FY Dolls

Plate 330
Doll, 10" tall, bisque socket head on composition toddler body with painted shoes and socks, brown sleep eyes, open mouth with four upper teeth, original wig, original clothes, mark BHS-18, $200.00 – $250.00.

Plate 329
Doll, 17" tall, bisque shoulderplate, cloth body with bisque arms, replaced clothes, an unusual doll, marked FY Nippon H148, $325.00 – $375.00.

Plate 331
Doll, 15" tall, bisque socket head on a composition baby body, brown sleep eyes, open mouth with two bottom teeth (unusual to find bottom teeth), replaced wig, old clothes, mark BHS-19, $300.00 – $350.00.

Plate 332
Doll, 15" tall, bisque socket head on a composition baby body, brown sleep eyes, open mouth with two upper teeth, celluloid molded tongue, mohair wig, replaced clothes, mark BHS-21, $325.00 – $375.00.

204

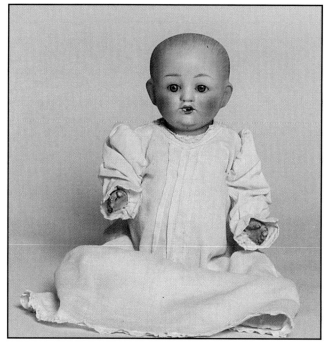

Plate 334
Doll, 12" tall, bisque socket head on a composition toddler body with painted stockings and shoes. The legs do not bend forward so the doll cannot be positioned to sit. Blue sleep eyes, open mouth with two upper teeth, original mohair wig, old clothes, an unusual doll but high cheek color detracts from the look of the doll and the value, mark BHS-24, $225.00 – $300.00.

Plate 333
Doll, 11" tall, bisque socket head on a composition baby body, blue sleep eyes, open mouth with two upper teeth, "breather" (pierced nostrils), brushstroke hair, old clothes, mark BHS-22, $250.00 – $300.00.

Plate 335
Group of Scrolled FY 400 series dolls showing three of the six different sizes.
Doll, 24" tall, described in Plate 338, mark BHS-405.
Doll, 20" tall, bisque socket head on a ball jointed composition body, blue sleep eyes, open mouth with four upper teeth, replaced wig, old dress, mark BHS-403, $300.00 – $350.00.
Doll, 25" tall, bisque socket head on a ball jointed composition body, blue set eyes (should have sleep eyes), open mouth with four upper teeth, new wig, new clothes, mark BHS-406, $500.00 – $550.00 if in good condition.

Plate 336
Doll, 20" tall, bisque socket head on a ball jointed composition body, sleep eyes, open mouth with four upper teeth, old wig, old clothes, mark BHS-25, size 403, $350.00 – $400.00.

Bisque-Head Dolls

A large sized doll of unusual loveliness. The Papier-Mache body makes her extremely light and strong. You can hug and squeeze it just as hard as you please. Her head, limbs and body are carefully moulded along life-like lines. And the bisque head, girls, is a perfect dream! The realistic eyelashes drop over the moving eyes when this dolly goes to sleep. And she has a row of the nicest little teeth. The mohair wig is curled in a becoming manner.

Spring jointings in neck, shoulders, elbows, hands, hips and knees will not deteriorate. The long-lasting qualities of this doll make it an exceptionally good value at the price we ask. Ball joints at elbows and knees. Height, 23 in. Ship. wt., 3¼ lbs.

149C2913—
Price..... **$6.50**

Plate 337
Doll, 24" tall, bisque socket head on a ball jointed composition body, blue sleep eyes, open mouth with four upper teeth, replaced wig, old clothes, mark BHS-25, size 405, $450.00 – $500.00.

Plate 338
Doll, 24" tall, bisque socket head on a ball jointed composition body, blue sleep eyes, open mouth with four upper teeth, mohair wig, new clothes, mark BHS-25, size 405, $450.00 – $500.00.

Plate 340
1920 Montgomery Ward catalog ad.

Plate 339
Close-up of the dolls in Plates 337 and 338. Even though these two dolls have the same mark, the head molds are slightly different and are different sizes. The doll's head on the left is 5½" tall with an 11¾" head circumference. The doll's head on the right is 5¼" tall with an 11¼" head circumference. At some point during the production of these dolls, the mold of the head was changed, perhaps to give the face a fuller, more child-like look.

Plate 342
Doll, 16" tall, bisque socket head on a composition toddler body, blue sleep eyes, open mouth with two painted upper teeth, brushstroke hair, old romper, mark BHS-26, size 504, $350.00 – $400.00.

Plate 341
Doll, 15" tall, bisque socket head on an unusual body made of wood and composition with coarse muslin covering the wood, dark brown sleep eyes, original human hair wig, original kimono, probably sold as a souvenir, mark BHS-25, size 402, $275.00 – $325.00.

Plate 344
Doll, 13¼" tall, bisque socket head on a composition toddler body, sleep eyes, open mouth with two upper teeth, mohair wig, old clothes, mark BHS-27, size 601, $275.00 – $325.00.

Plate 343
Doll, 13" tall, bisque socket head on a composition baby body, blue sleep eyes, open mouth with two painted upper teeth, brushstroke hair, replaced clothes, mark BHS-26, size 502, $250.00 – $300.00.

207

Plate 345
Doll, 13" tall, bisque socket head on a composition baby body, blue sleep eyes, open mouth with two upper teeth, old wig, old clothes, mark BHS-27, size 602, $275.00 – $325.00.

Plate 346
Doll, 14½" tall, bisque socket head on a composition baby body, brown sleep eyes, open mouth with two upper teeth, replaced wig, new clothes, mark BHS-27, size 603, $300.00 – $350.00.

Plate 347
Doll, 12" tall, bisque socket head on a composition baby body, blue sleep eyes, open mouth with four upper teeth, mohair wig, old clothes, mark BHS-28, size 902, $300.00 – $350.00.
Doll, 15" tall, bisque socket head on a composition baby body, blue sleep eyes, open mouth with four upper teeth, mohair wig, old clothes, mark BHS-28, size 904, $350.00 – $400.00.
Doll bottle is marked "Nippon," $15.00 – $20.00.

Plate 348
Close-up of 12" doll in Plate 347. This is an uncommon doll; note the fullness of the face.

Plate 350
Close-up of 16" doll in Plate 349.

Plate 349
Doll, 13" tall, bisque socket head on a ball jointed composition body, blue sleep eyes, open mouth with two upper teeth, old wig, old dress, mark BHS-29, size 2001, $250.00 – $300.00.
Doll, 16" tall, bisque socket head on a ball jointed composition body, blue sleep eyes, open mouth with two upper teeth, old wig, old clothes, mark BHS-29, size 2002, $300.00 – $350.00.

RE in Diamond Dolls

Plate 352
Sticker found on doll in Plate 351.

Plate 351
Doll by Louis Wolf & Company, 17" tall, bisque head, shoulder-plate on imitation kid body with lower bisque arms, blue sleep eyes, open mouth with four upper teeth, original mohair wig, original clothes, in unplayed with condition, original sticker on chest (see Plate 352), rare to find in original, unplayed with condition, mark BHS-30, $450.00 – $550.00.

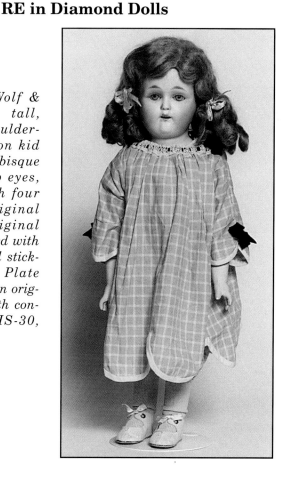

Plate 353
Close-up of doll in Plate 351 showing the beautiful blue eyes and excellent bisque.

Plate 354
Doll, 24" tall, bisque head, shoulderplate on imitation kid body with lower bisque arms, brown sleep eyes, open mouth with four upper teeth, original mohair wig, old clothes, mark BHS-30, $375.00 – $425.00.

Plate 355
1919 Montgomery Ward catalog ad.

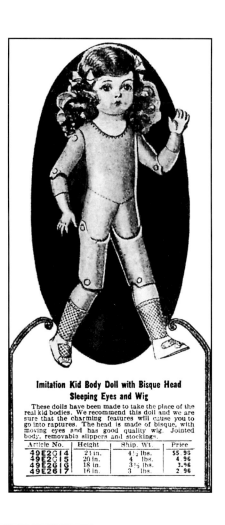

Imitation Kid Body Doll with Bisque Head Sleeping Eyes and Wig

These dolls have been made to take the place of the real kid bodies. We recommend this doll and we are sure that the charming features will cause you to go into raptures. The head is made of bisque, with moving eyes and has good quality wig. Jointed body, removable slippers and stockings.

Article No.	Height	Ship. Wt.	Price
49E2G14	21 in.	4½ lbs.	$5.96
49E2G15	20 in.	4 lbs.	4.96
49E2G16	18 in.	3½ lbs.	3.96
49E2617	16 in.	3 lbs.	2.96

Plate 356
Doll, 23" tall, bisque head, shoulderplate on imitation kid body with lower bisque arms, blue sleep eyes, open mouth with four upper teeth, old wig, old clothes, mark BHS-30, $375.00 – $425.00.

Plate 357
Doll, 19" tall, bisque head, shoulderplate on imitation kid body with lower bisque arms, sleep eyes, open mouth with four upper teeth, old wig, replaced clothes, mark BHS-30, $350.00 – $400.00.
Doll, 18" tall, bisque head, shoulderplate on imitation kid body with lower bisque arms, sleep eyes, open mouth with four upper teeth, old wig, old clothes, mark BHS-30, $350.00 – $400.00.

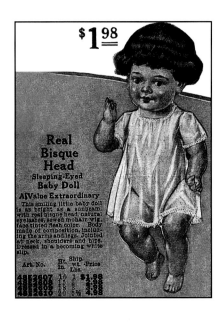

Plate 358
Doll, 8½" tall, bisque socket head on composition toddler body, blue sleep eyes, open mouth with two upper teeth, replaced mohair wig, old clothes, unusual small size, mark BHS-30, $200.00 – $250.00.

Plate 359
Doll, 12" tall, bisque socket head on a composition baby body, blue sleep eyes, open mouth with two upper teeth, brushstroke hair, single stroke eyebrows, old clothes, mark BHS-30, $250.00 – $300.00.

Plate 360
1919 Montgomery Ward catalog ad.

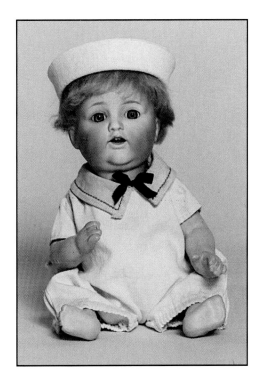

Plate 362
Doll, 10¼" tall, bisque socket head on an oyster shell composition baby body, blue sleep eyes, open mouth with two upper teeth, replaced mohair wig, old romper, mark BHS-33, size 3, $250.00 – $300.00.

Plate 361
Doll, 8½" tall, bisque socket head on an oyster shell composition baby body, blue sleep eyes, open mouth with two upper teeth, original mohair wig, old clothes, mark BHS-33, size 2, $225.00 – $275.00.

211

Plate 364

Doll, 16" tall, bisque socket head on a composition baby body, blue sleep eyes, open mouth with two upper teeth, fur wig (notice that the wig color matches the eyebrow color), new clothes, mark BHS-33, size 7, $325.00 – $375.00.

Plate 363

Doll, 11½" tall, bisque socket head on an oyster shell composition baby body, blue sleep eyes, open mouth with two upper teeth, molded tongue, original mohair wig, old clothes, mark BHS-33, size 4, $275.00 – $325.00.

Plate 366

Doll, 18" tall, bisque socket head on a composition baby body, brown sleep eyes, open mouth with two upper teeth, replaced wig, old dress and baby pin, mark BHS-33, size 8, $400.00 – $450.00.

Doll, 8" tall, bisque socket head on an oyster shell composition baby body, brown sleep eyes, open mouth with two upper teeth, original mohair wig, old clothes, mark BHS-33, size 1, $225.00 – $275.00.

Plate 365

Blue Ribbon Baby, 12" tall, bisque socket head on a composition baby body, sleep eyes, open mouth with two upper teeth, old wig, rare to find in original box (see page 96 for a photo of box), mark BHS-33, size 4, $500.00 – $550.00.

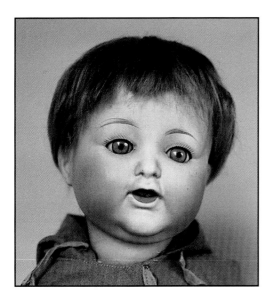

Plate 368
Doll, 22" tall, bisque socket head on a composition baby body, brown sleep eyes, open mouth with two upper teeth, molded tongue, human hair wig, replaced clothes, mark BHS-33, size 10, $650.00 – $700.00.

Plate 367
Doll, 20" tall, bisque socket head on an oyster shell composition baby body, blue sleep eyes, open mouth with two upper teeth, molded tongue, original mohair wig, old clothes, mark BHS-33, size 9, $600.00 – $650.00.

Plate 369
Doll (Hilda look alike), 14" tall, bisque socket head on a composition baby body, blue sleep eyes, open mouth with two upper teeth, molded tongue, mohair wig, old clothes, mark BHS-34, size 5, $600.00 – $700.00.

Plate 370
Group of three Nippon Hilda look alike dolls, showing three of the sizes available.

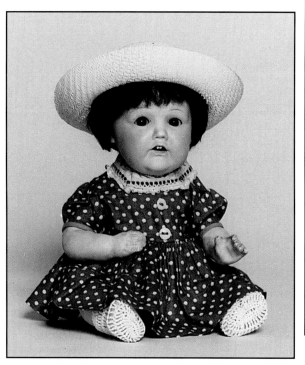

Plate 372
Doll (Hilda look alike), 16" tall, bisque socket head on a composition baby body, blue sleep eyes, open mouth with two upper teeth, replaced wig and clothes, mark BHS-34, size 7, $600.00 – $700.00.

Plate 371
Doll (Hilda look alike), 11½" tall, bisque socket head on a composition baby body, brown sleep eyes, open mouth with two upper teeth, mohair wig, replaced clothes, mark BHS-34, size 3, $450.00 – $550.00.

Plate 374
Doll (Hilda look alike), 19" tall, bisque socket head on an oyster shell composition baby body, blue sleep eyes with eyelashes, open mouth with two upper teeth, molded tongue, original mohair wig, old clothes are probably original, in unplayed with condition, mark BHS-34, size 8, $750.00 – $850.00.

Plate 373
Doll (Hilda look alike), 17" tall, bisque socket head on a composition baby body, blue sleep eyes, open mouth with two upper teeth, replaced wig and clothes, mark BHS-34, size 8, $600.00 – $700.00.

Plate 376
1919 Montgomery Ward catalog ad.

Plate 375
Doll (Hilda look alike), 20½" tall, bisque socket head on an oyster shell composition baby body, blue sleep eyes with eyelashes, open mouth with two upper teeth, molded tongue, original mohair wig, old clothes, original box (with no markings or label on it) mark BHS-34, size 9, $800.00 – $900.00.

Plate 377
Doll (Hilda look alike), 22" tall, bisque socket head on an oyster shell composition baby body, blue sleep eyes with eyelashes, open mouth with one upper tooth (one tooth missing), molded tongue, original mohair wig, old clothes are probably original, unusual BE in a Diamond mark, mark BHS-34, size 10, $900.00 – $1,000.00.

Plate 378
Close-up of the BE in a Diamond mark found on doll in Plate 377.

Plate 379
Full photo of Hilda look alike in Plate 377.

Bisque-Head Dolls

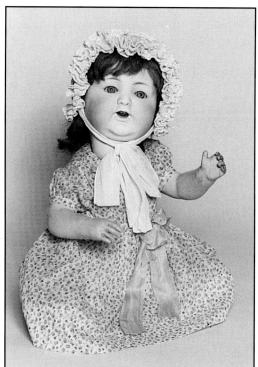

Plate 381
Doll, 20" tall, bisque socket head on a composition baby body, blue sleep eyes, open mouth with two upper teeth, molded tongue, old wig, old clothes, mark BHS-35, size 9, $600.00 – $650.00.

Plate 380
Doll, 18½" tall, bisque socket head on a composition baby body, brown sleep eyes, open mouth with two upper teeth, molded plaster tongue, replaced wig, new clothes, mark BHS-35, size 8, $500.00 – $550.00.

Plate 383
Doll, 20" tall, bisque socket head on a composition baby body, brown sleep eyes, open mouth with two upper teeth, brushstroke hair, old clothes, mark BHS-36, size 20, $500.00 – $550.00.

Plate 382
Doll, 16" tall, bisque socket head on an oyster shell composition baby body, blue sleep eyes, open mouth with two upper teeth, brushstroke hair, old clothes, mark BHS-36, size 16, $350.00 – $400.00.

Bisque Head Doll. Jointed

Wonderful Value Bisque Head Dolls. Painted Hair

Girls! Notice the charming smiling face on this little doll. Your heart will surely leap with joy to have her for your very own, to dress to love and fondle. The head is made of bisque with sleeping eyes, eyes that seem to say "Let me be your playmate always." Body made of composition jointed at neck shoulders and hips. Dressed in becoming white slip.

Article Number	Height Inches	Ship. Wt. Pounds	Price
49E2601	12½ in.	3 lbs.	$1.95
49E2602	15 in.	4 lbs.	2.95
49E2603	17½ in.	6 lbs.	3.95
49E2604	19 in.	6½ lbs.	4.95
49E2605	22 in.	7 lbs.	5.95

Plate 384
1919 Montgomery Ward catalog ad.

Plate 385
Doll, 18" tall, bisque socket head on an oyster shell composition baby body, brown sleep flirty-type eyes, open mouth with two upper teeth, brushstroke hair, old clothes, mark BHS-36, size 18, $475.00 – $525.00.

Plate 386
Doll, 22" tall, bisque socket head on a composition baby body, blue sleep eyes, open mouth with two upper teeth, brushstroke hair, new clothes, mark BHS-36, size 22, $550.00 – $600.00.

Plate 387
Doll, 11" tall, bisque socket head on a composition toddler body, blue sleep eyes, open mouth with four upper teeth, old wig, old clothes, mark BHS-37, size 1, $250.00 – $300.00.
Doll, 13" tall, bisque socket head on an oyster shell ball jointed composition body, blue sleep eyes, open mouth with four upper teeth, original wig, all original clothes, mark BHS-37, size 1, $325.00 – $375.00.
These two dolls have the same size head; the height difference is due to the different body types. This is often the case with bisque-head dolls where the size or type of body affects the over-all height of the doll. Collectors need to make sure that the head looks appropriate to the body in terms of size and type of body.

Plate 389
Doll, 21" tall, bisque socket head on a ball jointed composition body, sleep eyes, open mouth with two upper teeth, replaced wig, old clothes, mark BHS-37, size 5, $375.00 – $425.00.

Plate 388
Doll, 17" tall, bisque socket head on a ball jointed composition body, blue sleep eyes, open mouth with four upper teeth, new mohair wig, new clothes, mark BHS-37, size 4, $300.00 – $350.00.

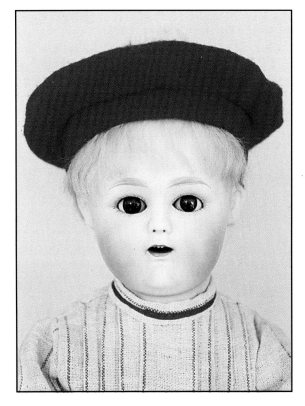

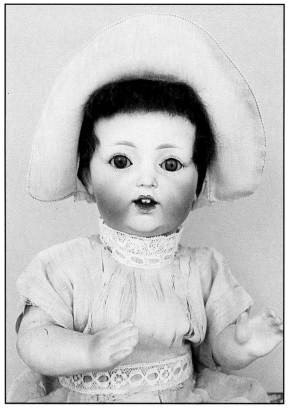

Plate 391
Doll, 15" tall, bisque socket head on an oyster shell composition baby body, blue sleep eyes, open mouth with two upper teeth, original mohair wig, original clothes, mark BHS-38, $400.00 – $450.00.

Plate 390
Doll, 24" tall, bisque socket head on a ball jointed composition body, brown sleep eyes, open mouth with four upper teeth, mohair wig, replaced clothes, mark BHS-38, $500.00 – $550.00.

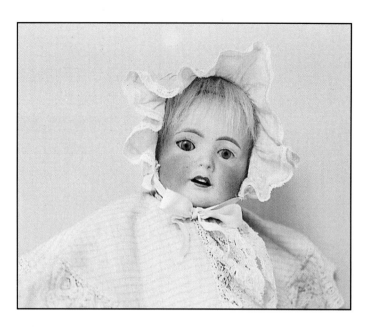

Plate 392
Doll, 12" tall, bisque socket head on a composition baby body, blue sleep eyes, open mouth with four upper teeth, mohair wig, old clothes, mark BHS-46, size 12, $250.00 – $300.00.

Plate 393
Doll, 14" tall, bisque socket head on a composition baby body, blue sleep eyes, open mouth with four upper teeth, original mohair wig, original clothes, mark BHS-46, size 14, $325.00 – $375.00.

Plate 395
Doll, 18" tall, bisque socket head on a composition baby body, blue sleep eyes, open mouth with four upper teeth, original mohair wig, old clothes, mark BHS-48, size 18, $550.00 – $600.00.

Plate 394
Doll, 14" tall, bisque socket head on a composition baby body, blue sleep eyes, open mouth with four upper teeth (1 chipped), replaced mohair wig, new clothes, mark BHS-47, size 14, $300.00 – $350.00.

H in Diamond Dolls

Plate 396
Doll, 14" tall, bisque socket head on a composition toddler body, blue sleep eyes, open mouth with four upper teeth, mohair wig, old clothes, a rare mark, mark BHS-45, $400.00 – $450.00.

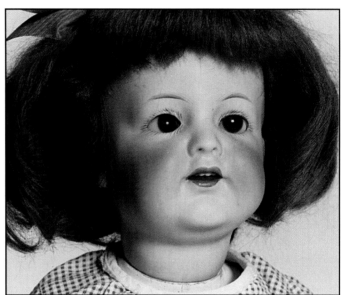

Plate 397
Close-up of doll in Plate 396.

KKS in Star Dolls

Plate 398
Doll, 14½" tall, bisque socket head on a composition baby body, brown sleep eyes, open mouth with four upper teeth, molded tongue, mohair wig, old clothes, rare mark BHS-49, $400.00 – $450.00.

Plate 399
Doll, 14" tall, bisque socket head on a composition baby body, brown sleep eyes, open mouth with four upper teeth (one chipped), old wig, old clothes, rare mark BHS-48, $400.00 – $450.00.

JW Dolls

Plate 400
Doll, 15" tall, bisque socket head on a ball jointed composition body, blue sleep eyes, open mouth with two upper teeth, mohair wig, new clothes, mark BHS-44, size 601, $275.00 – $325.00.

Plate 401
Doll, 21" tall, bisque socket head on a ball jointed composition body, blue sleep eyes, open mouth with two upper teeth, replaced wig, new clothes, mark BHS-44, size 605, $400.00 – $450.00.

Plate 402
Doll, 16" tall, bisque socket head on a composition baby body, sleep eyes, open mouth with two upper teeth, mohair wig, old clothes, mark BHS-44, size 604, $375.00 – $425.00.

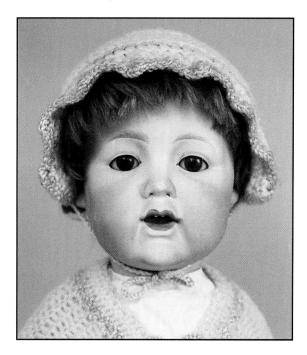

Plate 403
Doll, 20" tall, bisque socket head on a composition baby body, brown sleep eyes, open mouth with two upper teeth, mohair wig, old clothes, mark BHS-44, size 606, $450.00 – $500.00.

Bisque-Head Dolls

Horsman Dolls

Plate 404
Group of three Horsman dolls showing three of the four sizes.
Doll, 14" tall, bisque socket head on a composition baby body, brown sleep eyes, open mouth with two upper teeth, original mohair wig, old clothes, mark BHS-39, No. 1, $400.00 – $500.00.
Doll, 22" tall, bisque socket head on a composition baby body, brown sleep eyes, open mouth with two upper teeth, molded tongue original mohair wig, old clothes, mark BHS-39, No. 4, $700.00 – $800.00.
Doll, 16" tall, bisque socket head on a composition baby body, brown sleep eyes, open mouth with two upper teeth, original mohair wig, new clothes, mark BHS-39, No. 2, $500.00 – $600.00.

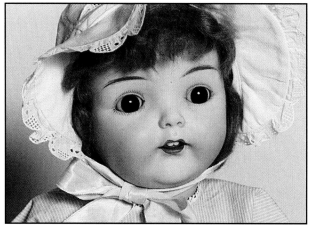

Plate 407
Close-up of 22" doll in Plate 404 showing wonderful expression and quality of bisque.

Plate 405
Doll, 17" tall, bisque socket head on a composition baby body, brown sleep eyes, open mouth with two upper teeth, molded tongue, original mohair wig, old clothes, mark BHS-39, No. 3, $600.00 – $700.00.

Plate 406
Doll, 16" tall, bisque socket head on a composition baby body, blue sleep eyes, open mouth with two upper teeth, mohair wig, new clothes, mark BHS-42, $500.00 – $600.00.

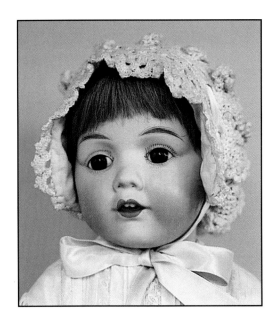

Plate 408
Doll, 22" tall, bisque socket head on a composition baby body, brown sleep eyes, open mouth with two upper teeth, human hair wig, old clothes, mark BHS-40, $700.00 – $800.00.

Plate 409
Doll, 21" tall, bisque socket head on a ball jointed composition body, blue sleep eyes, open mouth with four upper teeth, human hair wig, old clothes, mark BHS-41, $550.00 – $650.00.

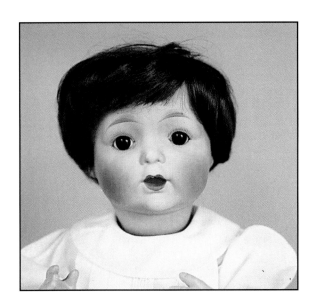

Plate 411
Doll, 17" tall, bisque socket head on a new composition toddler body, brown sleep eyes, open mouth with two upper teeth, new wig, new clothes, mark BHS-43, $350.00 – $400.00 as is.

Plate 410
Close-up of doll in Plate 409.

M in a Blossom Dolls

Plate 412
Doll, 22" tall, bisque socket head on ball jointed composition body, blue sleep eyes, open mouth with four upper teeth, human hair wig, old clothes, mark BHS-51, #18, $450.00 – $550.00.
Doll, 16" tall, bisque socket head on ball jointed composition body, blue sleep eyes, open mouth with four upper teeth, original mohair wig, original shoes, new dress/hat, old purse, mark BHS-51, #12, $350.00 – $400.00.

Plate 413
Close-up of 16" doll shown in Plate 412.

Plate 414
Close-up of 22" doll shown in Plate 412.

Plate 415
Googly doll, 11½" tall, bisque socket head on a composition toddler body, blue sleep googly eyes, closed smiling mouth, painted hair (bow added), old clothes, a very rare doll, mark BHS-50, $1,300.00 – $1,500.00 (see Glossary, page 316, for close-up of this doll).

Plate 417
Doll, 14" tall, bisque socket head on a ball jointed composition body, brown sleep eyes, open mouth with four upper teeth, mohair wig, old dress, mark BHS-52, $300.00 – $350.00.

Plate 416
Doll, 24" tall, bisque socket head on a ball jointed composition body, blue sleep eyes, open mouth with two upper teeth, new mohair wig, old dress, mark BHS-51 (size number unreadable), $450.00 – $500.00.

M (no Blossom) Doll

Plate 418
Doll, 23" tall, bisque socket head on a ball jointed composition body, blue sleep eyes, open mouth with four upper teeth, replaced wig, old clothes, mark BHS-53, $375.00 – $425.00.

Plate 419
Doll, 12" tall, bisque socket head on a composition baby body, blue/gray sleep eyes, open mouth with two upper teeth, new wig, old dress, mark BHS-54, $200.00 – $250.00.

M in a Circle Dolls

Plate 420
Doll, 28" tall, bisque socket head on a ball jointed composition body, blue sleep eyes, open mouth with four upper teeth, human hair wig, unusual oily bisque finish, old clothes may be original, mark BHS-56, $750.00 – $850.00.

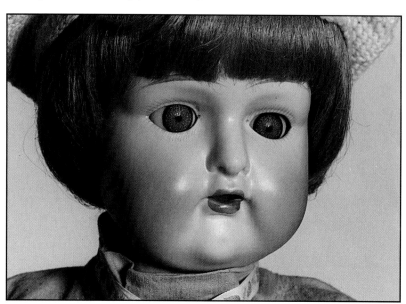

Plate 421
Close-up of doll in Plate 420 showing oily bisque finish. This is a unique doll that would be a wonderful addition to any doll collection.

Plate 423
Doll, 28" tall, bisque socket head on a ball jointed composition body, blue sleep eyes, open mouth with four upper teeth, replaced human hair wig, old clothes, mark BHS-56, $700.00 – $800.00.

Plate 422
Doll, 28" tall, bisque socket head on a ball jointed composition body, brown sleep eyes, open mouth with four upper teeth, replaced wig, old dress, mark BHS-56, $700.00 – $800.00.

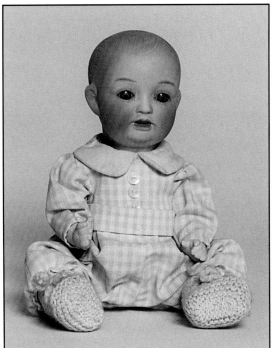

Plate 425
Doll, 11" tall, bisque socket head on a composition baby body, blue sleep eyes, open mouth with painted teeth, brushstroke hair, old clothes, mark BHS-58 (mold / size number unreadable), $225.00 – $275.00.

Plate 424
Doll, 19" tall, bisque socket head on a composition baby body, dark brown sleep eyes, open mouth with two upper teeth, molded tongue, painted hair, old clothes, unusual doll, mark BHS-59, $550.00 – $650.00.

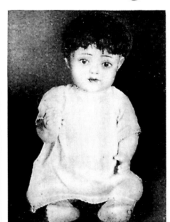

Plate 427
Doll, 12" tall, bisque socket head on a composition baby body, blue sleep eyes, open mouth with two upper teeth, molded tongue, replaced wig, new clothes, mark BHS-58, #80 / 1, $250.00 – $300.00.

Plate 426
1919 Playthings *ad.*

Deciphering Nippon Bisque-Head Doll Marks

Most Nippon doll manufacturers used some type of letters or numbers to designate the particular doll type (socket head or shoulderplate), mold (breather, pouty, dolly-face, etc.), and size of the doll. Unfortunately, none of this is documented anywhere, and it's only when a large collection of dolls is gathered that it's possible to make some sense of these marks. Even then, there are inconsistencies and variations that make it difficult to provide collectors with a completely accurate listing of the marks. Sometimes there are just not enough dolls found with a particular mark to understand the meaning of the mark; sometimes the mark on the doll is so light that we can't fully recognize the marking. We have provided as much information as we currently have on the marks. No doubt there are other marks yet to be discovered, and other information about the marks to be found. This listing is merely a starting point for collectors as to the marks that were used on Nippon bisque-head dolls.

The marks are normally found on the back of the head (sometimes on the neck) or the back of the shoulderplate. The marks are often not uniform even for those used by the same maker or distributor for identical dolls. As you go through this listing, you will see that there are instances where two different dolls have the same mark.

Letters and/or numbers are often used to indicate the size and/or mold type. Many times it is hard to decipher the exact letter or number on the doll because the mark is so worn or because of the way the letters or numbers were formed. For example, a 1 is sometimes confused with a 7 or a 6 is confused with a 0. Small sizes are often indicated by a fraction with a zero denominator such as $\frac{2}{0}$ or $\frac{4}{0}$. The higher the numerator, the smaller the doll. Therefore, $\frac{4}{0}$ is a smaller doll than $\frac{2}{0}$. Morimura Brothers used this type of size identification on several of their molds.

The symbols may represent the manufacturer, importer, or even the owner of the mold. For bisque-head dolls there were two types of molds — the master mold and the pouring mold. The master mold often belonged to either the importer or buyer of the doll head. For example, it's likely that Horsman owned the molds for their line of bisque-head dolls. When they contracted with a Japanese firm to make the heads, it was the Horsman mark that went on the head. The pouring mold was made from the master mold. The first heads out of the mold were more sharply defined than the later heads, which is why some of the marks are very clear and others are almost obliterated. The pouring mold could be used about 50 times and then a new one had to be made.

Marks: (BHS = Bisque Head with Symbol)

Note: For each mark we have included an example of only one size. In the narrative we provide information as to the different production sizes of the dolls. Also, these marks are hand-drawn and may differ slightly from the actual mark.

MORIMURA BROTHERS

Because Morimura Brothers produced a lot of dolls, it is a little easier to decipher some of their marks. They normally used their spider symbol on their dolls that makes it easier for collectors to identify them. The top number is always the mold number, and the bottom number is always the size number. They marked their dolls "JAPAN" instead of "NIPPON" even though their dolls were all made during the Nippon era.

BHS-1

Mold number 1 is for Morimura Brothers Full Jointed Doll, a dolly-faced child doll on composition body. It comes in 16 sizes — ⁴⁄₀, ³⁄₀, ²⁄₀, ¹⁄₀, 0, 1, 2, 3, 4, 5, 6, 7, 8, 9, 10, and 11. ⁴⁄₀ is the smallest and 11 is the largest. It is a commonly found mold.

BHS-2

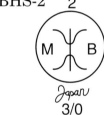

Mold number 2 is for Morimura Brothers Baby Ella doll, a character baby on a composition body. It was produced in sizes ⁴⁄₀ through 12 for the glass eye version. There is a painted eye version that was not made in as many sizes. It is a commonly found mold.

BHS-3

3 - 4/0

through

3 - 12

This mark shows an inconsistency in the way Morimura Brothers marked their dolls as this mark does not have their symbol on it. We have been able to determine this mark because we have a doll with its original Morimura Brothers tag that bears this mark. We know that Morimura Brothers was producing a solid dome head character baby as early as 1917 and they continued to advertise this doll up through 1921 yet none has turned up with the Morimura Brothers mark on them.

The mold number 3 is for their My Darling doll, a solid dome head character baby. The 3 is followed by a dash which is then followed by the size number. It probably came in sizes 4/0 through 12 and was made with either glass or painted eyes.

With no manufacturer's symbol on it, these dolls are often misidentified as German dolls which speaks volumes for their quality. However, it is possible that German companies used this same type of marking on their dolls.

BHS-4

Mold number 4 is a character baby on a composition body. It may have been made in sizes 1 through 12 but not all have been documented. This is one of the harder Morimura Brothers mold numbers to find.

BHS-5

Mold number 5 is for Morimura Brothers shoulderplate dolly-faced doll on an imitation kid (kidaline) body. The doll is a lot like their Full Jointed Doll, and they usually advertised this doll with the Full Jointed Doll. This shoulderplate doll does not come in as many sizes as the Full Jointed Doll, but it is a commonly found mold.

BHS-6

Mold number 6 is for a character baby with Asian features. It is on a composition body. This is a rare mold number, and we have only been able to document the size 1 in this doll.

BHS-7

Mold number 8 is for a character baby on a composition body. It is a hard to find mold number. The probable sizes are 1 through 12, but we have not been able document all of them.

BHS-8

Mold number 22 is for a character baby on a composition body. This mark shows up frequently on Morimura Brothers dolls and appears to have been made in the same sizes as mold number 2 (% through 12). Like mold number 2, it also was produced in both a glass eye and painted eye version.

BHS-9

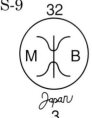

Mold number 32 is for a character baby on a composition body. This is a hard to find mold number, and only the size 3 has been documented.

FY

BHS-10

The FY mark is often attributed to Yamato Importing, and we have no information to either validate or dispute that. We do know that Foulds and Freure was importing these dolls as early as 1917. There is sometimes a period after the F and the Y. The mold number identifies both the type of doll and the size. For instance, 401 is the smallest size of the dolly-faced child doll; 400 identifies it as the dolly-faced doll and 1 is the size. The FY with no mold number has been found on a 13" character baby with a 5-piece composition baby body.

BHS-11

The 100 series is found on a solid dome head "breather" character baby. It was probably made in six sizes, 101 through 106.

BHS-12

The 200 series is found on a character baby. It was probably made in six sizes, 201 through 206.

BHS-13

The 300 series is the much sought after "pouty"/character baby. It is a rare doll, probably made in six sizes, 301 through 306.

BHS-14

The 400 series is a dolly-faced child doll on a composition body. This is a commonly found mold number and was made in six sizes, 401 through 406.

BHS-15

The 500 series is a solid dome head character baby. It is a commonly found mold number and was probably made in six sizes 501 through 506.

BHS-16

NIPPON
602

The 600 series is a character baby. It was probably made in sizes 601 through 606.

BHS-17

NIPPON
1604

The 1600 series is for a shoulderplate child doll on a cloth body. We have been able to document four sizes, 1601 through 1604.

SCROLLED FY

BHS-18

NO 76018
NIPPON

The Scrolled FY mark has also been attributed to Yamato Importing and, again, we have no information to verify or dispute that. We do know that the Scrolled FY mark can be found on some of the same molds as the FY mark, so there was definitely some relationship between the two marks.

For some reason the Scrolled FY mark is followed by a 5-digit number, usually No. 76018. We don't know what that number is meant to identify, maybe a patent number or some type of importer's number.

The Scrolled FY with no mold number has been found on a 10" dolly-faced child doll on a toddler body.

BHS-19

NO 76018
NIPPON
30/3

This mold number has been found on a 15" character baby.

BHS-20

NO 76018
NIPPON
30/6

This mold number has been found on a 19½" character baby.

BHS-21

NO 76018
NIPPON
30/8

This mold number has been found on a 15" character baby.

BHS-22

NO 76018
NIPPON
20/0

This mold number has been found on an 11" solid domehead breather character baby. It is the same mold as the FY 100 series.

BHS-23

NO 76018
103
NIPPON

The 100 series is a solid dome head breather character baby; it is the same mold as the FY 100 series and was probably made in six sizes, 101 through 106.

BHS-24

NO 76018
NIPPON
301

The 300 series is a character face doll on a composition body. We have not documented any other dolls with this mark.

BHS-25

NO 76018
NIPPON
405

The 400 series is a dolly-faced child doll on a composition body. This is a commonly found mold number and was probably made in six sizes, 401 through 406. This is the same mold as the FY 400 series. Note: It is possible to find this mark on two different dolly-faced dolls, indicating that sometime during its production they changed the sculpture of the mold.

BHS-26

NO 76018
NIPPON
502

The 500 series is a solid dome head character baby. It is a commonly found mold number and was probably made in six sizes, 501 through 506. It is the same mold as the FY 500 series.

BHS-27

NO 76018
NIPPON
601

The 600 series is for a character baby. It was probably made in six sizes, 601 through 606. It is the same mold as the FY 600 series.

BHS-28

NO 76018
NIPPON
902

This 900 series is for a character baby. it was probably made in six sizes 901 through 906. It is a scarce mold.

BHS-29

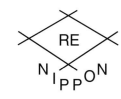

NO 76018
NIPPON
2001

The 2000 series is for a dolly-face child doll on a composition body. It is a harder to find mold number than the 400 series. It was probably made in 4 sizes, 2001 through 2004.

BHS-30

BHS-31

BHS-32

RE IN A DIAMOND
BE IN A DIAMOND

The RE in a Diamond mark usually uses a letter to denote the type of doll and a number to denote the size. The mark can be found with either NIPPON or MADE IN NIPPON. This country designation does not seem to make any difference in the appearance, quality, or mold of the doll. Sometimes there are lines through the RE or there is a mark with the RE but no diamond. It is not clear if this variation makes any difference in the mold or quality of the doll.

Also found are dolls bearing a BE in a Diamond mark. These appear to be the same molds as the RE in a Diamond dolls. It is not known why some are marked RE and some are marked BE, but the BE mark is scarce.

The RE in a Diamond with no mold number is found on several different dolls:

1) a shoulderplate dolly-faced child doll on an imitation kid body. This doll has been found in several sizes including 24" and 17" tall; the 17" doll has been found with a Louis Wolf & Company Superba sticker on it.

2) a 12" solid dome head character baby. This solid dome head is a different mold than the M series solid dome head.

3) an 8" dolly-faced child doll on toddler body.

4) a 30" show doll in the B series (Hilda look alike) mold.

BHS-33

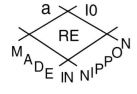

The A series is the mold letter for a character baby on a composition body. It was probably made in 10 sizes with size 1 being the smallest and size 10 being the largest. Occasionally the A has a period behind it or the A is lower case. This is one of the more commonly found RE in a Diamond molds.

In some sizes this mold appears to be a copy of the Kammer and Reinhardt 126 mold. It can be found with either the RE or BE in a Diamond mark.

BHS-34

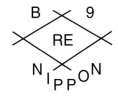

The B series is the mold letter for a character baby on a composition body. It was probably made in 10 sizes with size 1 being the smallest and size 10 being the largest. This mold is considered to be the Nippon version of the Kestner Hilda. It was a popular doll and even today is fairly easy to find. It can be found with either the RE or BE in a Diamond mark.

BHS-35

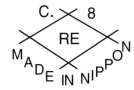

The C series is the mold letter for a character baby on a composition body. It was probably made in multiple sizes but not enough of them have been found to document this. It is a hard to find mold.

BHS-36

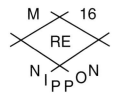

The M series is the mold letter for a solid dome head character baby on a composition body. The number denotes the total height of the doll in inches. Therefore, a 16 indicates the doll is 16" tall. It was made in at least 4 sizes — 16", 18", 20", and 22".

BHS-37

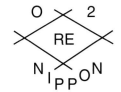

The O series is the mold letter for a dolly-faced child doll on a composition body. It was probably made in five sizes with 1 being the smallest and 5 being the largest.

BHS-38

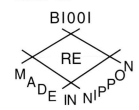

This mark is found on three different RE in a Diamond dolls:
1) a 15" character baby on a 5-piece composition body.
2) a 24" dolly-faced child doll on a composition body.
3) a 15" dolly-faced shoulderplate doll an on imitation kid body.
Since this mold number is completely different from the other RE in a Diamond marks, we are not sure why this mark was used. It could have been used for a particular line of dolls or for a particular store.

HORSMAN

There are several different marks used on the Horsman Nippon dolls. This mark is similar to the one used on the Fulper-made Horsman dolls. We do not know who made these dolls for Horsman. Horsman Nippon dolls are scarce.

BHS-39

1) No. 1 through No. 4 is for a character baby on a composition body. No. 1 is the smallest in the series and No. 4 is the largest.

BHS-40

2) B.9 is for a character baby on a composition body. It is assumed that other sizes were made.

BHS-41

3) No. 11 is a dolly-faced child doll on a composition body. It is assumed that various sizes were made.

BHS-42

This mark is for a character baby on a composition body. Note that "NIPPON" is misspelled.

BHS-43

This mark is found on a character head doll on a composition body. The top number or letters of the mark are unreadable. This is an unusual Horsman mark. Note that the "N" is backwards.

JW

BHS-44

JW
NIPPON
603

The JW mark is found on character head dolls with composition bodies. The only documented mold number is the 600 series with 601 being the smallest and 606 being the largest. It is a scarce mold mark.

H IN A DIAMOND

BHS-45

The H in a Diamond mark is found on a character head doll with a toddler body. It is assumed that the 14 indicates the size and B is the mold. However, no other examples of this doll have been documented. It is a rare mark. It is not known what the P.4 stands for.

HS IN AN OVAL

The HS in an Oval mark is sometimes attributed to Herman Steiner, a German doll maker, because it is very similar to a mark used by his firm. This may not be the case though, since most doll references put his firm as being in business from 1921 – 1925. It could be that the Japanese were copying the SH from the Simon & Halbig trademark. Notice how the word "NIPPON" is done in script.

BHS-46

The A series is a character baby on a composition body. The number indicates the height of the doll in inches. This mold was probably made in five sizes, 10", 12", 14", 16", and 18".

BHS-47

The C series is a character baby on a composition body. The number indicates the height of the doll in inches. We did not have enough dolls to know the sizes it was made in. It is harder to find than the A series.

It is likely there was also a B series but we have no documentation on this.

KKS IN A STAR

The KKS in a Star mark is done in a similar manner to the HS in an Oval mark. Notice that both marks have the word "NIPPON" in script. This star is the same as the star in the Kammer & Reinhardt, and it may be that the Japanese copied their mark. This is a rare mark.

BHS-48

The 3000 series is a character baby on a composition body. It is assumed that the 3 indicates the size but not enough dolls have been found to verify this. It is not known what the P.47 stands for.

BHS-49

The 4000 series is a character baby on a composition body. It is assumed that the 3 indicates the size but not enough dolls have been found to verify this. It is not known what the P.53 stands for.

M IN A BLOSSOM

BHS-50

The M in the Blossom mark has been attributed to Morimura Brothers since they used a similar mark on their porcelain products. We have not been able to verify this. Note that the "N" is backwards.

The M in the Blossom mark with no mold number is found on a solid domehead character doll with closed smiling mouth, googly eyes, and a toddler composition body. It is a rare mold.

BHS-51

This M in the Blossom mark with a number below the word "NIPPON" has been found on several sizes of dolly-faced child dolls. Two of the numbers found on this mark are 12 and 18. The number appears to be an indication of the size, but it does not correlate to the overall height of the doll in inches. It may be the height of the doll's composition body.

BHS-52

This M in the Blossom mark is found on a dolly-faced doll with a composition body. It is not clear what the number stands for.

BHS-53

This M in the Blossom mark with a letter and/or number below the trademark is found on two completely different types of dolls:
1) a dolly-faced child doll with a composition body. It is not clear what the letter and number stand for.
2) a solid dome head character doll with a closed smiling mouth; the 12 may stand for the height of the doll. It is a rare mold.

M

BHS-54

The M mark may be related to the M in the Blossom mark. Both M's are done in the same style. Only one doll has been documented with the mark, a character doll on a composition body. The 12 stands for the height of the doll. Doll has been found in two sizes — 10" and 12."

M IN A CIRCLE

The M in the Circle mark is similar in design to the Horsman marks.

BHS-56

The E24 is for a dolly-faced child doll on a composition body. The 24 does not correlate to the height of the doll as this mark is found on dolls 28 inches in height. This doll was made in other sizes. It is a rare mold.

BHS-57

The W10 is for a 10" character baby on a composition baby body. The 10 appears to be the height of the doll in inches. It is not known if other sizes were made. It is a rare mold.

BHS-58

OTHER

This mark does not include the name of the country that made the doll, but it is generally thought to be made in Japan. The country of origin designation must have been on a tag or sticker attached to the doll. This mark usually has a mold number under it.

BHS-59

This mark does not include the name of the country that made the doll, but the symbol is similar to the Scrolled FY. The N may stand for Nippon.

China Glazed Dolls

Nippon-marked china glazed dolls fall into two categories: china heads that were used on cloth bodies, and half-dolls which are sometimes referred to as "pincushion dolls." China glazed dolls are made of glazed porcelain and have a shiny finish. It is usually only the head or head and limbs that are china glazed.

Made by a variety of European porcelain companies, china head dolls were available as early as 1750 but reached popularity in the 1840s. These early china head dolls were put on a number of different body types including cloth, kid, and wood. Nearly all of the early china head dolls had black hair, but during the 1880s blond china head dolls had started to become popular and, according to the *Collector's Encyclopedia of Dolls*, by 1900 one out of three of the common-type china heads with wavy hair, was blond. By the early 1900s the popularity of china head dolls was declining and that likely explains why Nippon china head dolls are hard to find.

During the Nippon doll era, Butler Brothers continued to advertise china limb dolls and in September 1919, Morimura Brothers advertised "China limb dolls: Repeating our excellent line of 1919." This implies that Morimura Brothers made them for at least two years — 1919 and 1920. It should be noted, however, that there is the possibility that these china limb dolls are not glazed china and, therefore, do not have the shiny finish. It appears from old catalog ads that cloth body dolls with bisque heads and limbs were also called "china limb dolls" probably because they were made in the same manner and style as the china glazed dolls.

Nippon era china dolls were made by pouring slip into a mold, leaving it in the mold for an allotted time, and then pouring out the remaining slip. These were then left to dry in large heated rooms. After drying, they were cleaned and fired in large kilns. Once cooled, the molded hair, eyes, mouth, and, if a half-doll, clothes were painted. A feldspatic glaze was then applied and another firing took place. This left the item with a high gloss finish.

Nippon china head dolls have blond hair molded in what is called a low-brow hairstyle — wavy hair parted in the middle that comes down onto the forehead. To date, no Nippon china head dolls have surfaced that have any other color of hair.

They could be purchased as either a complete doll with cloth body and china limbs or the head only. These are shoulderplate heads that were attached to the body either with glue or stitches. There are two sew holes on both sides of the shoulderplate. A price tag found on a Nippon china head indicates that it sold originally for 40¢. Those who bought just the heads usually put them on a home-made body or used them as replacements for broken ones.

*Two sizes of glazed china; holes are for sewing head to the cloth body. Left: 4",
right: 4¼".*

Nippon china heads come in at least three different sizes — 3½", 4", and 4¼". There may be other sizes but these dolls are uncommon and it's difficult to find enough of them to make a definitive statement. They are usually incised "NIPPON" on the back outside of the shoulderplate, but this author has seen one example where "NIPPON" was inside the shoulderplate. This, of course, means that if the head is on a body, the mark is impossible to see. It may be that many Nippon china head dolls are marked in this manner, and we just can't see the mark.

While Nippon china head dolls are hard to find because of declining popularity, Nippon china glazed half-dolls are hard to find because by 1921 half-dolls had not yet reached their full popularity.

Called "pincushion dolls" by many collectors, they were not used solely for pincushions. They could be found on a variety of items including powder boxes, clothes brushes, even small lamps. They were produced by a number of European firms, and they may have been produced as early as the 1880s. However, it was not until the early 1900s that they started to have some measure of popularity in the United States. They enjoyed their greatest popularity from the 1920s through the 1930s — well after the Nippon era.

It may also be hard to find Nippon-marked half-dolls because of the way they were marked — in black lettering over the glaze on the back of the flange (the lower area of the half-doll where the sew holes are). Over-glaze marks are applied after the glaze has been fired and then fired again, at a lower temperature, to set the mark. Unfortunately, this type of mark can probably be removed either intentionally or by accident. Also, if the half-doll still has its original pincushion or other dressing on it, it may be impossible to see the mark since it is on the flange.

Mark found on the half-doll.

The Japanese did copy German designs for their china half-dolls, and some designs were popular for years so it's possible to find the same style half-doll marked Germany, Nippon, and Japan. Nippon half-dolls were also made in different sizes but like the china head, there are so few available that it's impossible to make any type of definitive statement about the sizes made. They also came in different colors; the Charles William Stores in 1920 advertised a Dutch girl pincushion in two colors — blue and pink — for $1.19.

Occasionally a collector is lucky enough to find one with its original dressing or pincushion still attached. This original dressing should not be removed because it adds to the value to the half-doll.

Because of their uniqueness, all Nippon china glazed dolls are highly sought after by Nippon doll collectors.

1920 Charles William Stores ad.

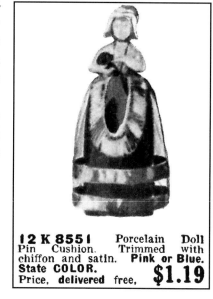

12 K 8551 Porcelain Doll Pin Cushion. Trimmed with chiffon and satin. **Pink or Blue.** State COLOR. Price, delivered free, **$1.19**

Some china glazed figures were made during the Nippon era that were not technically dolls. The example shown here is marked on the bottom in red lettering. Because these figures are rare, it's impossible to know exactly what figures were made.

China glazed figurine marked "NIPPON" in red on bottom. 4" tall.
Note: The coloring and faces are done the same as the half-dolls.

Design patent using doll shown in Plate 433 (page 245).

DESIGN.

C. LAFITTE.

PINCUSHION.

APPLICATION FILED MAY 16, 1919.

54,853.

Patented Apr. 13, 1920.

WITNESSES
Edw. Thorpe.
J. H. ___

INVENTOR
Cecile Lafitte
BY *___ Co*
ATTORNEYS

UNITED STATES PATENT OFFICE.

CECILE LAFITTE, OF NEW YORK, N. Y.

DESIGN FOR A PINCUSHION.

54,853.   Specification for Design.   **Patented Apr. 13, 1920**

Application filed May 16, 1919.   Serial No. 297,709.   Term of patent 14 years.

To all whom it may concern:
Be it known that I, CECILE LAFITTE, a citizen of France, residing at New York, borough of Manhattan, in the county and State of New York, have invented a new, original, and ornamental Design for a Pin-cushion, of which the following is a specification, reference being had to the accompanying drawings, forming part thereof.

The figure is a perspective view of a pin cushion, showing my new design.
I claim:
The ornamental design for a pincushion as shown.

CECILE LAFITTE.

Text to patent number 54,853 (page 243).

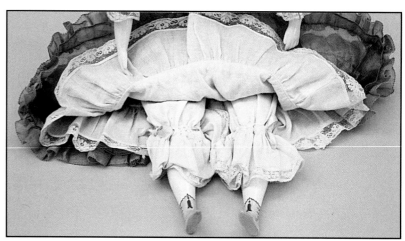

Plate 428
Doll, 15" tall, replaced cloth body with china arms and legs, replaced clothes, incised "NIPPON," $175.00 – $225.00.

Plate 430
Doll, 19½" tall, replaced cloth body with china arms and legs (shown in Plate 431), replaced dress that is wonderfully done with underslip and bloomers, incised "NIPPON," $250.00 – $325.00.

Plate 429
Doll, 19½" tall, cloth body with china arms only, old clothes, incised "NIPPON," $250.00 – $325.00.

Plate 431
Photo showing china legs and underclothes of doll in Plate 430.

Plate 434
Pincushion doll with replaced brush, doll 3¼" tall, over-all 8" tall, "NIP-PON" on flange, $90.00 – $140.00.

Plate 432
Pincushion doll, 3½" tall, "NIPPON" on flange, $110.00 – $160.00.
Pincushion doll, 3¾" tall, "NIPPON" on flange, $110.00 – $160.00.
Pincushion doll, 3½" tall, "NIPPON" on flange, $110.00 – $160.00.

Plate 433
Pincushion doll, 3¼" tall, "NIPPON" on flange, $90.00 – $140.00.
Pincushion doll, 3" tall, "NIPPON" on flange, $90.00 – $140.00.
Pincushion doll, 3¼" tall, "NIPPON" on flange, $90.00 – $140.00.

Plate 435
Pincushion doll with original silk covered pin-cushion, doll 3" tall, "NIPPON" on flange, $250.00 – $300.00.

Plate 438
Pincushion doll with origi-nal silk covered pincushion, 9½" tall over-all, doll 3½" tall, "NIPPON" on flange, celluloid. $300.00 – $350.00.

Plate 436
1919 Charles William Stores catalog ad.

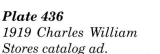

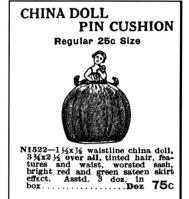

Plate 437
1920 Butler Brothers catalog ad.

Celluloid Dolls and Toys

Celluloid is a synthetic material composed of cellulose nitrate (pyroxylin), camphor, alcohol, and pigments. It is an early form of plastic and was invented by John Wesley Hyatt and his brother, Isaiah, in 1869. Over the years many patents were issued for improvements in making celluloid and for celluloid products including dolls. It is unknown when the first celluloid doll was made, but in 1880 a U.S. patent was issued for improving celluloid doll heads, and in 1881 another U.S. patent was issued for celluloid dolls.

While today we think of celluloid dolls as cheaper than bisque, initially celluloid dolls cost about the same as bisque. Celluloid, as a material, was a natural choice for dolls and toys since it was washable, did not shatter as bisque and china did, and didn't flake or peel like composition. Celluloid bath toys became popular. Celluloid had drawbacks however. It was flammable, faded easily, and was fragile, especially in items made of thin pieces. Many of the early celluloid dolls were designed to look like and made in a similar manner as bisque-head dolls. Celluloid doll heads were put on cloth, kid, and composition bodies. Celluloid character babies were also popular. Figural-type celluloid dolls, just like their all-bisque counterparts, became popular in the early teens with the introduction of the Kewpie doll. A variety of American, Germany, and French companies were making celluloid dolls prior to World War I.

It is hard to say exactly when the Japanese began producing celluloid dolls and toys, but there are records of celluloid toys being sold in Japan in 1913. Because it was cheap for them to make celluloid, the Japanese had a significant advantage in marketing celluloid products. An essential ingredient of celluloid is camphor, and the Japanese had ready access to large supplies of camphor since it's a product of Taiwan. In fact, there are reports that Japan had a monopoly on the world's supply of camphor, and they controlled the market price of camphor, even putting some American companies out of business. Based on the information available in *Playthings*, it is evident that celluloid dolls and toys were a leading Japanese export.

For example, in 1918 the production of celluloid toys was valued at $2,191,822.00, porcelain toys at $808,267.00, wooden toys at $782,220.00, and metal toys at $723,580.00.

There were many different Japanese compa-

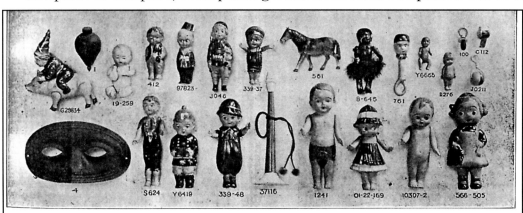

nies producing celluloid items. Some of the Japanese companies that have been identified are Aiba Kintoro, Sekiguchi Co. Ltd., Ando Togoro, and Yoshino Sangyo. Nippon celluloid dolls and toys have been found with these manufacturer's trademarks or similar ones.

Morimura Brothers also sold celluloid items, and their celluloid Dolly doll has the MB symbol on the bottom of its feet. In 1919 Morimura Brothers advertised celluloid novelties including trumpets, floating animals, roly-polys, and funny figures. The Takito, Ogawa & Company also advertised celluloid dolls. It's likely that neither Morimura Brothers nor Takito, Ogawa & Company made their own dolls but instead had a celluloid company make them.

The making of celluloid items required specialized materials and equipment, making it necessary for celluloid items to be produced in a factory environment. Also, the making of celluloid items was dangerous because of the highly flammable nature of cellulose nitrate. Many celluloid factories here in the U.S. became victims of explosions and fires, and it's probable that some Japanese factories met that same fate. Other hazards associated with the making of celluloid included acid burns and breathing difficulties due to nitric acid and wood alcohol fumes.

Nippon celluloid dolls and toys are hollow, made in a process called blow molding. *Celluloid, A Collector's Reference and Value Guide* describes the process this way: "First, two halves of a metal mold are coated with soapy water or glycerin, then a thin sheet of celluloid is placed on each side. Next, the mold is clamped shut and steam or heated air is forced between the celluloid sheets, softening the material and causing it to conform to the mold. Finally, the hot mold is immersed in cold water, then opened, and the hollow celluloid object removed." After the item is removed from the mold, excess celluloid along the seams had to be trimmed by hand — a tedious and time consuming process.

Because blow-molded dolls and toys are thin and hollow, they are especially susceptible to dents and cracks. Also, because they are molded in two parts, they sometimes split at the seams. As was discussed under "Care and Handling of Your Dolls," it's almost impossible to repair dents and cracks. Collectors should expect a decrease in price if the item is less than perfect.

The arms and legs on most Nippon celluloid dolls were strung with elastic by knotting the ends of the elastic and pushing the knots through small holes in the limbs. Over time, the elastic starts to disintegrate and the limbs hang loosely or fall completely off. This can be repaired, but you must use patience and a light touch. Directions for making this type of repair can also be found under "Care and Handling of Your Dolls."

Most Nippon celluloid dolls and toys were not molded in color. Instead, the items came out of the mold an ivory, cream, or flesh color and were then hand painted. Accent colors would have been spray painted on the item through fitted stencils with details like the eyes and mouth hand painted. Therefore, just like the porcelain items, each celluloid item can be painted just a little differently. Because the color is not incorporated into the celluloid, paint can sometimes rub or flake off. Collectors should pay attention to this when purchasing celluloid items.

During the Nippon era, the Japanese made a wide range of celluloid figural dolls and characters, toy animals, rattles, even holiday items (see chapter on "Holiday Items"). Montgomery Ward in 1919 advertised a celluloid toy set consisting of a jointed doll, red hunting horn, and a figural donkey for 75¢. You could have bought a set of bath toys for 65¢ and in 1920, an 8½" celluloid doll with mohair wig sold for $1.29.

Today, these items, like all celluloid dolls and toys, are becoming more expensive. The supply of good items is dwindling and the number of collectors increasing. Nippon collectors often find themselves competing with celluloid or specialized collectors for the unusual items. Especially sought after are those items depicting well-known characters such as Buster Brown and Charlie Chaplin. Rattles and roly-polys are also popular with collectors, and this is reflected in their prices. The larger fully jointed baby dolls are harder to find than the smaller figural dolls.

Celluloid Dolls and Toys

A final word of caution about celluloid dolls and toys. Because they are made of cellulose nitrate they are flammable and should be kept away from flames and excessive heat. Celluloid items should be stored in a well-ventilated place, not in tightly closed containers.

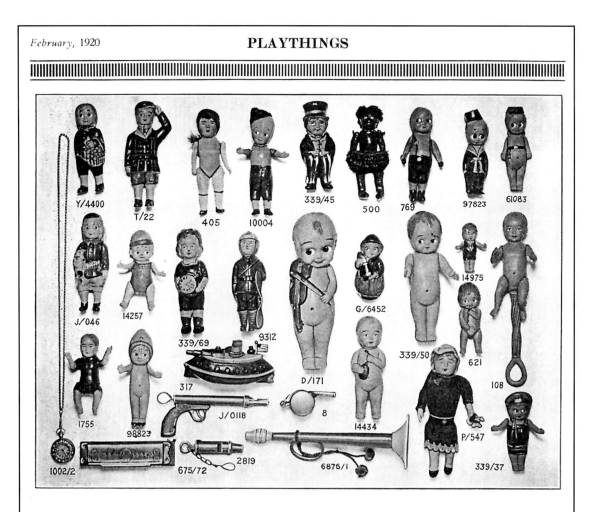

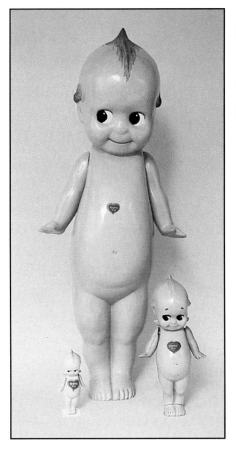

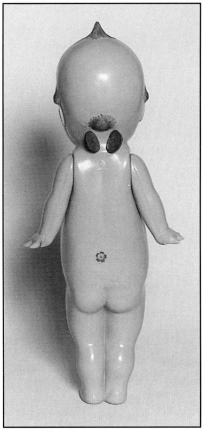

Plate 439
Kewpie doll, 3½" tall, mark CL-4, original sticker, $60.00 – $90.00.
Kewpie doll, 22" tall, mark CL-4, original stickers on chest and bottom of feet, an extraordinary doll, rare, $800.00 – $900.00.
Kewpie doll, 7¾" tall, mark CL-4, original sticker, $150.00 – $200.00.

Plate 440
Back view of 22" Kewpie shown in Plate 439. Sticker seen on back is an inspection sticker found on many Nippon-era celluloid dolls.

Plate 441
Kewpie doll, 4" tall, old crepe paper clothes, mark CL-4, $80.00 – $120.00.

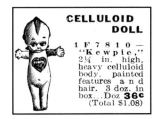

Plate 442
Old Butler Brothers ad.

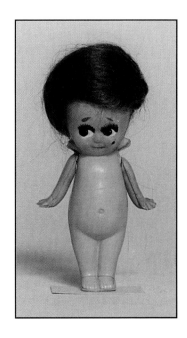

Plate 443
Kewpie doll, 3½" tall, original wig, mark CL-4, $80.00 – $120.00.

249

Celluloid Dolls and Toys

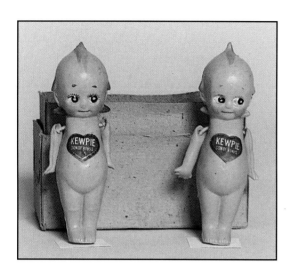

Plate 444
Kewpie "Son of Venus" doll, 4" tall, original box marked "Made in Japan;" "25" penciled on box which may be the original price, mark CL-1, $70.00 – $110.00 each.
These are copies of the authentic Kewpie doll. From the sticker it is obvious they were made to cash in on the popularity of Kewpie.

Plate 445
Kewpie look alike, 2¼" tall, mark CL-22, $30.00 – $40.00.

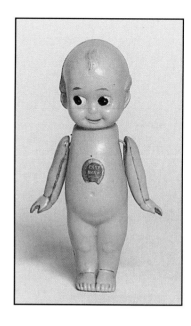

Plate 446
Best Baby doll, 6" tall, mark CL-15, original sticker, $70.00 – $100.00.

Plate 448
Back view of Best Baby shown in Plate 449.

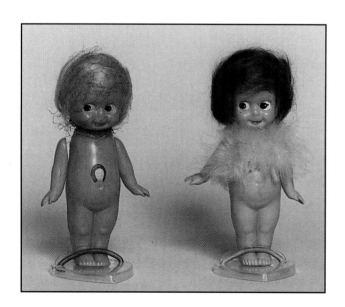

Plate 447
Best Baby dolls, 6" tall, both dolls have original wig, mark CL-15, original sticker, $80.00 – $110.00.

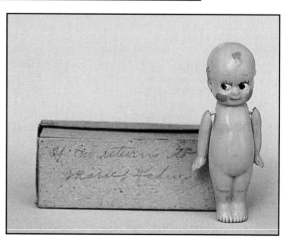

Plate 449
Best Baby doll, 3½" tall, original box, note on box says "If lost return to Marie Kahne," mark CL-15, $60.00 – $90.00.

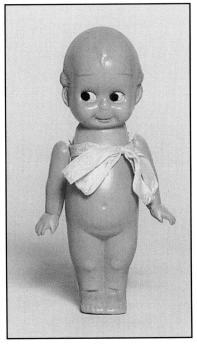

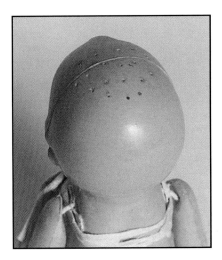

Plate 451
Top view of Plate 450 showing shaker holes in head. This is a home-made item. Since celluloid could easily be pierced and cut, it lent itself to this type of conversion.

Plate 450
Best Baby doll made into a talcum powder shaker, 6" tall, mark CL-15, $80.00 – $120.00.

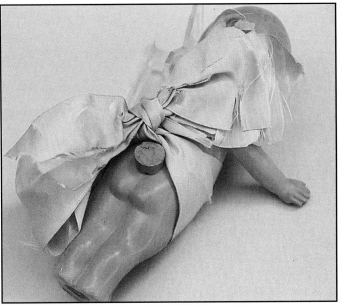

Plate 452
Back view of Plate 453 showing cork stopper for the talcum powder shaker.

Plate 454
Figural dolls, 2¼" tall, mark CL-1, $30.00 – $50.00 each.

Plate 453
Best Baby doll made into talcum powder shaker, 6" tall, mark CL-15, $80.00 – $120.00.

Plate 455
1920 Montgomery Ward catalog ad.

Plate 458
Dolly figural (Morimura Brothers), 3½" tall, mark CL-3, $100.00 – $125.00.

Plate 457
Dolly (Morimura Brothers), 4¾" tall, mark CL-3, original sticker on back, $125.00 – $150.00.

**EXCEPTIONAL VALUE
CELLULOID DOLL**

F7809—6 in., well proportioned heavy celluloid body, excellent modeled head, embossed hair, painted features, jointed at shoulders, blue or brown painted molded "stork effect" panties, rattle body, will stand. 1 doz. in box.......... Doz. $2.15

Plate 461
August 1919 Butler Brothers catalog ad.

Plate 456
Charlie Chaplin as "The Tramp," 5¼" tall, Charlie Chaplin first played The Tramp character in 1914 and it was immediately popular, very rare, mark CL-12, $200.00 – $250.00.

N3506   N3519
No. N3506. Celluloid Soldier Boy, flesh tinted body, painted cap, sword, gun and features, rattle inside, 3½ inches high. One dozen in box. Per dozen .... .80
No. N3519. Celluloid Boy, with red fez, attractively colored in bright combinations, painted features, rattle inside, 3½ inches high. One dozen in box. Per dozen... .80

Plate 460
1919 Shure Winner catalog ad.

Plate 459
Figural doll (rattle), 3¼" tall, small dent in head, mark CL-1, $40.00 – $60.00 without the dent. Figural doll, 3⅛" tall, mark CL-5, $40.00 – $60.00.

Plate 462
Figural doll (rattle), 5" tall, mark CL-13, $100.00 – $125.00.
Figural doll, 4¼" tall, mark CL-6, $80.00 – $110.00.
Figural doll (rattle), 5" tall, mark CL-13, $100.00 – $125.00.

Plate 465
*Figural doll, 4"
tall, mark CL-1,
$70.00 – $100.00.*

Plate 463
*Figural doll, 3¾" tall, mark CL-21,
$70.00 – $100.00.
Figural doll, 3¾" tall, mark CL-23,
$70.00 – $100.00.*

Plate 464
*Old Butler Brothers cata-
log ad.*

Plate 466
*Figural doll, 3¾" tall,
mark CL-2, $70.00 –
$100.00.
Figural doll, 3¾" tall,
mark CL-8, $70.00 –
$100.00.*

Plate 468
*Figural doll (rattle), 4" tall, mark
CL-1, $90.00 – $115.00.
Figural doll (rattle), 4" tall, mark
CL-2, $90.00 – $115.00.*

Plate 467
*Doll, 4" tall, mark CL-1,
$70.00 – $100.00.*

Plate 469
*Figural doll (rattle), 4½" tall,
mark CL-9, $115.00 – $140.00.*

Celluloid Dolls and Toys

Plate 470
Figural dolls, 3" tall, mark CL-7, $40.00 – $60.00 each.

Plate 471
Doll, jointed arms, 5¾" tall, dent in hat, mark CL-2, $110.00 – $140.00 without the dent.

Plate 472
Figural doll, 5¼" tall, mark CL-14, $100.00 – $125.00. Figural doll (rattle), 4⅞" tall, mark CL-12, $100.00 – $125.00.

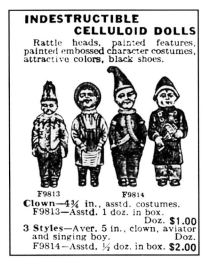

Plate 473
1917 Butler Brothers catalog ad.

Plate 474
1919 Montgomery Ward catalog ad.

Plate 476
*Doll, jointed arms, 5¾" tall, CL-18, $110.00 – $140.00.
Doll, jointed arms, 4⅞" tall, CL-1, $90.00 – $110.00.*

Plate 475
1920 Montgomery Ward catalog ad.

Plate 479
Roly-poly (set of 6), 2½" tall, mark CL-5, metal bottom keeps dolls upright and allows rolling action, rare, $90.00 – $110.00 each.

Plate 477
Figural doll (rattle), rare Buster Brown holding Tige, 5½" tall, mark CL-11, $175.00 – $225.00.

Plate 478
Doll (rattle), jointed arms, 6" tall, mark CL-12, $120.00 – $150.00.

12D8672   Rose Color Pin Cushion. Celluloid doll. nestled in Old Rose Satin. Price. del'd free. each.... **49c**

Plate 480
1919 Charles William Stores catalog ad.

Plate 482
Group of Nippon-era celluloid dolls in original box, these dolls are unmarked except for a Japanese Design Patent Registration No. 13758 sticker that is on one of the dolls; these dolls are pictured in the 1920 Foulds and Freure Plaything *ads shown earlier in this chapter; 4" tall, $50.00 – $70.00 each.*

Plate 481
Mark found on pincushion in Plate 484.

Plate 483
Photocopy of sticker found on dolls in Plate 482.

Plate 484
Pincushion, celluloid head, over-all height 2¾" tall, marked on bottom (see Plate 481), unusual item, $125.00 – $150.00.

Celluloid Dolls and Toys

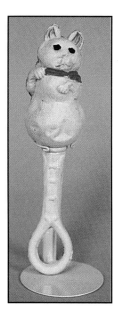

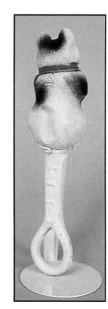

No. N3180. Celluloid Baby Rattles, assorted styles with fancy ball and animal head top, cats dogs, etc., with ring, and long handles with teething ring end. In assorted colors. Large size, average length 4 to 7 inches. A handsome and popular assortment.

Per dozen assorted.......... 1.95

Plate 487
1919 Shure Winner catalog ad.

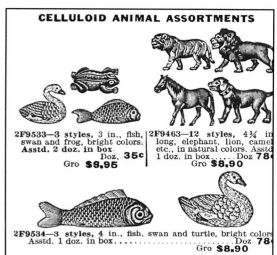

Plate 488
Old Butler Brothers ad.

Plate 485
Rattle, 5½" tall, some dents, mark CL-19, unusual item, $125.00 – $150.00 with no dents.

Plate 486
Back view of rattle shown in Plate 485.

Plate 490
Figural dogs, 3½" long, mark CL-17, note color variations, $25.00 – $35.00 each.

Plate 489
Figural swan, 2" long, mark CL-1, $15.00 – $20.00.
Figural swan, 1½" long, mark CL-2, $10.00 – $15.00.

Plate 492
Figural lion, 2½" long, mark CL-1, $15.00 – $20.00.

Plate 491
Figural tigers, 4" long, mark CL-17, note color variations, $25.00 – $35.00 each.

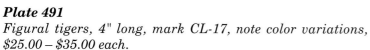

Plate 493
Figural bear, 2⅝" long, mark CL-1, $15.00 – $20.00.

256

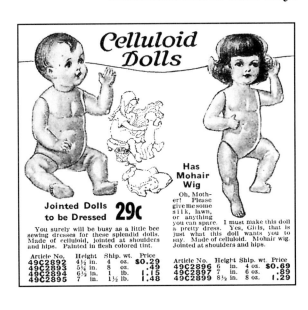

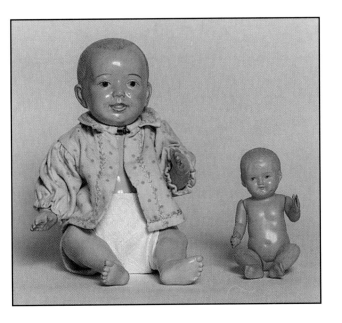

Plate 494
*Doll, jointed arms and legs, swivel head, 11½" tall,
old clothes, mark CL-16, $175.00 – $200.00.
Doll, jointed arms and legs, 6½" tall, mark CL-10,
$60.00 – $80.00.*

Plate 495
1920 Montgomery Ward catalog ad.

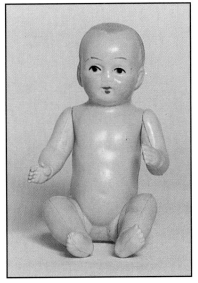

Plate 497
*Doll, jointed arms and legs, 6"
tall, good coloring, mark CL-1 in
purple ink on bottom on doll,
$80.00 – $110.00.*

Plate 496
*Doll, jointed arms and legs, 5¾" tall, origi-
nal clothes and baby bottle, mark CL-10,
$125.00 – $150.00.*

Plate 498
*Doll, jointed arms and
legs, 8" tall, old clothes,
mark CL-24, $135.00 –
$165.00.*

Celluloid Doll and Toy Marks

The marks found on the back of Nippon celluloid dolls and toys are varied and many. This listing is only those marks we have been able to document. No doubt there are many other marks that were used on Nippon celluloid dolls and toys that we have not yet documented. Where possible, we have identified the company that the mark belongs to but in most cases this information is just not available. Please note that many of these marks are hand-drawn and may differ slightly from the actual mark. At the end of this listing we have provided a picture of the stickers that have been documented to date on Nippon celluloid dolls and toys.

Marks: (CL = Celluloid)

CL-1   **NIPPON**   molded on the back or in ink on the back

CL-2   **MADE IN NIPPON**   molded on back

or

**MADE
IN
NIPPON**

CL-3   found on Morimura Brothers Dolly on bottom of feet

CL-4   molded; often found on Kewpies

CL-5   molded

CL-6   molded

CL-7   molded

CL-8   molded; mark of Yoshino Sangyo

CL-9   molded

CL-10   molded; mark of Ando Togoro, Tokyo, Japan

CL-11   molded

CL-12   molded

CL-13   molded

CL-14   molded

CL-15   molded; found on Haber Brothers Best Baby

CL-16   molded; mark of Sekiguchi Co. Ltd., Tokyo, Japan

CL-17   molded

CL-18   molded; mark of Aiba Kintoro, Marugane, Tokyo, Japan

CL-19   molded

CL-20   molded

CL-21   molded

CL-22   molded

CL-23   molded

CL-24   molded

Stickers

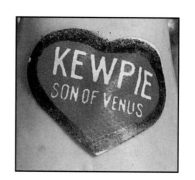

Sticker found on the feet of Kewpie.

Sticker found on Morimura Brothers celluloid Dolly.

Inspection sticker found on celluloid doll.

Composition Dolls

It is rare to find a Nippon-marked composition doll. It appears that the manufacture of composition dolls was either not a priority of the Japanese or they were not imported in large numbers.

Composition is a material usually made from a wood pulp and glue mixture although other materials such as rags were sometimes thrown in. Papier-mache is a form of composition with paper or rag fiber as its primary ingredient. Many collectors do not differentiate between the two compositions and often refer to papier-mache doll bodies as composition. Each doll maker usually had his or her own formula for the composition mixture. Dolls or doll heads made from composition or papier-mache were produced in molds similar to those used for the bisque-head dolls.

By the time of the World War I era, composition and papier- mache doll heads had been manufactured for many years. According to *Collector's Encyclopedia of Dolls,* papier-mache was being used as a material for dolls as early as the 1500s. Composition dolls became available in the late 1800s with Lazarus Reichman being credited with the invention of composition in 1877. It was during the World War I era that composition dolls started to gain in popularity. One reason, of course, was the inability to procure bisque-head dolls from Europe. Secondly, doll makers in the United States were able to produce composition dolls much easier than bisque-head dolls. Therefore, they concentrated on improving the processes for making composition dolls.

It may be for this reason that the Japanese did not produce many composition dolls. Perhaps they did not think there was a market here for them or that they could compete with American doll makers. The composition doll pictured in Plate 499 is actually made of oyster shells, and the body is very much like those oyster shell bodies used on the Nippon bisque-head dolls. The only difference is that the socket head on this doll is also made of oyster shells. We have included it in this chapter because using oyster shells as the base ingredient is a form of composition, replacing wood pulp composition.

The doll itself is not marked in any way. The only way we have been able to determine that this is a Nippon doll is from the tag attached to it. It's interesting to note that the doll was made by the same firm that used the RE in a Diamond mark on the bisque-head dolls. Also interesting is that oyster shell bodies are primarily found on RE in a Diamond dolls. From this we can surmise that this firm may have had prior expertise in making oyster shell dolls and doll bodies. It also appears that from the use of the crown on the tag, they were trying to copy the Kestner crown mark. We have not been able to find any advertisements for this type of Nippon doll.

It is unfortunate that the doll itself is not marked in any way since this makes it hard to identify these dolls. We don't know if other types of oyster shell composition dolls were made although it seems unlikely that only one style of doll was produced. Hopefully, in the future, we will find other dolls with their original tags intact. It is definitely a unique doll to have in one's collection.

The Nippon papier-mache nodders are comic characters that were popular during the World War I era. The boy and girl pair looks like the googly dolls produced by many German firms and are copies of the German-produced Peek-A-Boo dolls designed by Chloe Preston, an illustrator whose drawings of round-faced, round-eyed, and plump children appeared in a book called *The Peek A Boos.* The German Peek-A-Boo dolls were also made in a boy and a girl version. The dolls' heads are attached to the bodies by a spring that allows them to nod or bob. They are marked on the bottom of the doll with the word "NIP-PON" in ink on the paper label. To date, only a few examples of the Nippon papier-mache nodders have been documented.

From looking at these nodders it's obvious they were cheaply made and inexpensive to buy. Purchased as novelty items or maybe even given away as carnival prizes, when the buyer tired of them they were often disposed of. On those that have survived it's not unusual to find chips, cracks, and flaking paint. These, too, are unique dolls to have in a Nippon doll collection.

If you are fortunate enough to have either type of Nippon composition doll in your collection, you will need to take some precautions with it. Composition is sensitive to changes in temperature and humidity, and these environmental factors can cause it to crack and flake. Cleaning is difficult because you cannot get composition wet — it will disintegrate. If you have one of these dolls, it is best to leave it as is and take care of it so that no further damage is done.

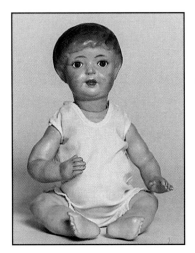

Plate 499
Oyster shell composition doll, 11½" tall, jointed arms and legs, swivel head, painted blue eyes, open-closed mouth, molded and painted hair, unmarked, same doll has been found with a Baby King tag on it (see Plate 501), rare and unusual doll, $195.00 – $225.00. The body of this doll is the same body that is used on the bisque-head dolls.

Plate 501
Tag of Baby King. Note that the tag has an RE in a Diamond on it indicating that it was made by the same company that made the bisque-head dolls.

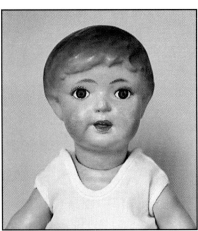

Plate 502
Papier-mache nodders, 4½" tall, paper label on bottom has "NIPPON" in blue ink, $145.00 – $195.00 each.

Plate 500
Close-up of Plate 499.

Plate 503
Papier-mache nodder, 4½" tall, paper label on bottom has "NIPPON" in blue ink, $145.00 – $195.00.

Children's Porcelain Items

For centuries toys reflecting adult pursuits have been made for children. Even today you can walk down the aisles of a toy store and find items that allow children to play as adults and learn to be adults. And so, too, in the Nippon era items were produced that allowed children to play but also learn to act as adults. In those days it was expected that boys would learn about the business world from their fathers. Girls were expected to learn the art of good housekeeping and social graces from their mothers. And porcelain made specifically for children was one means for preparing them for these important aspects of adult life. This is not to say that children did not play with these items. They certainly did. But adults expected that such play would be a learning experience as well.

Today most of us associate children's porcelain with toy tea sets and they are the most readily available items in Nippon children's porcelain. Children's tea sets came in different sizes and the size depended on their intended use. The larger sets were meant to be used by girls having tea parties with their friends. These larger sets were often of a good quality porcelain and many of the Nippon ones have the Rising Sun mark. When looking at these sets, it's not hard to imagine a child having a very proper tea with her friends or even her mother. Some of the children's tea sets were decorated with a floral or scenic design similar to the adult tea sets. However, many were made in a variety of designs that would appeal to children including Sunbonnet Babies, animals, and children playing. One rather unusual set shows a rabbit pulling a cart with painted eggs and the words "Going to Market." Most Nippon tea sets do not have any wording on them and this set, while of a poor quality porcelain, definitely has a certain appeal to it.

As an example of how important the teaching of etiquette was, Morimura Brothers published 10 rules of table etiquette on the box of their The Little Hostess tea set and, in a 1919 ad made note that their tea set was "instructive." The 10 rules are:

1 - *Seating the Guests* — The places can be designated by place cards or as arranged by the Hostess. After the guests are all seated the Hostess takes her seat.

2 - *Serving (A)* — Ladies should always be served before Gentlemen.

3 - *Serving (B)* — The plate or cup should be passed to the guest nearest the hostess to her right, who in turn passes it along until it reaches the one for whom it is intended.

4 - *Use of Utensils* — The knife should be used for cutting only, and never to carry food to the mouth. Only the spoon or fork should be so used. Between the mouthfuls, the utensils should be placed on the plate until ready to use again, and not kept in the hands continually.

5 - *Use of Fingers* — The fingers can be used in handling the bone of a bird, or for asparagus, radishes, celery or olives.

6 - *Conversation* — The guest should never criticize the food nor praise it unless asked for an opinion by the Hostess.

Children's Porcelain Items

7 - *Cleanliness* — Guests should always come to the table with hands and face clean, the hair in order, and clothes tidy.

8 - *Use of the Napkin* — The Napkin should be held on the lap and not tucked under the chin; when through, fold it and place it on the table.

9 - *Leaving the Table* — The Hostess gives the signal by rising first; all the guests then rise and carefully lift the chair back so they can leave without making a noise.

10 - *General Rule* — The main object of Etiquette is to avoid causing displeasure or annoyance to others. By carefully watching, one soon learns to become a pleasing and welcome guest, and will always be included when the list of invitations are being made out for the next party.

While The Little Hostess tea set is marked Japan, Morimura Brothers was selling these sets as early as 1917 (the year they registered "The Little Hostess" as a trademark). They produced The Little Hostess tea set in at least two different sizes. In the larger size the teapot is 3¼" high; in the smaller size the teapot is only 2" high. Even though Morimura Brothers was an importer for Noritake Company porcelain, The Little Hostess set is not a Noritake product. The quality of the porcelain is too poor for it to have been manufactured by Noritake. Morimura Brothers was, however, importing Noritake children's tea sets at the same time as The Little Hostess tea set.

Those sets that were produced in a smaller size were made for girls to have parties with their dolls or for dolls to have parties among themselves. One of the more popular small size Nippon sets is the child's face pattern. This tea set came in several different sizes, but all are in what would be considered a small size with the largest cup being only 1¼" tall! Notice just how little the teacup is when placed next to an adult's and a child's teacup in photo at right.

Child's face pattern tea set.

Three teacup sizes, adult, child, and doll.

It is not unusual to find children's tea sets that were made with two, four, or six cups and saucers. There are even advertisements in old trade catalogs that picture children's tea sets with three cups and saucers! It was also possible to buy just a teapot, sugar, and creamer. Nippon children's tea sets display a variety of quality in the porcelain and decoration. The sets made by the Noritake Company are definitely of higher quality than many of the sets by unknown manufacturers. There was little concern by many manufacturers or importers about the overall quality of the sets. After all, these sets were for children, and it was expected that some would ultimately be broken.

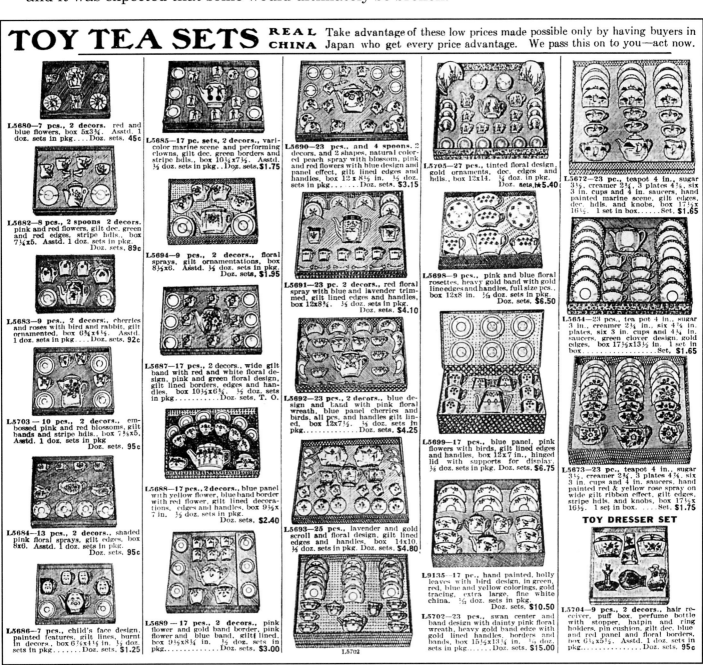

1917 Butler Brothers ad.

With a variety of quality and number of pieces, there was also a wide range of prices. A seven-piece tea set could be purchased in 1919 from Sears for 67¢. Sears also sold a 21-piece set (6 cups/saucers and 6 plates) for $2.98, a 15-piece set (6 cups/saucers but no

Children's Porcelain Items

plates) for $1.98, and an 11-piece set (4 cups/saucers) for $1.47. Obviously, something for every mother's pocketbook.

One of the uncommon types of child-size teapots is one with a wicker handle instead of a porcelain handle. These are hard to find and locating a tea set with a pot of this type is rare.

Of course, you can't have a proper tea party without serving dishes. Unfortunately for Nippon collectors, child-sized serving dishes with a Nippon mark are rare. It appears that many of the serving dishes are marked with the Noritake Made in Japan mark and in some Noritake Japan tea sets, it's possible to find handled cake plates, covered serving dishes, and platters. Small tureens are the most common of the Nippon child-sized serving pieces, and there is also a child-sized cheese and cracker server. A young girl must have been delighted to be able to serve her family, friends, and dolls with such elegant pieces.

Today children's tea sets and serving items are sought by Nippon collectors, doll collectors, and those who collect children's porcelain items. Therefore, these sets are becoming harder to find and expensive. Many collectors look for those tea sets with animals, children playing, or unusual decorations such as antique cars. Of course, any tea set decorated with Kewpies or Sunbonnet Babies is highly sought after and commands high prices.

Those sets that still have their original boxes are also sought after. These boxes, like The Little Hostess set, can often provide important information to the collector and researcher. For example, The Little Hostess box indicates that Morimura Brothers copyrighted it in 1917 and that they also trademarked the term "The Little Hostess," that the original price was $1.00 (marked on the bottom of the

Serving pieces of a rare Nippon child's dinner set. Tureen is 6" by 3", platter is 4½" by 3", gravy (with attached tray) is 3" by 2", relish tray is 3¼" by 2" and the plates and bowls are 3¼" across. All pieces are marked with the blue Rising Sun mark.

box), and that K.S. Co. of New York was the importer or seller.

Not only were children's tea sets produced during the 1891 – 1921 period, but miniatures of popular adult items were also manufactured. One can find small dresser items, chambersticks, and candlesticks made in sizes for children. A comparison of how they differ in size can best be shown when adult items are placed next to those intended for children. These adorable dresser sets are a little girl's version of her mother's set. Like the tea sets, children's dresser sets were designed to give young girls the opportunity to emulate their mothers. Today, these miniature items are rare, and it's a lucky collector who has one in their collection.

Children's feeding dishes and mugs were also produced during the Nippon era (1891 – 1921). These were decorated in whimsical designs, all to appeal to the small child. Both adult's and children's breakfast and oatmeal (sometimes called porridge) sets were manu-

Adult size open hatpin holder and child-sized open hatpin holder.

factured. Old ads indicate that an oatmeal set consisted of a matching bowl, plate, and small pitcher. The breakfast set consisted of a matching bowl, plate, and mug. Mugs, feeding dishes, and even eggcups were produced in matching designs.

Adult's and child's ring trees.

One capricious scene features two little girls wearing large hats and evidently playing a game of badminton. The game has temporarily stopped when a dog chews up one of the girls' shuttlecocks. Badminton was first played in Badminton, Gloucestershire, England, in 1873, and was still a popular game during the Nippon era. Evidently sets with this scene were popular because it was used on a variety of pieces and is rather common today.

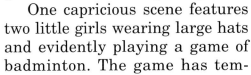

Comical baseball players wearing baggy wool uniforms and baseball caps reminiscent of this time are on other pieces.

Football players and sailors can also be found on a few. Animals of all kinds are featured on many items — bunnies, ducks, and chickens are just a few. One favorite is of a small girl playing with her cat. Very few domesticated cats are featured on Nippon wares, so this is a rare find. There are pieces painted with clowns and even people motoring in old-fash-

ioned cars. A pin box, which was originally part of a set for a baby's room, displays a stork carrying a newborn high over rooftops, certainly a unique Nippon item.

Most of the porcelain children's items bear the Rising Sun backstamp which indicates that they were manufactured by the Noritake Company on or after 1911. To date, a total of 14 backstamps have been located on children's wares, and four are products of the Noritake Company

and its forerunner, Morimura Brothers, which has been producing fine porcelain for over 100 years. Approximately 85% of the Nippon era porcelain pieces (this includes all porcelain items, not just children's items) found in today's collections were originally manufactured by the Noritake Company or its forerunner, Morimura Brothers.

Plate 504
Child's tea set by Louis Wolf & Company, in original box, marked on lid, dishes are unmarked, quality of porcelain is poor, pot is 3½" tall, box is 14⅝" x 10⅝", $150.00 – $200.00.

Plate 505
Close-up of tea set in Plate 504.

Plate 506
Close-up of label on lid of box of Louis Wolf & Company tea set, showing mark in lower left corner.

Plate 507
1917 Playthings *ad.*

Children's Porcelain Items

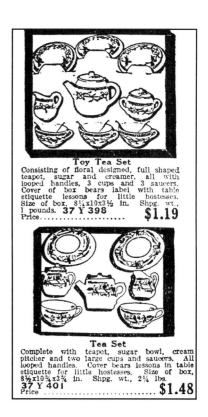

Plate 508
The Little Hostess child's tea set by Morimura Brothers, in original box, marked on lid (lid shown on page 264), dishes are unmarked, porcelain quality is poor, pot is 2" tall, box is 9⅝" by 7½", $135.00 – $185.00.

Plate 509
1920 Charles William Stores catalog ad for Little Hostess tea sets.

Plate 510
Child's tea set, consists of teapot, creamer, sugar, two cups, saucers, and plates, pot is 3" tall, mark POR-8, $175.00 – $200.00.

Plate 511
Child's tea set, unusual pumpkin design, consists of teapot, creamer, sugar, two cups, saucers, and plates, pot is 3" tall, mark POR-8, $225.00 – $250.00.

Plate 512
Child's tea set, automobile design, consists of teapot, creamer, sugar, four cups and saucers, pot is 3" tall, mark POR-8, $350.00 – $400.00.

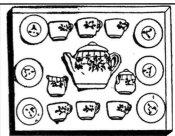

Floral Design Tea Set
Consisting of teapot, sugar bowl, cream pitcher, and 6 large cups and saucers. A set like this brings endless amusement and good times to little girls. Size of box, 8¾x11½x2¼ in. Shpg. wt., 2 lbs.
37 Y 396   Price **92c**

Tea Set
This Tea Set that will appeal to any small girl and bring her the means of having many good times and endless enjoyment. Set consists of teapot, sugar bowl, cream pitcher and two large cups and saucers. Packed in box, 7x9x2 inches. Shipping weight, 1¼ pounds.
37 Y 394   Price, complete.... **58c**

Plate 514
Child's plate, 6½" across, mark POR-8, $30.00 – $40.00.

Plate 513
1920 Charles William Stores catalog ad.

Plate 515
Child's sugar and creamer, snow scene, sugar is 2½" tall, mark POR-8, $75.00 – $100.00.

Plate 516
Child's tea set, consisting of teapot, sugar and creamer, pot is 4" tall, mark POR-8, $110.00 – $150.00.

Children's Porcelain Items

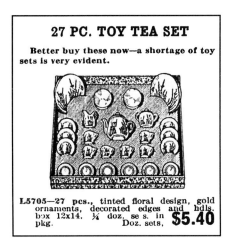

Plate 517
1917 Butler Brothers catalog ad.

Plate 518
Child's tea set, consisting of teapot, sugar, creamer, four cups and saucers and plates, pot is 3½" tall, mark POR-8, $325.00 – $375.00.

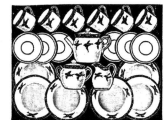

Plate 519
1918 November-December Montgomery Ward grocery catalog ad.

Plate 520
Child's tea set, consisting of teapot, sugar, creamer, four cups and saucers and plates, pot is 3½" tall, mark POR-1, $275.00 – $ 300.00.

Note: Even though the designs are similar and they have the same number of pieces, the tea set in Plate 518 is more expensive. The price difference between Plates 518 and 520 is due to the quality of the porcelain, and the fact that Plate 518 was made by the Noritake Company. Generally, those children's tea sets made by the Noritake Company carry a higher value.

Plate 521
1919 Montgomery Ward catalog ad.

Plate 522
*Child's tea set, consisting of teapot, sugar, creamer, six cups and saucers, pot is ¾"
tall, mark POR-8, $325.00 – $375.00.*

Plate 524
*Close-up of design in Plate
525.*

Our Cute Doll Design
23-Piece China Tea Set

This pretty tea set for our little
Miss is decorated with a doll
and rabbit design. Set consists of
6 cups, 1⅜ in. high, 6 saucers,
2¼ in. diam.; 6 plates, 3⅛ in. diam.;
creamer, covered sugar bowl, 2¾
in. high and covered tea pot, 3½
in. high. Ship. wt., 6 lbs.
49E3387 — Price, set.....**75c**

Plate 523
*1919 Montgomery Ward
catalog ad.*

Plate 525
*Child's tea set, consisting of teapot, sugar,
creamer, four cups, saucers, and plates, pot
is 3½" tall, mark POR-8, $325.00 – $375.00.*

E5668

E5668—23 pcs., 2 decors., one allover
green landscape scene, other pink
and blue oriental flowers, blue
enameled border, 10½x6¾ parti-
tioned box. Asstd. ⅓ doz. sets in
pkg.............Doz. sets, **$6.75**

Plate 527
1917 Butler Brothers catalog ad.

Plate 526
*Child's tea set, consisting of teapot, sugar, creamer, four cups,
saucers, and plates, pot is 3½" tall, mark POR-8, $325.00 –
$375.00.*

Children's Porcelain Items

Plate 528
Child's tea set, consisting of teapot, sugar, creamer, four cups, saucers, and plates, pot is 3½" tall, mark POR-8, $325.00 – $375.00.

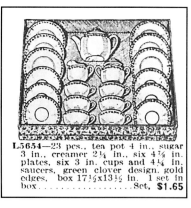

Plate 529
1917 Butler Brothers catalog ad.

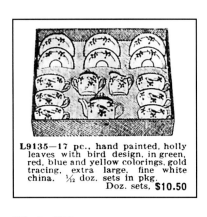

Plate 530
1917 Butler Brothers catalog ad.

Plate 531
Child's tea set pieces consisting of plate, cup and saucer, plate 4¼" across, mark POR-8, $30.00 – $50.00.

Plate 532
Child's tea set, consisting of teapot, sugar, creamer, six cups and saucers, mark POR-8, $325.00 – $375.00.

Plate 533
1917 Butler Brothers catalog ad.

17-Piece Tea Set
A very dainty little set decorated with flying bluebirds on a sunset background. Burnished gold on edges and handles. Consists of six cups and saucers, tea pot, 3¼ inches high, sugar bowl and creamer. Diameter of saucer, 2¾ inches. Shipping weight, 3½ lbs.

49C3393—Price......... **$2.98**

Plate 534
Child's tea set, consisting of teapot, creamer, two cups, saucers, and plates, sugar missing, pot is 3½" tall, mark POR-1, $200.00 – $225.00.

Plate 535
1920 Montgomery Ward catalog ad.

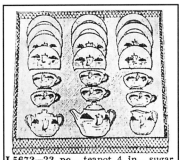

L5672—23 pc., teapot 4 in., sugar 3½, creamer 2¾, 3 plates 4¾, six 3 in. cups and 4 in. saucers, hand painted marine scene, gilt edges, dec. hdls. and knobs, box 17½x 16½. 1 set in box......Set. **$1.65**

Plate 536
1917 Butler Brothers catalog ad.

Plate 537
Child's tea set, consisting of teapot, sugar, creamer, four cups and saucers, pot is 3½" tall, mark POR-8, $300.00 – $350.00.

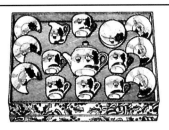

REAL CHINA 16 PC.
TOY TEA SET
Extra large pieces. Suitable for regular use. Will appeal strongly to your juvenile trade.

L5706—Cup 2¼x2¼, saucer 3¾, teapot 3½, sugar 3¼, creamer 2½, swan and lake scene decor., bright colorings, gilt edges and stripe handles. Each set in 18x12 spaced holly box.
SET (16 pcs.). Temp. Out

Plate 539
1917 Butler Brothers catalog ad.

Plate 538
Child's tea set, consisting of teapot, sugar, creamer, four cups and saucers, pot is 3½" tall, mark POR-8, $300.00 – $350.00.

Children's Porcelain Items

Plate 540
Close-up of design in Plate 541.

Plate 543
Child's plates, 5" across, mark POR-13, $10.00 –
$15.00 each.

Plate 541
Child's tea set, consisting of teapot, sugar, creamer, four cups,
saucers, and plates, pot is 3¾" tall, mark POR-8, $325.00 – $375.00.

Plate 542
Child's tea set, consisting of teapot, sugar, creamer, four cups
and saucers, pot is 3½" tall, mark POR-8, $300.00 – $350.00.

Plate 544
Child's tea set, consisting of teapot, sugar, creamer, four cups,
saucers, and plates, pot is 3¾" tall, mark POR-8, $325.00 – $375.00.

Plate 545
Child's plate, 4¼" across, promotional give-away
from Hahne & Co., mark POR-1, $25.00 – $35.00.

Plate 547
1920 Butler Brothers catalog ad.

Plate 546
Child's chocolate set, consisting of chocolate pot, sugar, creamer, four cups, saucers, and plates, pot is 4¼" tall, mark POR-8, unusual, $350.00 – $400.00.

Plate 549
1917 Butler Brothers catalog ad.

Plate 548
Child's tea set, consisting of teapot, sugar, creamer, two cups and saucers, pot is 3½" tall, mark POR-8, $250.00 – $300.00.

Plate 550
Child's tea set, consisting of teapot, sugar, creamer, four cups, saucers, and plates, pot is 4" tall, mark POR-8, $325.00 – $375.00.

Children's Porcelain Items

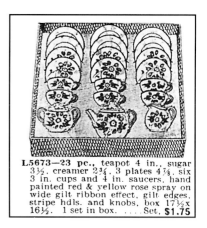

Plate 551
Child's tea set, consisting of teapot, sugar, creamer, four cups, saucers, and plates, pot is 3½" tall, mark POR-8, $300.00 – $350.00.

Plate 552
1917 Butler Brothers catalog ad.

L5673—23 pc., teapot 4 in., sugar 3½, creamer 2¾, 3 plates 4⅞, six 3 in. cups and 4 in. saucers, hand painted red & yellow rose spray on wide gilt ribbon effect, gilt edges, stripe hdls. and knobs, box 17½ x 16½. 1 set in box. . . . . Set, **$1.75**

Plate 553
Child's tea set, consisting of teapot, sugar, creamer, six cups, saucers, and plates, pot is 3½" tall, mark POR – 8, $325.00 – $375.00.

L5690—23 pcs., and 4 spoons. 2 decors. and 2 shapes, natural colored peach spray with blossom, pink and red flowers with blue design and panel effect, gilt lined edges and handles, box 12 x 8½ in. ¼ doz. sets in pkg. . . . . . Doz. sets, **$3.15**

Plate 554
1917 Butler Brothers catalog ad.

Plate 555
Child's tea set, consisting of teapot, sugar, creamer, two cups, saucers, and plates, pot is 4" tall, mark POR-8, $275.00 – $300.00.

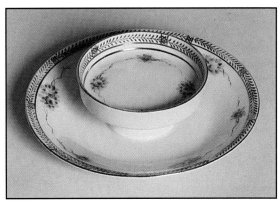

Plate 556
Child's teapot with bamboo handle, 3" tall (excluding handle), mark POR-8, $45.00 – $65.00.
Child's teapot with bamboo handle, 3" tall (excluding handle), blue mark POR-5, $45.00 – $65.00.
Child's teapot with bamboo handle, 3" tall (excluding handle), mark POR-8, $45.00 – $65.00.

Plate 557
Child's cheese and cracker server, 6" across, mark POR-8, $60.00 – $80.00.

Plate 558
Child's tureen with attached underplate, 5¼" long, green mark POR-5, $80.00 – $100.00.
Child's tureen with attached underplate, 5½" long, green mark POR-4, $80.00 – $100.00.
Child's tureen, 6" long, mark POR-8 (also marked "Made in Japan"), $90.00 – $110.00.

Plate 559
Child's tea set, consisting of teapot, sugar, creamer, four cups and saucers, pot is 4" tall, mark POR-8, $275.00 – $300.00.

Plate 560
Child's tea set, consisting of teapot, sugar, creamer, four cups, saucers, and plates, pot is 3½" tall, mark POR-8, $275.00 – $300.00.

Children's Porcelain Items

Plate 562
1917 Butler Brothers catalog ad.

Plate 561
Child's tea set, consisting of teapot, sugar and creamer, pot is 3½" tall, mark POR-8, $100.00 – $140.00.

Plate 564
Child's feeding dish, 7" across, mark POR-8, $75.00 – $100.00.

Plate 563
Child's tea set, consisting of teapot, sugar, creamer, four cups, saucers, and plates, pot is 3¼" tall, mark POR-8, $325.00 – $375.00.

Plate 566
Child's mug, 2½" tall, mark POR-8, $65.00 – $95.00.

Plate 565
Child's oatmeal set, all pieces marked POR-8:
Plate, 6½" across, $40.00 – $60.00.
Bowl, 5½" across, $40.00 – $60.00.
Pitcher, 3¼" tall, $50.00 – $75.00.

Plate 567
Child's tea set, consisting of tea pot, sugar, creamer, four cups, saucers, and plates, pot is 3½" tall, mark POR-6, Sunbonnet Baby decoration is highly collectible, $450.00 – $500.00.

Plate 568
Mark found on Sunbonnet Baby tea set above. Mark is similar to but not exactly like mark POR-6.

Plate 569
Picture from the 1907 book The Sunbonnet Twins.

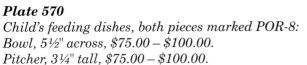

Plate 570
Child's feeding dishes, both pieces marked POR-8: Bowl, 5½" across, $75.00 – $100.00. Pitcher, 3¼" tall, $75.00 – $100.00.

Plate 571
Hanging plaque, 7½" across, green mark POR-4, $275.00 – $350.00.

Children's Porcelain Items

Plate 572
Child's face (also called doll face or googly) tea set, in original box, molded in relief, pot is 2¾" tall, box is 6⅜" by 5⅝", unmarked, rare to find this tea set in the original box, $275.00 – $350.00.

Plate 573
Child's face hanging plaque, molded in relief, 6⅛" across, mark POR-8, $100.00 – $125.00.

Plate 575
Child's face heart-shaped trinket dish, molded in relief, 5¼" across, mark POR-8, $125.00 – $150.00.
Child's face powder or trinket box, molded in relief, 3½" across, mark POR-8, $125.00 – $150.00.

Plate 574
Child's face cup and saucer, molded in relief, cup is 2½" tall, saucer is 5" across, mark POR-8, $100.00 – $125.00.

Plate 576
Child's face feeding dish, molded in relief, mark POR-8, hard to find, $175.00 – $225.00.

Plate 578
Child's face salt and pepper with tray, molded in relief, salt and pepper are 1½" tall, tray only marked POR-8, hard to find, $150.00 – $200.00.

Plate 577
Child's face plate, molded in relief, 6¾" across, mark POR-8, $75.00 – $100.00.
Child's face pitcher, molded in relief, 3" tall, mark POR-8, $75.00 – $100.00.

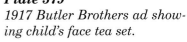

Plate 579
1917 Butler Brothers ad showing child's face tea set.

Plate 580
Child's face doll-size tea set, molded in relief, pot is 2¾" tall, sugar is missing lid, unmarked, $150.00 – $175.00 as is.

Plate 582
Child's face cereal bowl, molded in relief, 5¾" across, mark POR-8, $75.00 – $100.00.

Plate 581
Child's face egg cup, molded in relief, 3⅜" tall, mark POR-8 $100.00 – $125.00.
Child's face mug, molded in relief, 3" tall, mark POR-8, $100.00 – $125.00.
Child's face mug, molded in relief, 2½" tall, mark POR-8, $100.00 – $125.00.
Child's face mug, molded in relief, 2¼" tall, mark POR-8, $100.00 – $125.00.

Children's Porcelain Items

Plate 584
Reverse of mug in Plate 583, showing doll, an unusual item to be found on a baseball player mug!

Plate 583
Child's feeding dishes, all marked POR-8:
Bowl, 5½" across, $60.00 – $80.00.
Mug, 2½" tall, $75.00 – $100.00.
Feeding dish, 7" across, $75.00 – $100.00.
Pitcher, 3" tall, $50.00 – $75.00. Items with baseball players featured on them are sought after.

Plate 585
Figural trinket dish with the same baseball player that is shown on the child's feeding dishes in Plate 583, mark POR-8, $225.00 – $275.00.

Plate 588
Child's egg cup, 2½" tall, mark POR-8, $60.00 – $80.00.

Plate 586
Child's feeding dishes, all marked POR-8:
Pitcher, 3¼" tall, $60.00 – $80.00.
Plate, 6½" across, $60.00 – $80.00.
Mug, 2½" tall, $75.00 – $100.00.
Feeding dishes and child's tea sets with patriotic decorations such as the sailor pictured here or the World War I dough boy are popular with collectors.

Plate 587
Child's feeding dishes, all marked POR-8:
Mug, 2½" tall, $65.00 – $95.00.
Feeding dish, 8" across, $75.00 – $100.00.

Plate 590
Child's feeding dish, blue background, marked POR-8, $75.00 – $100.00.

Plate 589
Child's feeding dishes, white background, both marked POR-8:
Feeding dish, 6¾" across, $75.00 – $100.00.
Mug, 2⅝" tall, $65.00 – $95.00.

Plate 591
Child's oatmeal set, blue background, all pieces marked POR-8:
Plate, 6½" across, $40.00 – $60.00.
Bowl, 4¾" across, $40.00 – $60.00.
Pitcher, 3" tall, $50.00 – $75.00.

Plate 592
Child's breakfast set, white background, all pieces marked POR-8: Plate, 6¾" across, $40.00 – $60.00. Cup and saucer, cup 2¼" tall, saucer 5¼" across, $75.00 – $100.00. Note that the saucer is deep, almost like a bowl.

Plate 593
Child's oatmeal set, white background, all pieces marked POR-8: Bowl, 5¾" across, $40.00 – $60.00. Plate, 6½" across, $40.00 – $60.00. Pitcher, 3⅜" tall, $50.00 – $75.00.

Children's Porcelain Items

Plate 594
Child's feeding dishes, both marked POR-8:
Plate, 6½" across, $50.00 – $70.00.
Cup and saucer, cup 2¼" tall, $75.00 – $100.00.

Plate 595
Child's mug, 2⅜" tall, marked POR-8,
$65.00 – $95.00.

Plate 596
Close-up of decoration in Plates 594 and 595.

Plate 597
Child's pitcher, 3¼" tall, marked POR-8,
$50.00 – $75.00.

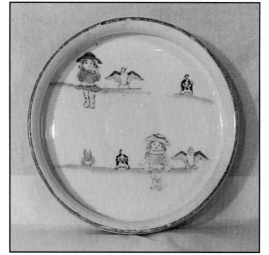

Plate 598
Child's feeding dish, 7" across, marked POR-8, $75.00 – $100.00.

Plate 599
Child's feeding dish, 7" across, marked POR-8, $75.00 – $100.00.

Plate 600
Child's oatmeal set, all pieces are green mark POR-8:
Plate, 6¼" across, $40.00 – $60.00.
Bowl, 5½" across, $40.00 – $60.00.
Pitcher, 3" tall, $50.00 – $75.00.

BABY SETS

L6560—Plate 7 in., bowl 6, pitcher 3½, clear white china, blue forget-me-not band between gold lines, maroon dotted border, gold striped edges and handle. ⅙ doz. sets in pkg............Doz. sets, $5.50

L6561—Tray 7 in., bowl 4⅜ in., cup 2½ in., pure white china, famous "Blue Bird" decor., gold line edges. 2 sets in pkg.....Set, 57c (Total $1.14)

L6562—Tray 6¾ in., bowl 4⅜ in., cup 2¾ in., hand painted Holland scenes and figures in green, blue, yellow and old ivory finish. 2 sets in pkg................Set, 65c (Total $1.30)

Plate 601
1917   Butler Brothers catalog ad.

Plate 602
Child's feeding dishes, both pieces marked POR-10: Bowl, 5⅜" across, $40.00 – $60.00. Pitcher, 3½" tall, $50.00 – $75.00.

Plate 603
Child's mug, 2½" tall, mark POR-8, $65.00 – $95.00.

Plate 604
Child's mug, 3¾" tall, mark POR-8, $85.00 – $110.00.

Plate 605
Child's pitcher, 3½" tall, mark POR-8, unusual design, $65.00 – $95.00.

287

Children's Porcelain Items

Plate 609
Mark found on bowl in Plate 611, inscription says "To Francis From Anna Xmas 1907."

Plate 606
Child's pitcher, Kewpie decoration, 3" tall, mark POR-8, $100.00 – $125.00.
This Kewpie pitcher, the Kewpie pin box (Plate 607), and the Kewpie bowl (Plate 611) were sold as undecorated blanks and then decorated in the United States by china painters. China painting was a popular pastime during the early 1900s.

Plate 607
Child's pin box, Kewpie decoration, 2" tall, mark POR-8, $100.00 – $125.00.

Plate 608
Another view of Plate 606.

Plate 610
Another view of Plate 606.

Plate 611
Child's bowl, Kewpie decoration, 6⅛" across, mark POR-14, $75.00 – $100.00.

Plate 612
Child-size dresser shown with Nippon child's dresser set (Plate 613) and chamberstick (Plate 618). The doll is also Nippon (Plate 412).

Plate 613
Child's dresser set, tray 6" by 4¼", hatpin holder 2" tall, hair receiver 2⅝" across, mark POR-9, rare, $225.00 – $275.00.

Plate 614
Child's trinket box, 4" wide, blue mark POR-4, $200.00 – $250.00.

Plate 616
1917 Butler Brothers ad.

Plate 615
Child's dresser set, hatpin holder is 2" tall, mark POR-8, rare, $300.00 – $400.00.

Children's Porcelain Items

Plate 617
Child's trinket box, 4" wide, green mark POR-4, rare, $300.00 – $375 00.

Plate 618
Child's chamberstick, 3¼" across, green mark POR-4, $85.00 – $120.00. Child's chamberstick, 3½" across, green mark POR-4, $85.00 – $120.00.

Plate 620
Child's dresser set, tray 6" x 4¼", powder jar 2⅝" across, hair receiver 2⅝" across, mark POR-9, rare, $225.00 – $275.00.

Plate 619
Child's hair receiver, 2¾" across, red mark POR-4, $100.00 – $135.00.

Plate 621
Child's dresser jar (lid missing), 3" tall, green mark POR-4, unusual decoration, $125.00 – $150.00 with lid.

Plate 622
Child's dresser set, powder box and hair receiver 2¾" across, green mark POR-8, rare, $200.00 – $285.00.

Porcelain Backstamps

This listing provides those backstamps that, to date, we have been able to document on Nippon children's porcelain items. Because of the number of porcelain backstamps used during the Nippon era, there are likely children's porcelain items that have other backstamps that we have not yet documented. Please note that some of these backstamps were hand-drawn and may differ slightly from the actual backstamp.

(POR = Porcelain)

POR-1   **NIPPON**   Stamped on items; found primarily in black but also blue and red.

POR-2  Crown (pointed), hand painted Nippon; found in green and blue.

POR-3  Crown (square), hand painted Nippon; found in green and green with red.

POR-4  M-in-wreath, hand-painted Nippon; M stands for the importer, Morimura Bros.; found in green, blue, magenta, and gold; used since 1911; it is a backstamp of the Noritake Company.

POR-5  Maple leaf Nippon; found in green, blue, and magenta; dates back to 1891; used by Morimura Brothers, forerunner to the Noritake Co.

Porcelain Backstamps

POR-6

Noritake M-in-wreath Nippon; M stands for the importer, Morimura Bros.; found in green, blue, and magenta; used since 1912; it is a backstamp of the Noritake Co.

POR-7

Pagoda hand-painted Nippon.

POR-8

Rising Sun Nippon; used since 1911; it is a backstamp of the Noritake Co.

POR-9

Torii hand-painted Nippon.

POR-10

Elite hand-painted Nippon.

POR-11

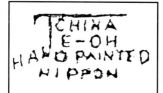

China E-OH hand-painted Nippon; found in blue and green.

POR-12

Cherry blossom hand-painted Nippon; found in blue, green, and magenta.

POR-13

RC Noritake Nippon hand painted; found in green and blue; RC stands for Royal Crockery (fine china). This mark has been in existence since 1911.

POR-14

Noritake Nippon, found in green, blue, and magenta. Mark dates from 1911; used on blank pieces (undecorated) of Nippon.

The Noritake Company

The following is an excerpt of information provided by the Noritake Co., Limited, regarding their history:

The founder of Noritake was Baron Ichizaemon Morimura who was born in 1893 in a family of merchants who acted as purveyors to feudal lords. In 1860, when he was twenty years old, the shogunate decided that a delegation be sent to the United States to return the courtesy visit of Commodore Perry. Baron Morimura was ordered to change Japanese money into American coin in the Yokohama foreign concession for the delegation to carry to the United States.

Japanese money to be exchanged was gold coin of high purity, while the currency to be received was coin of very low quality called Mexican silver.

Baron Morimura felt that it was a great loss to the country to allow gold of such high purity to flow out of Japan and spoke about the matter to Yukichi Fukuzawa, one of the great leaders in the modernization of new Japan from the feudal shogunate governing era.

Fukuzawa told Morimura that it was necessary to promote export trade so that the gold coin that went out of Japan would flow back into the country.

Ichizaemon Morimura and his young brother Toyo founded Morimura Gumi (Morimura Company) at Ginza in Tokyo in 1876, and, in the same year, Toyo formed a Japanese retail shop 'Hinode' (later this became Morimura Brothers, Inc.) at 6th Avenue, New York. Then the two brothers started a trade business between Tokyo and New York and exported traditional Japanese style pottery, bamboo works, other Japanese gift items, and so-called Japanese sundry goods to the United States.

This business transaction was the first trade between Japan and the United States after Japan opened its door with the Western countries.

During expansion of its export business, Morimura Brothers decided to change from retail to a wholesale business and to concentrate on ceramics. Thus Nippon Toki Kaisha (later this became the Noritake Company, Limited) was founded on January 1, 1904, at Noritake village which is the present site of the main factory. This factory's primary purpose was manufacturing and exporting high quality china mainly to the United States. Since then, the United States has been the greatest supporter and biggest customer for Noritake.

The founders were Ichizaemon Morimura, Mogobei Okura, Saneyoshi Hirose, Yasukata Murai, Kazuchika Okura, and Kotaro Asukai. The technique to manufacture high quality dinnerware was mastered in the 1910s. Noritake adopted a streamlined mass production system in the twenties and thirties and enjoyed the high reputation of Noritake china all over the world.

During World War II, the Noritake factory produced abrasive grinding wheels for heavy industries instead of chinaware. Although Noritake's old main office building was burned in World War II, the factory buildings suffered almost no damage. Therefore, Noritake could start the production of chinaware sooner than other factories. However, the quality of china was not up to pre-war standards because of the lack of high technology and superior materials and the equipment shortages at that time. In order to maintain the reputation of Noritake China, which meant quality products, the trademark "Rose China" was adopted temporarily before a satisfactory level of quality was restored. In 1948 the trademark "Noritake" was employed again, and the Noritake Company is still in operation today.

The Noritake Company

Photo of old Noritake factory in Nagoya, Japan.

Modern day decorating studio at Noritake Company in Nagoya, Japan.

Nippon-era dolls on display at Noritake Museum in Nagoya, Japan.

Toys

As was described in the *Playthings* article, "The Toy Industry in Japan," the Japanese toy industry did not begin to flourish until after 1913. In fact, prior to 1915 there is practically no mention of Japanese toys in *Playthings*. However, with the advent of World War I Japan stepped up its toy production, and by 1918 the Japanese were making toys out of all types of materials including wood, rubber, metal (including mechanical), cotton, paper, even earthenware.

Advertisements found in *Playthings* indicate that during the Nippon era, the Japanese were producing many different types of toys. In 1915 Morimura Brothers advertised such items as doll furniture, toy boats, games, wooden toys, mechanical toys, puzzle banks, musical toys, military sets, and stuffed animals. These were apparently popular items since Louis Wolf & Co. advertised many of the same items as well as toy watches, tennis rackets, and stuffed toys of all kinds. In 1919 Morimura Brothers advertised that they had papier-mache animals — horses, dogs, cows, and donkeys — on wood platforms with wheels and sitting dogs, cats, and monkeys with voice. The Taiyo Trading Company noted that as part of their import line for 1921 they had harmonicas, metal whistles, and "many other toy novelties." This paragraph from a July 1920 *Playthings* article gives us a small glimpse into the type of toy that was popular and how the toy was constructed:

JAPANESE TOYS

We are in a Position to Supply
the American Trade with

ORIGINAL, QUAINT, WELL MADE and PROFITABLE
MERCHANDISE FROM JAPAN

CHARACTER DOLLS	WOODEN TOYS
TOY PARASOLS	MECHANICAL TOYS
TOY TEA SETS	PUZZLE BANKS
DOLL FURNITURE	MUSICAL TOYS
TOY BOATS	MILITARY SETS
GAMES	STUFFED ANIMALS
HOLIDAY NOVELTIES	CELLULOID TOYS

Our Toy Department has been greatly enlarged to
accommodate the enormous demand for these goods.

MORIMURA BROS.

546 and 548 Broadway

BOSTON
144 Congress St.   NEW YORK   CHICAGO
220 So. State St.

June 1915

The aero line has made such a hit that large shipments are being sent to New York, Boston, Chicago, and other eastern centers. The Soloman-Heineman Company practically controls the output of two Japanese factories which are devoting themselves to aerial toys which retail from twenty-five cents to $10. There are bi-planes, aeroplanes and mono-planes with wings made of silk, stretched on when it is wet. The machines fly on the principle of the gyroscope. The wings are "knock-down," and can be folded up, but the body of the machine is not collapsible.

The toy trade in Japan was mainly a household industry with many of the toys made by hand, not machine. This led to the manufacture of toys that were not of uniform quality, and subsequently, led many to the belief that Japanese-made toys were cheap. It was seldom that the toys were designed in Japan and rarely were any kept in stock. Most were made upon individual order from a sample and immediately shipped either directly from the manufacturer or through middle men. As noted in a number of trade advertisements, many in the toy trade went to Japan to direct the production and shipment of toys. No doubt those who went to Japan took samples with them.

Toys

In this December 1917 excerpt from a *Playthings* article, the author, who has interviewed Mr. R.C. Gibson a buyer for Marshall Field & Co., describes the situation:

> *Questioned regarding the reported release from Holland of a large shipment of German toys destined for this country, he said that no part of such a shipment had reached Field's, and this statement was confirmed by other toy buyers interviewed.*
>
> *Japan, he thought, would be an increasing factor in the toy manufacturing trade. Mr. Gibson has been there every year since the war began, and while at first they had nothing to offer but the well-known Japanese specialties, usually poorly made and unsuitable in any large measure for American needs, now he was getting large supplies from there. He estimated that the volume of Japanese toys in his department this season represented about one-third what he formerly secured from Germany. The difference in language and the lack of knowledge of American life and conditions had made it very difficult to teach the Japanese workmen just what was wanted, and samples had been returned as many as eight times, but as soon as they thoroughly understood he was confident they could successfully reproduce most of the toys formerly obtained from the Germans.*

Whether well-made or not, the Japanese toy trade continued to grow mainly because of World War I and anti-German sentiment after the war. Many in the toy trade advertised that they had "no German toys," and it was not until after 1920 that German toys came back on the market in the United States.

Today toys marked "NIPPON" are rare. For one reason, they were items that were meant to be played with and then, if broken, thrown out. Another is that the toys were often marked on a box that was usually destroyed or a paper label that was removed. This left many Nippon-era toys as unmarked. Of course, many were probably originally marked "JAPAN" which makes it impossible to differentiate between those made during the Nippon era and those made after the Nippon era. Because of this rarity,

Above Is Shown a Straight-from-the-Shoulder Toy Advertisement Run in the Newspapers of Vancouver, B. C., During the Recent Holiday Season

it is difficult to offer a realistic evaluation of what collectors look for or the prices they are willing to pay. On certain items, specialized toy collectors might be willing to pay more than a Nippon collector might pay.

One example of this is with Nippon-marked mechanical toys. Examples marked "Nippon" are rare and their prices reflect that rarity. Recently (August 1999), a tin windup motorcycle that was marked "Made in Nippon" on the wheels was auctioned on the Internet. This wind-up

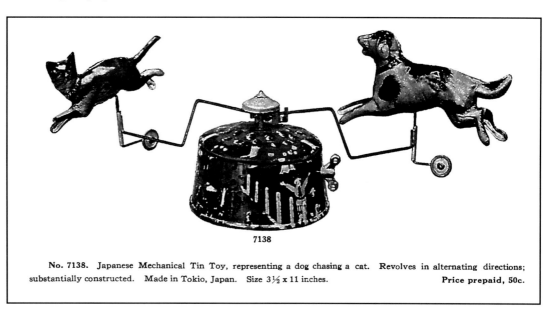

No. 7138. Japanese Mechanical Tin Toy, representing a dog chasing a cat. Revolves in alternating directions; substantially constructed. Made in Tokio, Japan. Size 3½ x 11 inches. Price prepaid, 50c.

1916 A. A. Vantine catalog ad.

toy was in excellent condition with good coloring and minimal rust. The toy featured a motorcycle being driven by a young boy in brown soldier's clothing and a girl, also in soldier's clothing, riding on the back. A teddy bear was riding on the back, and a toy soldier doll was riding on the front bumper. In addition to "Made in Nippon" the motorcycle was marked:

 MADE IN JAPAN

When the auction ended, the bid had reached over $3,500, but the reserve was not met. While this price is not indicative of the value of most Nippon toys, it does provide collectors some idea as to the rarity and price of certain Nippon-marked toys.

1916 A. A. Vantine catalog ad for Japanese wooden toys.

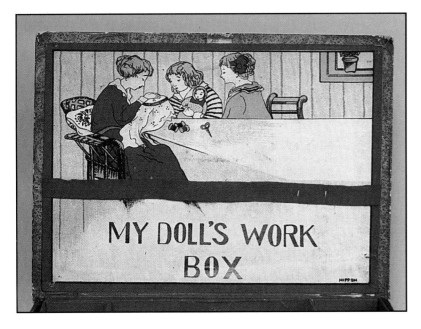

Plate 623
Inside lid of Plate 624 showing "NIPPON" in lower right corner.

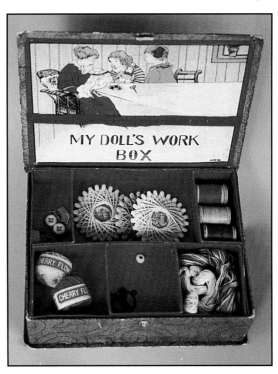

Plate 624
Child's sewing set, box is 6" x 8" by 2¼" tall, covered in imitation leather; divided tray lifts out; contents include three spools of sewing thread, 2 spools of embroidery floss, several other types of floss, 2 old buttons, a snap, a horse charm, a blue glass bead, and some partially completed doll clothes (see Plate 625); at one time the kit probably had scissors and sewing needles, $65.00 – $100.00.

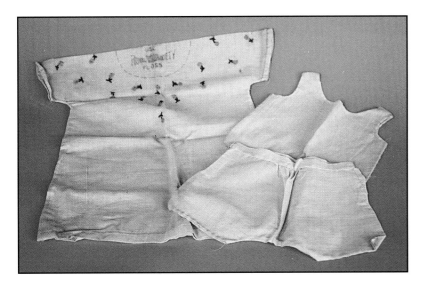

Plate 625
Doll clothes found under the tray of the sewing kit; includes underclothes, a partially completed dress, a partially completed dressing sacque, a partially completed boudoir cap, and a partially completed apron. Printing on dress is "No. 370 Doll's Outfit- Use Royal Society Floss."

Plate 627
Child-size sewing basket, 4" across, basket is 2" tall (excluding gauze top), drawstring closure, marked "NIP-PON" on bottom, $30.00 – $40.00.

Plate 626
Wooden dominoes, box is 4⅛" by 2⅜", marked "NIPPON" on bottom of box, box has a domino painted on the top and sides, $10.00 – $15.00.

Toys

Plate 629
Original sticker found on wooden duck.

Plate 630
Wooden bird rolling toy, as wheels roll, the bird bobs up and down, 4" long x 3" tall, marked "NIPPON" inside wheel, $50.00 – $80.00.

Plate 628
Wooden duck pull toy, as duck rolls, the head bobs up and down and the beak opens and closes, 6½" long x 6" tall, original sticker (see Plate 629), $75.00 – $100.00.

Noisy Quacker Ducks 25c

Quacker Ducks of fine quality heavy hardwood, beautifully painted in blue, black and silver colors that won't come off. 3¾-in. solid hardwood wheels decorated in various colors and a 1-inch rear guide wheel. As the toy is drawn along the floor there is a grotesque up and down movement of the head and neck, and the long yellow bill opens and closes, producing a most unusual appearance. Regular $1.00 toy. Length, 5½ in.; height, 5 in. 3-in. wheels. Shpg. wt., 1½ pounds. **25c**
37Y5068 Price, each **25c**
37Y5069 Length, 6 inches; height, 6½ inches. Shpg. wt., 2½ lbs. Price, each....................................**40c**

Plate 631
1917 Charles William Stores catalog ad for the wooden duck shown in Plate 628.

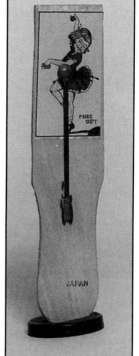

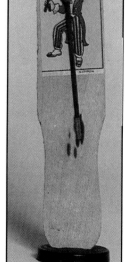

Plate 632
Wooden gymnasts, when knob is turned the men tumble over the bar, 3½" tall by 4½" long, marked "NIPPON," handwritten on bottom "R. Edward Airis / 1918. St. Paul, Minn.," $80.00 – $120.00.

Plate 633
Clapper-type noise maker, 6" tall, marked "NIPPON" on one side, "JAPAN" on the other, probably a transitional item used as a give-away, $10.00 – $15.00.

Plate 634
Reverse of Plate 633, "NIPPON" marked in lower right corner.

Plate 635
Wooden doll furniture, in original box that is marked with the Morimura Brothers spider symbol (see chapter on Morimura Brothers for an explanation of this symbol) and "Made in Japan." Box label obviously plays on a patriotic theme, chairs are 3" tall, table is 2¼" tall and 3⅛" square, $40.00 – $60.00.

Plate 636
1916 A. A. Vantine & Co. catalog ad.

No. 15216. Japanese Inlaid Wood Toy Furniture Set, consisting of two large chairs, two small chairs, two benches, one table, one vase, one bottle, two cups and two plates; packed in a box; size 4½ x 2¼ x 3⅜ inches.

Price per set, prepaid, 50c.

No. 15217. Child's Japanese Folding Furniture Set, consisting of table, two chairs, vase, bottle, two cups and two plates; table top is inlaid with wood in attractive designs. The entire set folds up and packs into a box; size 3½ x 2⅝ x 2⅞ inches. Price per set, prepaid, 50c.

Plate 637
1916 A. A. Vantine & Co. catalog ad.

Plate 638
Wooden doll furniture, in original box that is marked "Made in Nagoya Nippon," box has original price of 10¢ written on it, lounge is 5" long, chairs are 3" tall, table is 3½" square, furniture marked "Made in Japan," rug may be original to set, $40.00 – $60.00.

A·A·VANTINE·&·CO·Inc·

6000

No. 6000. Japanese Crying Bear. Has a papier mache head and cloth body. Feet and hands are movable. Size (as in cut) 4¾ x 6½ inches.

Price prepaid, 35c.

Plate 639
1916 A. A. Vantine & Co. catalog ad.

Plate 640
Wooden boat, 7½" long, marked "NIPPON" on bottom, note the faded American flags on the poles, $15.00 – $25.00.

Plate 641
Mark found on the bottom of the boat in Plate 640.

301

Toys

Plate 643
Metal whistle, 3¼" long, marked "NIPPON," $20.00 – $30.00.

Plate 642
Composition animals, in original box marked "NIPPON" in lower right corner, animals approximately 2" tall each, $80.00 – $120.00.

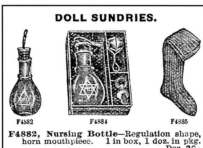

DOLL SUNDRIES.

F4882   F4884   F4885

F4882, Nursing Bottle—Regulation shape, horn mouthpiece.   1 in box, 1 doz. in pkg.
Doz. **36c**

F4884, Doll Baby Set—Nursing bottle with horn mouthpiece, cork stopper and glass top, small babies' rattle, and bone rubber teething ring with nipple or pacifier. All 3 in spaced box. 1 doz. sets in pkg.
Doz. sets, **39c**

F4885, Stockings—Openwork, asstd. sizes, 1½ to 2½ in. foot, 3 to 6 in. leg, half black, half asstd. white, pink and blue. 1 doz. prs. in envelope......................Doz. prs. **40c**

Plate 644
1917 Butler Brothers catalog ad with doll bottle set shown in Plate 647.

1307

No. 1307.   The Oriental people furnish more comic as well as curious playthings to delight their children than any other nation.   By pressing the head of this little dog the mouth opens and the dog barks; made of white flannel with metal collar, bell and chain.   **Price each, 35c.**

Plate 646
1916 A. A. Vantine & Co. catalog ad.

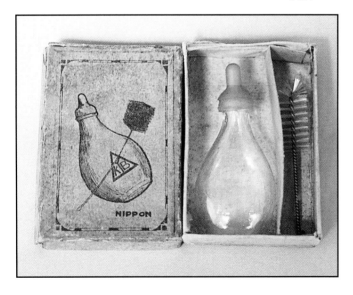

Plate 645
Doll bottle set, in original box, box is 2¼" x 3" tall, bottle embossed with "La Petite Alpha" on one size and "NIP-PON" on the other size, brush not original, and nipple has been replaced, $75.00 – $100.00.

Plate 647
Doll bottle set, in original box, box is 2⅝" x 3⅛", bottle is 2¼" tall, bottle marked "NIPPON," box marked "MADE IN JAPAN," rubber nipples on bottle and pacifier have totally deteriorated, as is often the case, $75.00 – $100.00.

Holiday Items

A review of old trade catalogs indicates that the Japanese were producing some holiday decorations as early as 1908 and possibly earlier than that. In 1908 Butler Brothers was advertising Japanese Easter novelties consisting of cotton chicks and rabbits, straw and bamboo candy baskets adorned with a variety of cotton chicks and rabbits, cardboard-trimmed candy containers also with cotton chicks and rabbits, and figural rooster and duck candy containers. They even advertised china chick-shaped salt and pepper shakers and china toys consisting of a rabbit, duck, hen, and rooster.

SPECIAL 10 CENT ASSORTMENT OF

Japanese Easter Novelties.

Unequaled variety of the best sellers at small cost.

L6108—18 pcs. 4¾x6½ cotton chicks and rabbits, 3 styles; 10 pcs. 5½x8¾ papier mache and leather roosters, duck and goose candy boxes; 12 pcs. 2¾ to 5¼ in. 2 style handled candy baskets with cotton rabbit, chick, etc. 24 pcs. 3¼ to 5 in. 4 style covd. candy baskets asstd. colors, animal ornaments. 72 pcs. in case, NO LESS SOLD.   Each, 6½c

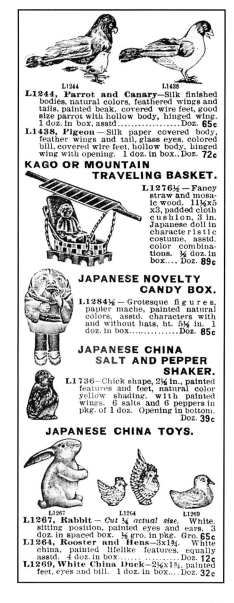

L1244, Parrot and Canary—Silk finished bodies, natural colors, feathered wings and tails, painted beak, covered wire feet, good size parrot with hollow body, hinged wing. 1 doz. in box, asstd..................Doz. **65c**

L1438, Pigeon—Silk paper covered body, feather wings and tail, glass eyes, colored bill, covered wire feet, hollow body, hinged wing with opening. 1 doz. in box..Doz. **72c**

**KAGO OR MOUNTAIN
TRAVELING BASKET.**

L1276½—Fancy straw and mosaic wood. 11½x5 x3, padded cloth cushion, 3 in. Japanese doll in characteristic costume, asstd. color combinations. ⅓ doz. in box.... Doz. **89c**

**JAPANESE NOVELTY
CANDY BOX.**

L1284½—Grotesque figures, papier mache, painted natural colors, asstd. characters with and without hats, ht. 5½ in. 1 doz. in box...............Doz. **85c**

**JAPANESE CHINA
SALT AND PEPPER
SHAKER.**

L1736—Chick shape, 2½ in., painted features and feet, natural color yellow shading, with painted wings. 6 salts and 6 peppers in pkg. of 1 doz. Opening in bottom.   Doz. **39c**

JAPANESE CHINA TOYS.

L1267, Rabbit — *Cut ¼ actual size.* White, sitting position, painted eyes and ears. 3 doz. in spaced box. ⅓ gro. in pkg. Gro. **65c**

L1264, Rooster and Hens—3x1¾. White china, painted lifelike features, equally asstd. 4 doz. in box.............Doz. **12c**

L1269, White China Duck—2½x1¾, painted feet, eyes and bill. 1 doz. in box....Doz. **32c**

"DISPLAY" ASST. OF JAPANESE EASTER TOYS AND CANDY BOXES.

Quick selling staples and newest novelties to retail at 5 and 10c. Selected and packed in our own warehouse in Japan.

Free with each asst. 2 Large Show Pieces.

LG107: Comprises the following:
```
 36 pcs. 2½ in. to 4¼ in. cotton rabbits, chicks and roosters, 5 styles.
 12  "   4 in. nodding head roosters and chicks, 2 styles.
 30  "   4 to 5¾ in. papier mache and feather roosters, ducks and geese candy boxes, 5
         styles.
 24  "   2¾ x 2½ in. handled candy baskets with rabbits, chicks, etc., 5 styles.
 42  "   2½ to 3½ in. candy baskets and boxes with cotton rabbits, chicks, etc., 7 styles.
144  "   in case (FREE: 11 in. feather rooster and 10 in. rabbit).
              (Asst. $4.68)
```
Each, **3¼c**

Although Japan was producing some holiday items in the early 1900s, prior to World War I, Germany was the producer of the vast majority of holiday decorations. Most German, and subsequently most Japanese, decorations centered around three holidays — Christmas, Easter, and Halloween. In fact, most of the major importers of Nippon dolls and toys were also advertising Christmas, Easter, and Halloween novelties and ornaments. This is not to say that other holidays were ignored but those three were the most popular and, if one can find Nippon marked holiday items, it is usually for one of those three holidays. Morimura Brothers did advertise that they had St. Patrick's Day, Washington's Birthday, and Independence Day novelties, and other importers such as the Taiyo Trading Company advertised Fourth of July novelties. Many of the holiday items produced were favors, candy boxes, lanterns, and ornaments.

SPECIAL 5c ASST. OF JAPANESE EASTER NOVELTIES.

Includes all the popular staple sellers as well as the latest novelties. With each assortment are given 2 large size show pieces free of charge.

LX1256—Assortment comprises 144 pieces, 24 styles as follows:

```
     only 4 in. white and yellow cotton chicks.       6 only cotton chicks in silk woven cage on
 6  "  3  "  white cotton roosters with chicks            bellows base. with voice.
            on back.                                  6  "  2¾ in. 4 wheel wood wagon with dressed
 6  "  4 in. cotton rabbits with carrot.                    cotton rabbit and chick.
 6  "  5  "  cotton rabbit, sitting position.         6  "  3¾ in. silk covered wire handled basket
 6  "  3  "  hollow body roosters with feath-               with hinged cover, floral spray and
            ered wings and tail.                            chick ornaments.
 6  "  asstd. color 3 in. birds.                      6  "  2¾ in. chair with 3 piece cotton
 6  "  4½ in. geese with hats.                              chick family.
 6  "  5½ in. white cotton dressed rabbits           12  "  2 styles cotton chicks and rabbits, orna-
            holding carrot.                                 mented bellow platform. with voice.
 6  "  cotton rabbits holding chick, on bellow      36  "  6 styles. asstd. shapes and size baskets,
            base with voice.                                one style with handle, all have cotton
 6  "  3 piece cotton rooster with chick sets.              rabbit, chicken or duck ornaments,
 6  "  2½ in. wood benches with 3 piece cotton              some with green moss, many will
            rooster and chick set.                          hold candy.
 6  "  4 in. wood bench with cotton rabbit
            and chick.
Total 144 pieces.        (Total for assortment, $5.04)      Each, 3½c
```

This paragraph from *Playthings* 1916 describes some of the Christmas items produced by Morimura Brothers:

> *When the war commenced to tighten the oversea (sic) Christmas tree ornament trade, L.W.G. (Louis W. Greeman of Morimura Brothers) at once asked himself if his house could not supply part of that need. With a mind trained to such a situation, he immediately decided that their well-known confectionary line which had previously never been sold to the toy trade was just the line to fit the needs of the hour. These articles, consisting of red brick candy boxes showing Santa Claus, reindeer Christmas trees, Santa autos and sleighs, snow topped houses and chimneys, snowballs, Santa Claus figures, etc., etc., with string attached, were immediately featured as Christmas tree ornaments with sensationally successful results — altogether as neat a little merchandising stroke as one might hope to encounter. Besides these tree ornaments, red and green roping is being offered for holiday decorarating, made of the well-known Hinoki wood fibre.*

It is not known what the Morimura Brothers "confectionary line" was, but it is likely that the items Mr. Greeman was describing were made of cardboard, crepe paper, cotton, and papier-mache.

The Japanese also made glass Christmas ornaments as indicated in this 1920 *Playthings* article:

> *The Soloman-Heineman Co. has a quantity of Japanese goods which are arriving in excellent shape. Much of this stock consists of tree ornaments, some of which are distinctly novel and attractive. Natives of the extreme Orient, especially the Japanese and Chinese, seem to possess a gift of handling a riot of colors and making them blend harmoniously, and this gift crops up very noticeably in the Christmas tree ornaments, made of beads and glass, that radiate vivid colors and harmony simultaneously.... The color combinations in these beads are beautiful.*

Unfortunately, little else is known about these Nippon-era holiday ornaments and novelties. Many of these items were made of inexpensive materials such as cardboard, crepe paper and cotton although a few are made of bisque and celluloid. Sometimes the holiday candy boxes are adorned with a papier-mache figural item. Most likely these items were assembled by at-home workers using samples supplied by the American importers.

It's also possible to find Nippon dolls that are decorated for the holidays. Some of the dolls were probably decorated in Japan, and others were likely decorated once they came to the United States. Interestingly, the Japanese did not advertise holiday-decorated dolls as part of their product lines although they may have considered decorated dolls to be party favors. From 1916 to 1917 *Good Housekeeping* ran a series with decorated Kewpies. In this series we can find Kewpies decorated for Halloween, Thanksgiving, Christmas, St. Patrick's Day, Easter, and the Fourth of July. These Kewpies were sold already dressed and could be bought for 50 to 60 cents each. Trade catalogs and advertisements from vendors specializing in holiday items also advertised Kewpies that were dressed for various holidays. Crepe paper companies provided instructions for decorating dolls as holiday centerpieces and party favors, so some dolls were decorated after they were bought.

Many of the cardboard and papier-mache items are marked in purple ink on the bottom of the item. This is especially true for the candy boxes. The cardboard Easter eggs are usually marked inside the egg. Unfortunately, many Nippon-era holiday items were either destroyed, not individually marked but marked by the box lot, or marked "Japan" making it impossible to differentiate between pre-1921 and post-1921 items. It's also likely that some had paper labels that have been removed. Therefore, it is difficult to find Nippon-marked holiday items, and those items that are available tend to be expensive. They are popular as holiday collectibles, and the candy boxes are sought after by both holiday and candy box collectors. Nippon collectors can expect to compete with holiday collectors for any Nippon holiday items available.

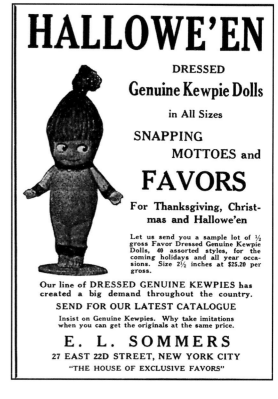

1920 Playthings *ad.*

For HALLOWEEN of 1918

Our Exclusive and Original Line of

Favors, Decorations, Lanterns, Candy Boxes, Hats and Noisemakers

Is Now Ready and on Display

An Early Inspection is Strongly Advised

MORIMURA BROS.

53-55-57 West 23d Street

NEW YORK

Holiday Items

Plate 648
Leprechaun, all bisque, 4¾" tall, incised "NIP-PON," hard to find, $140.00 – $190.00.

Patrick, pipe, and all is of china, and is wearin' o' the green in costume; 60 cents

Plate 649
1917 Good Housekeeping ad for a Kewpie dressed in St. Patrick's Day attire.

Plate 650
Paddy and the Pig, celluloid, 4½" tall x 4" long, marked "MADE IN NIPPON," old store stock from Pattersons, a wholesaler of novelty items and inexpensive toys (Salem, Massachusetts), in business from the 1800s through the 1940s, rare, $165.00 – $190.00.

JAPANESE EASTER BASKET NOVELTY.

One of the very best 10 centers you can find. Note remarkable price.

LX1446—About 4x4, 6 fancy shapes, wire, silk cord and fancy hinoki covering variegated, hinoki trimmed edges, cotton animals on each. 1 doz. in box. Per dozen. **48c**

Plate 651
1908 Butler Brothers catalog ad.

L7362, Airship —Net decorated papier mache telescope, wire frame, American flag chick and rabbit ornaments, cardboard, propeller, elastic cord and ring hanger. 1 doz. in box....Doz. **95c**

Plate 652
1908 Butler Brothers catalog ad.

Plate 653
Bisque doll head decorated in pink crepe paper, on a replaced candy box. Doll head was originally on a pink candy box but the dealer threw it out because the box was in such poor condition. Head 4" tall (not including box), marked 0 2, $90.00 – $120.00.
Note: Original boxes, clothing, parts, etc. should always be kept and never thrown out, even if in a total state of disrepair. Because the dealer threw out the original box, the value of this piece is diminished.

308

JAPANESE EASTER TOYS

Rooster—2 in., silk paper covered, feather tail and wings, red comb, wire feet.
F5546—1 gro. in box....Gro. **92c**

Nodding Head Toy Asst—6 styles, aver. ht. 5 in., birds, goose, duck and turkey, silk paper covered bodies, feather wings and tail, wire feet, wood bills.   Doz.
F3785—Asstd. 2 doz. in box.   **35c**
(Total for asst. 70c)

Flying Bird Asst—6 styles, aver. 6 in., asstd. colors, canaries, wild geese, pigeons, storks, etc., silk paper bodies, feather tails and wings, spring hanger.   Doz.
F6003—Asstd. 2 doz. in box...**42c**
(Total for asst. 84c)

Easter Toy Asst—Aver. 4 in., 6 styles, rooster, duck, goose, pigeon, parrot and stork, silk paper bodies, feather wings and tails, bead eyes, wire feet.   Doz.
F6006—Asstd. 2 doz. in box...**42c**
(Total for asst. 84c)

Rooster With Voice—6½ in., flannel covered body, feathered tail, red cloth comb, glass eyes, when back is pressed rooster opens bill and crows.
F3803—1 doz. in box....Doz. **69c**

Flying Bird Asst—6 styles, aver. 7 in., pigeons, wild geese and storks in asstd. bright colors, silk paper bodies, feather tails and weighted wings give appearance of flying, spring hanger.   Doz.
F6004—Asstd. 1 doz. in box...**72c**

Rocking Birds—6 styles, aver. 6¼, asstd. birds, silk paper bodies, glass eyes, feather wings and tails, wire and web feet, weighted for rocking.   Doz.
F6007—Asstd. 1 doz. in box...**79c**

Nodding Head Asst—4 styles, aver. 6¾ in., rooster, duck, swan and goose, asstd. color silk paper bodies, glass eyes, feather wings and tails, paper covered wire and web feet.
F6009—1 doz. in box....Doz. **84c**

Stuffed Flannel Rabbit and Rooster—Aver. ht. 7½ in., rabbit with flannel cutaway coat, trousers and high hat; rooster with soldier suit, tin sword and scabbard, bead eyes.
F3802—Asstd. 1 dz. in bx. Dz. **89c**

Stuffed Flannel Rabbit Asst — Length 8 in., extra good model, asstd. plain white, and brown & white spotted, bead eyes, blue ribbon collar.   Doz.
F3804—Asstd. 1 doz. in box.'..**89c**

Plate 654
1908 Butler Brothers catalog ad.

Holiday Items

Plate 655
Candy containers, all made of cardboard, crepe paper, and cotton, all marked "NIPPON" on bottom in ink.
4¾" tall, $150.00 – $175.00.
4¼" tall, $150.00 – $175.00.
6" tall, $175.00 – $200.00.

Plate 656
1908 Butler Brothers catalog ad.

Plate 657
Rabbit rattle, celluloid, 4½" tall, mark CL-20, $100.00 – $135.00.

Plate 658
Easter egg candy container, 4½" long, old grass and cotton chick inside, top and bottom do not match but fit together and have the same interior, $50.00 – $60.00.

Plate 659
Mark found inside containers in Plates 658 and 660.

Plate 660
Easter egg candy containers, 4½" long and 2¾" long, string loops allow for hanging, large $40.00 – $50.00, small $30.00 – $40.00.

Plate 662

All-bisque dolls dressed in home-made outfits of ribbon and netting, 4⅝" tall, boy incised "NIPPON," girl incised "MADE IN NIPPON," $100.00 – $125.00 each.

Plate 661

All-bisque doll dressed in crepe paper clothes, 4½" tall, incised "NIPPON," $165.00 – $200.00.

Plate 664

Type of mark found on Halloween candy containers in Plates 663 and 666. This same type of mark is also found on the Easter candy containers.

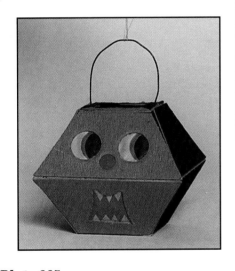

Plate 663

Candy containers, all made of cardboard, crepe paper, and papier-mache (cat), all marked "NIPPON" in ink on bottom, 2¼" tall, $100.00 – $125.00. 3½" tall, $150.00 – $200.00. 2½" tall, $100.00 – $125.00.

Plate 665

Jack-o'-lantern, made of cardboard and crepe paper, 3¼" tall (not including wire handle), folds flat for storage, has a metal candle holder inside bottom, marked "NIPPON" in ink on bottom, and has original price of 25¢, rare, $150.00 – $200.00.

Plate 666

Candy containers, all made of cardboard and crepe paper, all marked "NIPPON" in ink on bottom, 2" tall, $100.00 – $125.00. 4" tall, $175.00 – $225.00. 2" tall, $100.00 – $125.00.

Plate 667

View of jack-o'-lantern in Plate 665 folded flat for storage.

Holiday Items

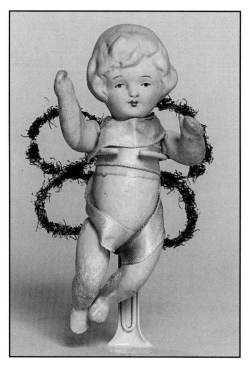

Plate 669
*Papier-mache Mrs. Santa Claus. 5½"
tall, marked "NIPPON" in red ink on
bottom, $90.00 – $120.00.*

Plate 668
*Bisque-head angel, composition body,
6" tall, incised "NIPPON" on head,
original ribbon and tinsel wings, the
shape and angle of the legs indicate
that this was originally intended to be
used as an angel not as a doll, an
unusual and hard to find item,
$150.00 – $200.00.*

Plate 671
*All-bisque doll in original Christmas
box, doll wears a blue and yellow silk
outfit and has a red pincushion with
it, doll incised "NIPPON," old Christmas tag has "Sylvia" written on it,
$90.00 – $120.00. Companies such as
Butler Brothers sold items pre-pack-
aged in Christmas boxes.*

Plate 670
*Celluloid Santa, jointed legs only, 4¾"
tall, marked "MADE IN NIPPON,"
hard to find, $125.00 – $160.00.*

Plate 672
1920 Playthings ad.

Glossary

-A-

ABC Bodies: Cloth bodies with the ABC's printed on them. These bodies were considered to be educational.

Age of Dolls: Advertisements, catalogs, illustrations are all helpful in determining the age of a doll. So also are patents, trademarks, copyrights, and the actual mark on the doll. Family history can often be used to date a doll. Because of the McKinley tariff act Nippon dolls are usually marked with the word "Nippon" indicating the country of origin, Japan. Nippon dolls were most popular from 1917 through 1921.

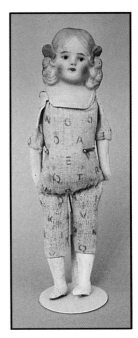

ABC cloth body.

All-bisque Dolls: Generally small dolls under 7" tall. Though popular for years, their greatest popularity came in the twentieth century Kewpie era. Many were not toys but were meant for the adult market to be used as party favors and decorative purposes. The majority of Nippon all-bisque dolls have shoulder joints; some are jointed at both the shoulder and the hip; and a few are not jointed at all (figural or statuette dolls). One unusual Nippon all-bisque doll is jointed only at the hips.

Group of all-bisque dolls.

Art Dolls: Dolls designed by well-known artists. Rose O'Neill of Kewpie doll fame was one of the many artists.

-B-

Baby Bodies: Also called bent limb or 5-piece baby body, the bodies are chubbier and have shorter limbs than the children or toddler dolls' bodies. At the beginning of the twentieth century as part of the trend toward making lifelike character dolls, composition baby bodies were introduced that really resembled a chubby baby. The hands were often molded in baby-like poses, one with the finger curved in, the other with the fingers stretching out. The big toe was usually turned up slightly.

Backstamp: The mark found on porcelain items identifying the manufacturer, exporter or importer, and the country of origin.

Ball-Jointed Body: A ball joint was composed of a ball (usually wooden) and two adjacent sockets strung with elastic to permit the doll joint to move in all directions. Mostly seen on composition child bodies, the joints were usually at the shoulder, hips, knees, and elbows. A ball jointed body doll was often referred to in the doll trade as fully jointed. (Note: Bent limb baby bodies do not use ball joints.)

German-type ball-jointed body; it has been repainted.

Bent limb baby body shows normal wear.

313

Glossary

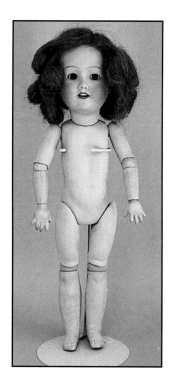

Morimura Bros. ball jointed body — notice that the hip joints are not ball jointed.

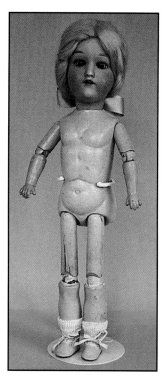

Ball jointed baby with broomstick legs; notice the wrists are not jointed.

Bathtub Baby: Small all-bisque doll in sitting position found in a small china-glazed tub.

Bisque: A ceramic material with hard matte or nonglossy surface that, in better grades, is translucent. Bisque heads may be pressed or poured into molds. Nippon dolls were mold poured as the pressed were generally used prior to 1890. Bisque dolls' heads vary in grade according to the ingredients, the firing techniques, the polishing, and the painting. Most bisque heads and all-bisque dolls are fired both before and after the color is applied. Bisque dolls made from the same mold can appear quite dissimilar if the eye sockets are cut out in different sizes or the mouth is open or closed. The coloration and decoration can also make them look different. Some lesser quality, all-bisque Nippon dolls do not have the second firing (after the color was applied) and, therefore, the paint can be rubbed or washed off. *See Painted Bisque.*

Blank: Greenware or bisque items devoid of decoration; Nippon blanks were used by decorating studios and china painters.

Bonnet Dolls: Dolls with molded bonnets or hats. Popular since the 1890s, Morimura Brothers advertised bonnet dolls in 1915 and 1916.

Breather: A term used by collectors for dolls with pierced nostrils.

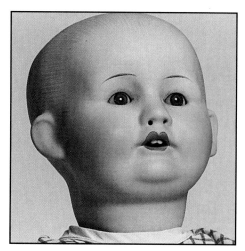

Pierced nostrils of breather doll.

- C -

Candy Store Dolls: Small, inexpensive, all-bisque dolls originally sold in candy stores.

Celluloid: A synthetic material composed of cellulose nitrate (pyroxylin), camphor, pigments, fillers, and alcohol. Celluloid products were first produced as early as 1863 although it is not known when the first celluloid dolls were produced. A celluloid doll is made by blowing steam or hot air into molds. During World War I celluloid was used for dolls' eyes, and there are celluloid dolls and toys marked "Nippon."

Character Dolls: Lifelike representations of babies and children, character dolls accounted for the majority of dolls produced in the twentieth century. Many of these dolls were modeled after actual children. Nippon character dolls can be found in a variety of facial expressions including a closed mouth pouty.

Group of celluloid dolls.

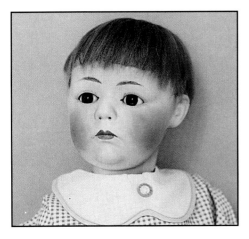

Character face.

Chemise: A garment that many Nippon dolls were originally sold in. It usually had sleeves, covered the doll to mid-calf, and tied in the back. It was often made of a cheap muslin or cheesecloth-like material and then trimmed with lace.

China Doll: Heads made of white clay, tinted, fired, dipped in glaze, and refired, they are sometimes referred to as glazed bisque. Generally, it is only the head or head and limbs that are made of china. Borgfeldt, Butler Brothers, and Morimura Brothers were distributors of china head dolls. Nippon half-dolls were also made of china.

Cloth body.

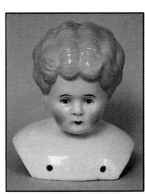

China glazed.

Cloth Bodies: Muslin (both in white and red) was often used for the Nippon china and bisque shoulderplate dolls. Cloth bodies have been popular since ancient times. *See ABC Bodies.*

Color Rubs: Places were cheek and nose color is rubbed off.

Composition: A wood pulp mixture most often used for ball jointed and baby bodies. Some Nippon composition bodies were actually made of papier-mache or a mixture made from oyster shells.

Crier: Mechanism within the doll that allows the doll to produce a cry sound. Morimura Brothers produced a crier doll that has a bellow in the head that produces a cry sound. Sometimes a crier mechanism is found in the torso of the doll.

White spot on right cheek is a color rub.

 - D -

Doll: This word appeared in an English dictionary around 1700. The word "doll" did not come into common usage in America until the mid-eighteenth century or later.

Dolls' House Dolls: Small dolls used in dolls' houses. Many of the Nippon all-bisque jointed dolls were probably used in WWI-era doll houses.

Dolly Face: A bisque doll head with a sweet, child-like face but no real expression.

Dolly face.

- E -

Eyes: Nippon doll eyes normally fall into two categories: painted and glass. The majority of all-bisque, china, and small bisque-head dolls have painted eyes, usually blue or brown in color with black pupils. Most bisque-head dolls have glass eyes that are either sleeping (will close shut when the doll is laid on its back) or set (do not close). Primarily found in blue or brown, eyes in any other color are rare. However, many shades of blue exist, from a blue-gray to a vivid bright blue. The many shades of blue eyes can possibly be attributed to the different formulas that made up the glass batch.

Eyebrows: Most eyebrows on Nippon bisque-head dolls are painted on using feathered brushstrokes in various shades of brown. Most all-bisque and china dolls, as well as some bisque-head dolls, have a simple line-type or single stroke eyebrow.

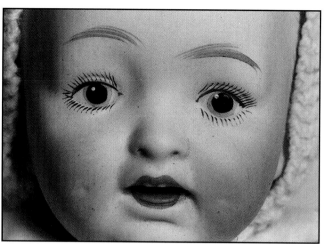

Painted eyes.

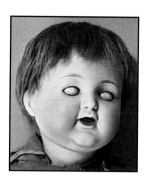

Bisque-head doll with sleeping eyes closed.

Actual eye mechanism from bisque-head Nippon doll.

Eyelashes: Usually both upper and lower lashes were painted on the bisque doll heads although there are some heads that do not have painted upper lashes. These heads would have had 'natural' or hair eyelashes that were attached to the upper part of the glass eye right before the lid. This type of eyelash could be easily removed by a child, and it is rare to find a Nippon doll with the natural eyelashes still intact. Nippon all-bisque and china dolls seldom have any type of eyelash.

- F -

Faces: Nippon dolls' are as varied as those of people. Even when dolls were made from the same mold, there were often slight differences due to the fact that each face was painted by hand. The shape of the doll's face and neck usually indicates the age of the person it represents. A round chubby face with a short neck usually indicates a baby doll; a longer face and neck, a child or toddler doll. *See Character Dolls, Dolly Face.*

Flange neck.

Flange Neck: Necks that open out at lower edge. They are generally found on small bisque heads and are used with cloth bodies or as pincushions. The cloth is sewed over the flange holding the head onto the body.

Flirty-type Eyes: Eyes that move from side to side, not up and down. Eyes of this type are not found on Nippon dolls; however, flirty-type eyes may be found on a few Nippon dolls. These flirty-type eyes are looking to the side but do not move from side to side. *See Googly.*

Flirty-type eyes.

- G -

Googly: Large, round eyes glancing to the side; found on both all-bisque and bisque-head dolls. See *Flirty Eyes.*

- H -

Hair: Most Nippon bisque-head dolls originally had wigs that were either made from human hair or mohair (fine glossy hair from the Angora or Tibetan goat). However, other materials such as wool, woolcrepe, or fur were sometimes used,

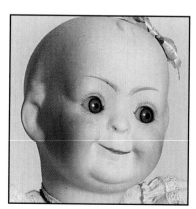

Googly eyes.

and during the war, mohair was often mixed with wool because of mohair shortages. The most popular hair colors were blonde, brown, auburn, and tosca (a dull gold). Because the wigs were easily dirtied and damaged, many dolls are now seen with new replacement wigs. Solid domehead dolls usually have painted-on brown brushstroke hair and sideburns. Some all-bisque and small bisque shoulderplate dolls also required wigs. *See Molded Hair, Painted Hair.*

Half-Dolls: Dolls, usually china, where the doll is modeled only from the waist up. Most have sew holes at the flange or waist area. These sew holes were used to attach material to the doll. Sometimes called pincushion dolls because they were most often used atop a pincushion. However, they also adorned such items as small lamps, powder boxes, candy boxes, clothes brushes, perfume bottles, etc. Nippon half-dolls are rare; the mark is on the flange in black lettering.

Half-doll.

Holes in Head: The crown of many bisque dolls' heads was sliced off to facilitate access to the inside of the head for setting of eyes, especially sleep eyes, and for attaching the head to the body. Cardboard pates (used to cover the crown opening) also permitted an easier method of attaching wigs. The small holes in the back of the head were used to secure eyes to the head so that the eyes would not rock back and forth and be damaged in transit.

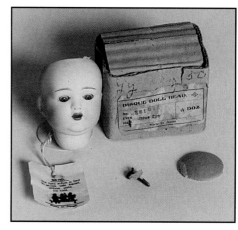

Doll head found in original box. Eyes still tied in place. Pieces in front of box are neck ring, hook, and pate.

Incised: Type of mark commonly found on Nippon dolls; the mark looks etched or cut into the doll's head or back. The mark was actually part of the doll mold, and because of this, if the doll is the first one out of the mold, the mark is very deep; if the doll is the last one out, the mark may be almost obliterated.

Intaglio Eyes: Painted eyes with the iris and pupil concave. Primarily used with German all-bisque dolls or small bisque-head dolls. Nippon dolls have painted but not intaglio eyes. *See Painted Eyes.*

- K -

Kid Bodies: Popular throughout the nineteenth and early twentieth centuries, kid bodies were primarily found on the large bisque-head shoulderplate dolls. Universal joints, Ne Plus Ultra joints, and other rivet-type joints were used to allow the bodies to move in a manner similar to the ball jointed composition bodies. Stuffed with sawdust or cork, kid becomes brittle and cracks as it ages. The Japanese primarily used imitation kid (oilcloth) for their bodies.

Imitation kid body; bisque lower arms; elbows, knees and hip joints are riveted; the owner sewed a muslin chemise onto the doll.

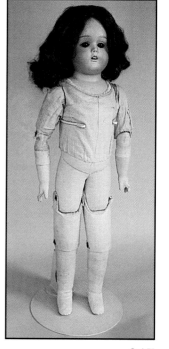

Kidaline (or Kidolyn) Bodies: Imitation kid bodies that Morimura Brothers advertised from 1919 through 1921.

Glossary

- L -

Large Dolls: Dolls 30" or more in height are called show dolls. Large dolls were primarily used for displays, carnivals, or premiums. *See Sizes.*

- M -

Marks: Nippon doll marks are usually found on the back of the head or the shoulders. The marks may be incised, stamped in ink, or attached to the doll with a tag or sticker. On the bisque-head dolls the mark is most often incised on the back of the head in the neck area. All-bisque dolls are usually incised on the back although sometimes the word "Nippon" can be found stamped in ink on the back or the bottom of the feet. The mark may only be the country of origin or may include a manufacturer's symbols and mold numbers. *See Incised, Numbers.*

Mint Condition: The state of a doll that has been preserved in its original box or container and never been played with. *See Original Condition.*

Molded Clothing: Clothing formed in the mold of the doll, not made of cloth. Nippon all-bisque dolls, celluloid dolls and toys, and papier-mache nodders can be found with molded clothing.

Molded Hair: Hairstyle is molded as part of the head, then painted. Seen on many Nippon all-bisque and small bisque-head dolls, sometimes bows, headbands, and hats are part of the molded hair. *See Hair.*

Molded in Relief: A technique used in making porcelain items where the pattern is embossed on the item by the mold in which the article is shaped. These items give the appearance that the pattern is caused by some type of upward pressure from the underside. Porcelain collectors sometimes call these types of items "blown-out."

Molded clothing.

Molds: For bisque-head dolls, molds were of two types, the master mold and the pouring mold. The master mold design often belonged to large companies such as Horsman or Borgfeldt, rather than to the porcelain factory. The pouring mold was made from the master mold. The first heads made in the pouring mold were usually more sharply defined than later ones, and by the time 50 heads had been made from a pouring mold, it had to be discarded and another one made from the master.

Molded in relief items.

Mouths: Bisque-head dolls' mouths fall into three categories: open, closed, and open-closed. The most prevalent is the open mouth with the lips parted and the teeth showing. Sometimes open mouths also have a molded tongue. Open mouth dolls became very popular at the end of the nineteenth century and in the twentieth century. These open mouths increased the expense of manufacture, but their popularity made them so prevalent that closed-mouth dolls, with the lips together, almost became non-existent. A few open-closed mouths are found; these had the tongue and teeth molded as part of the mouth and though the mouth had the appearance of being open, there was no hole in it. All-bisque and china dolls usually have closed mouths. *See Pouty.*

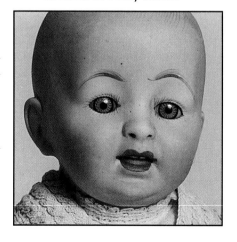

Example of open-closed mouth.

318

- N -

Names: Some Nippon dolls were given names, and these can sometimes be found on stickers, tags, or boxes still with the dolls. Of course, many of these have been removed or lost through the years. The creators of dolls often gave them trade names that were sometimes registered as trademarks, i.e., Kewpie, Baby Bud, Queue San Baby, etc. These trade names were used for lines of dolls as well as individual dolls.

Ne Plus Ultra Patent Joint: A rivet-type joint that was primarily used for the hips of kid dolls. *See Kid Bodies.*

Nodders: Dolls whose heads are loose, but held on by springs, elastic or other means so they nod or bob easily. Rare in Nippon dolls.

Nostrils: Two red dots usually indicated the nostrils on dolls. A few dolls have pierced nostrils. *See Breather.*

Numbers: Most bisque-head dolls' heads bear numbers. Some of them represent the size, some represent the mold number, and occasionally there are numbers that represent dates, etc. The size numbers on small-size bisque heads are often in the form of fractions. *See Marks.*

Example of papier-mache nodder.

- O -

Original Condition: The term used by doll collectors for dolls with all original parts including wig and clothes. This does not mean the doll is in mint condition, which implies the doll is in its original box or container and has never been played with. If a doll has all its parts, as originally made, with no substitutions or alterations, it can be designated as in original condition even though it may have lost a few strands of hair, its body may show some wear, or it may show a few similar ravages of time. *See Mint Condition.*

- P -

Painted Bisque: After painting, the bisque decorated in this manner is not given a second firing. Therefore, the paint eventually wears or washes off.

Painted Hair: Hair is painted on head with no molding. Often found on solid dome head dolls. *See Hair, Molded Hair, Solid Dome Head.*

Papier-Mache: A type of composition made from paper pulp, paste or glue for adhesion, and clay or flour for stiffness plus necessary chemicals. It was used for doll bodies and, rarely in Nippon, for complete dolls and toys.

Pate: The covering for the large hole found on the top of most bisque-head dolls. Generally, the wig is attached to the pate. Most Nippon doll pates are made from cardboard.

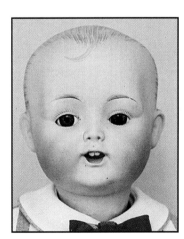

Solid dome head with painted hair; notice little bangs painted down on forehead.

Patents: Regular patents can be obtained for the materials of which a doll is composed, the articulation and assembling of the body, and for special functions such as sleeping, walking, and talking. Design patents can be obtained for the design or look of the doll. For instance, Rose O'Neill was issued a design patent for the Kewpie dolls.

Porcelain: A mixture composed mainly of kaolin and petuntse, which are fired at a high temperature and vitrified (changed into a glass-like substance by the application of heat).

Glossary

Pouty: Bisque-head doll with a closed mouth that has a somewhat sad look. Nippon closed-mouth dolls are rare in part because by the early 1900s, closed-mouth dolls were out of style. *See Mouths.*

-S-

Shoulderplate doll.

Shoulderplate dolls: One-piece molded construction of doll's head and shoulders.

Sizes: Nippon dolls vary in size from the small all-bisque ones less than 3" tall to bisque head babies that are almost life-size. All-bisque dolls over 7" tall are seldom found. The Nippon bisque-head babies are usually found in sizes 10" to 21" tall; child dolls in sizes 12" to 28" tall. The larger babies and child dolls are harder to find. Probably they were not as popular with children or, since they would have been harder for a child to handle, they may have been broken more often. *See Large Dolls.*

Sleep Eyes: Eyes that close as the doll is laid on its back (to show the eyelids) and open when the doll is upright usually by means of a counterweight. These are usually made of glass, but other materials such as celluloid were sometimes used. *See Eyes.*

Socket Head: An opening in the doll body into which the head and neck fit. This allows the head to turn from side to side. Except for Nippon shoulderplate dolls, all Nippon bisque-head dolls have socket heads.

Solid Dome Head: Term for bisque doll heads that do not have an opening in the crown. These generally have painted brushstroke hair and are most often found on baby bodies. *See Hair, Holes in Head.*

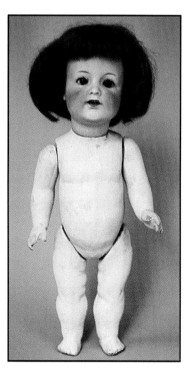

Toddler body, notice damage to toes and fingers. These were usually the first parts of a doll's body to be damaged.

Starfish Hands: Type of hand, with fingers apart, often found on all-bisque, cherub-type dolls such as Kewpie.

Stone Bisque: A heavy, nontranslucent type of bisque. Used for some all-bisque dolls and figures.

-T-

Teeth: Most open mouth bisque-head dolls were given ceramic upper teeth to add realism to the look of the doll. Teeth became popular in the late nineteenth and early twentieth century. Generally, Nippon dolls have teeth that were molded separately and inserted later. Some Nippon bisque-head dolls, as well as a few all-bisque dolls, have painted teeth. It is rare to find Nippon dolls with only lower teeth or both upper and lower teeth.

Example of starfish hands.

Toddler Body: A chubby composition body that is sometimes ball jointed but on Nippon dolls can usually be found with only five pieces. Toddler bodies have shorter thighs with a diagonal hip joint. The arms are usually curved instead of jointed, and the legs are straight and chubby.

Tongues: Many character dolls had molded tongues that were generally made of plaster, bisque, or celluloid. Molded tongues that move in or out as the doll is moved

320

are often referred to as "wobble" tongues. Sometimes felt or cardboard was used to cover the mouth opening from the inside of the doll head to simulate a tongue.

Trademarks: A word, name, symbol, or combination of these adopted and used by a manufacturer or merchant to identify their goods and distinguish them from those manufactured or sold by others. If a doll or toy is trademarked, it must have been made and distributed more than just locally, whereas patented dolls may never have been produced commercially.

- U -

Universal Joint: Used on kid and fabric bodies, the joint had three members held together by a bolt, which allowed the knuckle end to pivot within the concave area; at the same time, a swivel connection between the two parts of the knuckle permitted one of the members to rotate on the other members. *See Kid Bodies.*

- W -

Walker: Doll whose body has joints to simulate walking, the head usually moves in unison with the legs. It's very rare to find Nippon dolls on a walker body.

Wigs: Human hair and mohair were the principal materials for wigs although other materials such as lambs wool and fur were sometimes used. *See Hair.*

Wire-jointed: Dolls whose arms and legs are held on with wire. Many Nippon all-bisque dolls, especially those with jointed arms and legs, used wire.

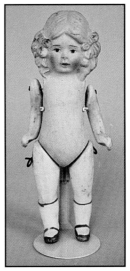

All-bisque doll with wire joints.

Bibliography

Books and Articles

Angione, Genevieve, *All-Bisque and Half-Bisque Dolls*, Schiffer Publishing Ltd., 1969.

Axe, John, *Kewpies — Dolls & Art*, Hobby House Press, Cumberland, Maryland, 1987.

Buchholtz, Shirley, *A Century of Celluloid Dolls*, Hobby House Press, 1983.

Coleman, Dorothy S., Elizabeth A., and Evelyn J., *The Collector's Encyclopedia of Dolls*, Crown Publishers, New York, 1968.

_____, *The Collector's Book of Dolls' Clothes*, Crown Publishers, New York, 1975.

Deefler, Leslie and Brace, *Harcourt, An Age of Conflict*, Jovanovich College Publishers, Ft. Worth, Texas, 1990.

Fainges, Marjory, *Antique Dolls of China and Bisque*, Kangaroo Press, Australia, 1991.

Gray, Gordon, "Porcelain at Fulper Pottery, Part 1," *The Stangl/Fulper Times,* January 1997.

Green, Bernard, *The Timetables of History*, Simon and Schuster, Inc., New York City.

Harris, Kristina, *Collector's Guide to Vintage Fashions*, Collector Books, Paducah, Kentucky, 1999.

Herlocker, Dawn, *200 Years of Dolls Identification and Price Guide*, Antique Trader Books, Dubuque, Iowa, 1996.

Herron, R. Lane, *Warman's Dolls, A Value and Identification Guide*, Krause Publications, Iola, Wisconsin.

Kirsch, Francine, *"The Well-Dressed Kewpie,"* Antiques and Collecting, date unknown.

Laubner, Ellie, *Fashions of the Roaring '20's*, Schiffer Publishing Ltd., Atglen, Pennsylvania, 1996.

Lauer, Keith and Julie Robinson, *Celluloid, Collector's Reference and Value Guide,* Collectors Books, Paducah, Kentucky, 1999.

May, Stella Burke, "Women and Dolls," *Everybody's Magazine*, November 1925, republished *Doll Reader,* November 1984.

Moyer, Patsy, *Doll Values Antique to Modern*, Collector Books, Paducah, Kentucky, 1999.

Noritake Company, Limited, *History of the Materials Development and Chronology of the Backstamps*, 1997.

Punchard, Lorraine, *Playtime Pottery and Porcelain from Europe and Asia*, Schiffer Publishing, 1996.

Seeley, Mildred and Colleen, *Doll Collecting for Fun and Profit*, HPBooks, Tucson, Arizona, 1983.

_____, *Doll Costuming*, HPBooks, Tucson, Arizona, 1984.

Smith, Patricia, *Oriental Dolls*, Collector Books, Paducah, Kentucky, 1979.

Van Patten, Joan, *Collector's Encyclopedia of Nippon Porcelain*, Collector Books, Paducah, Kentucky, 1979.

_____, *Collector's Encyclopedia of Nippon Porcelain, Second Series*, Collector Books, Paducah, Kentucky, 1982.

_____, *Collector's Encyclopedia of Nippon Porcelain, Third Series*, Collector Books, Paducah, Kentucky, 1986.

_____, *Collector's Encyclopedia of Nippon Porcelain, Fourth Series*, Collector Books, Paducah, Kentucky, 1997.

_____, *Collector's Encyclopedia of Nippon Porcelain, Fifth Series*, Collector Books, Paducah, Kentucky, 1998.

Van Patten, Joan and Williams, Peggy and Elmer, *Celluloid Treasures of the Victorian Era*, Collector Books, Paducah, Kentucky, 1999.

Wells, Richard A., Manners, *Customs and Dress*, King, Richardson & Company, Publishers, Springfield, Massachusetts, 1891.

Westbrook, Dorothy and Sherry Ehrhardt, *American Collector Dolls*, Heart of America Press, Kansas City, Missouri, 1975.

Wheeler, Beth, "Collecting Half Dolls," *Warman's Today's Collector*, September 1997.

Uncle Milton, *The Sunbonnet Twins, A Story in Verse and Music for Little Tots,* Cupples & Leon Company, New York, 1907.

Catalogs, Periodicals, Newspapers

A.A. Vantine & Co., The Oriental Store – 1916.

Butler Brothers – various years 1908 through 1921.

Baltimore Bargain House – June 1917.

Charles William Stores – Fall/Winter 1916/1917; Fall/Winter 1918/1919; Fall/Winter 1920/1921.

Dennison's Bogie Book, Dennison Manufacturing Company, date unknown.

How to Make Party Favors and Table Decorations, Dennison Manufacturing Company, 1928.

Good Housekeeping – 1916 through 1917.

Montgomery Ward – November/December 1918 (Pure Food Groceries catalog); Fall/Winter 1919 and 1920; 1920 sale catalog.

New York Times – December 1917.

Playthings – 1910 through 1921.

Sears Roebuck & Company – 1915 through 1921.

The Shure Winner – 1919.

Other

Guise and Dolls: The Rise of the Doll Industry and the Gender of Material Culture, 1830 – 1930; Miriam Formanek-Brunell, PhD; Degree date: 1990; Rutgers, N.J.

About the Authors

Joan Van Patten is the author of *Collector's Encyclopedia of Nippon Porcelain*, First through Sixth Series, *Nippon Price Guide, Collector's Encyclopedia of Noritake,* First and Second Series and *Celluloid Treasures of the Victorian Era*, all published by Collector Books. She is presently working on *Collector's Encyclopedia of Nippon Porcelain*, Seventh Series.

She has written hundreds of trade paper and magazine articles and is a contributor to *Schroeder's Antique Price Guide.*

Joan has been on the board of the INCC (International Nippon Collector's Club) since its inception. She served as its first president and was also the co-founder. She has served as a director of the club for many years. She has lectured on the subjects of Nippon, Noritake, and celluloid throughout the United States.

The research of antiques and collectibles, travel, and volunteer work are her other major interests.

Linda Lau has been a Nippon doll and toy collector for over 20 years. She has done extensive research on dolls and toys of the Nippon era and has written articles on Nippon-era dolls for the *Doll Reader, Doll World,* and *Antiques and Collectibles Magazine.* She is actively involved in the International Nippon Collectors' Club (INCC) and has served on the board of directors and as president. She is also a member of the United Federation of Doll Clubs (UFDC). In addition to Nippon dolls and porcelain, she is an avid collector of all things Victorian. In 1993 her home was featured in *Country Victorian Decorating and Lifestyle.*

Linda would like to dedicate this book to her family and thank them for their never-ending love, support, and encouragement.

Index

Index

Other Books by Joan Van Patten

Collector's Encyclopedia of Nippon Porcelain
Joan Van Patten

Today, Nippon porcelain is very popular with collectors. Joan Van Patten has compiled this important series of the *Collector's Encyclopedia of Nippon Porcelain*. Each deluxe hardbound volume in this popular series features this beautiful porcelain in full color. Thousands of pieces are illustrated and described with no pictures repeated. Detailed descriptions are provided, and there are helpful glossaries and current value guides. Marks, vintage ads, and hundreds of color photographs make each volume jam-packed with information. This series makes up the most complete reference on Nippon porcelain ever published.

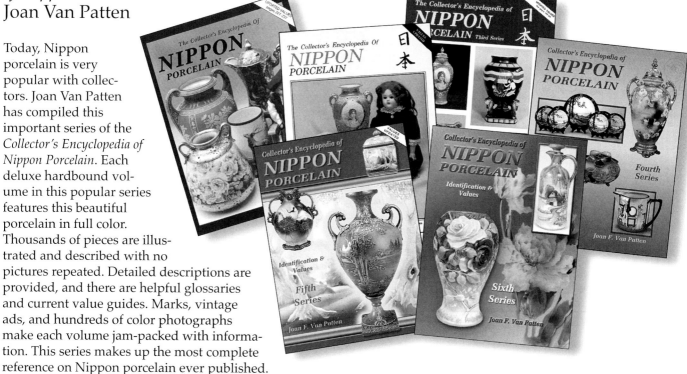

First Series • ISBN: 0-89145-108-0 • #3837 • 8½ x 11 • 238 Pgs. • HB • 2000 values • $24.95
Second Series • ISBN: 0-89145-186-2 • #2089 • 8½ x 11 • 256 Pgs. • HB • 1997 values • $24.95
Third Series • ISBN: 0-89145-308-3 • #1665 • 8½ x 11 • 336 Pgs. • HB • 2000 values • $24.95
Fourth Series • ISBN: 0-89145-719-4 • #4712 • 8½ x 11 • 288 Pgs. • HB • 1997 values • $24.95
Fifth Series • ISBN: 1-57432-056-4 • #5053 • 8½ x 11 • 336 Pgs. • HB • 2000 values • $24.95
Sixth Series • ISBN: 1-5743-191-9• #5678 • 8½ x 11 • 256 Pgs. • HB • 2001 values • $29.95

Celluloid Treasures of the Victorian Era
Joan Van Patten and Elmer & Peggy Williams

Encompassing what has been called the golden age of celluloid collectibles, *Celluloid Treasures of the Victorian Era* takes a look at the time period from 1885 to 1915. Photo albums; hat, glove, necktie, and handkerchief boxes; hand mirrors; brushes; autograph books; and prayer books featuring pastel portraits of beautiful Victorian women and children characterize this appealing book. 1999 values.
ISBN: 1-57432-077-7 • #5152 • 8½ x 11 • 232 Pgs. • HB • $24.95

Collector's Encyclopedia of Noritake
Joan Van Patten

This full-color value guide has over 450 photos along with a large section on marks, a history of Morimura Bros., as well as techniques used on Noritake wares. In addition, information on detection of damage, restoration, and insuring your pieces is provided. 2000 values.
ISBN: 0-89145-244-3 • #1447 • 8½ x 11 • 200 Pgs. • HB • $19.95

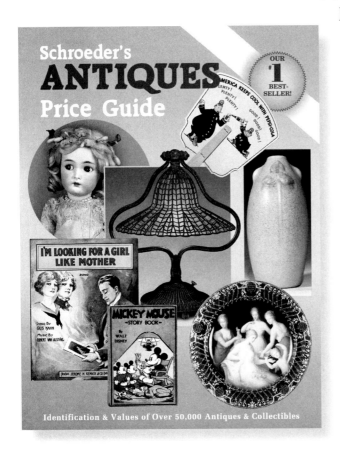